Schools at the centr

Educational management series
Series editor: Cyril Poster

Schools at the centre?

A study of decentralisation

Alison Bullock and Hywel Thomas

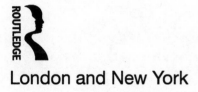

London and New York

First published 1997
by Routledge
11 New Fetter Lane, London EC4P 4EE

Simultaneously published in the USA and Canada
by Routledge
29 West 35th Street, New York, NY 10001

Typeset in Times by M Rules

Printed and bound in Great Britain by
Hartnolls Limited, Bodmin, Cornwall

British Library Cataloguing in Publication Data
A catalogue record for this book is available from the British Library

Library of Congress Cataloging in Publication Data
Bullock, Alison, 1962–
    Schools at the centre? : a study of decentralisation / Alison
Bullock and Hywel Thomas.
        p.   cm.
    Includes bibliographical references (p.   ) and index.
    1. Schools—Decentralization—Cross-cultural studies. 2. School-
based management—Cross-cultural studies.   I. Thomas, Hywel.
II. Title.
LB2862.B85   1997   96–26284
379.1'535—dc20   CIP

ISBN 0-415-12911-7

Contents

Figures

Tables

Acknowledgements

Much of the work in this book arose from two research studies, a three-year project funded by the National Association of Head Teachers on the impact of local management on schools, and a two-year project on the funding of schools made possible by a grant from The Leverhulme Trust. We are pleased to acknowledge their support and, in particular, the advice and comments received from the NAHT's steering group, which illustrated the value of such groups for researchers. As practitioners of local management they were colleagues of considerable knowledge and experience.

We thank all who responded to our requests for information. We are especially grateful to those head teachers who responded to three questionnaires and all those we met on our visits to schools.

Margaret Arnott, now at Glasgow Caledonian University, never tired in the year she worked on the NAHT study. We thank her for a contribution which was characterised by its energy, enthusiasm and efficiency.

We should also like to thank all those others who have supported the projects and the preparation of the book, notably the computing, reprographics and secretarial staff in the School of Education.

Abbreviations

AEN	Additional Educational Needs
ASB	Aggregated Schools' Budget
AWPU	Age-Weighted Pupil Unit
CCP	Chinese Communist Party
CTC	City Technology Colleges
DES	Department of Education and Science
DfE	Department for Education
DfEE	Department for Education and Employment
DP	Development Plan
FSM	Free School Meal
FTE	Full-time Equivalent
GEST	Grants for Education Support and Training
GM	Grant Maintained
GNP	Gross National Product
GSB	General Schools' Budget
HDI	Human Development Index
HMCI	Her Majesty's Chief Inspector
HMI	Her Majesty's Inspectorate
INSET	In-Service Training
IoW	Isle of Wight
LEA	Local Education Authority
LEAP	Local Education Authorities Project
LM	Locally Managed
LMS	Local Management of Schools
NNEB	National Nursery Examination Board
NoR	Number on Roll
NQT	Newly Qualified Teacher
NSW	New South Wales
OECD	Organisation for Economic Co-operation and Development
Ofsted	Office for Standards in Education
PSB	Potential Schools' Budget
PTA	Parent–Teacher Association

PTR	Pupil–Teacher Ratio
SAT	Standard Assessment Task
SDP	School Development Plan
SEN	Special Educational Needs
SMT	Senior Management Team
UNDP	United Nations Development Programme
USA	United States of America
WO	Welsh Office

Chapter 1

Adding value

'Then you should say what you mean,' the March Hare went on. 'I do,' Alice hastily replied; 'at least – at least I mean what I say – that's the same thing you know.' 'Not the same thing a bit!' said the Hatter. 'Why, you might just as well say that "I see what I eat" is the same thing as "I eat what I see!"' 'You might just as well say,' added the March Hare, 'that "I like what I get" is the same thing as "I get what I like!"'

(Alice's Adventures in Wonderland, 1865: 79–80)

Alice's Adventures in Wonderland and decentralised school management have much in common. They each contain phenomena – real and imagined – which are new to conventional experience. These phenomena are not always what they appear to be and are sometimes the opposite of their appearance. As you move from successive events – or countries – they undergo rapid and perplexing change. Finally, and in wonder, you ask whether and how it all matters to the 'real' world, in our case, of teaching and learning in schools.

It is all too evident that it does matter in some degree. Policies of decentralisation are being adopted in a great many countries, North and South. Despite a common language for describing these policies, however, even a cursory examination makes it apparent that their nature and purpose can differ substantially. The first purpose of this book, therefore, is to recognise this diversity and provide a framework for a clear *description* of the nature of decentralised management in schools. We support this description with our second purpose, which is to *analyse* these phenomena in different national settings and, drawing upon recent theoretical work and extensive evidence from one country, our third purpose is to *explain* these changes and evaluate their impact on schools. This provides the basis for our fourth purpose, which is to examine how decentralisation matters for schools, pupils and communities. It leads to our final purpose, which is to consider what directions decentralisation might take in future. During its preparation we were aware that we are adding yet another book to a rapidly growing literature, and we hope, therefore, that we are *adding value* as well as volume to that field: it is for readers to decide whether we have done so.

The remainder of the book is organised into three parts and nine further chapters. Part I, 'Understanding decentralisation', sets out the conceptual frameworks that we use in our descriptive and explanatory analysis. In Chapter 2, The nature of decentralised school management, we describe and discuss the factors associated with the concept of decentralised management, thereby outlining the diversity of factors included in international experience in this area. It will illustrate, for example, how the curriculum is the focus of greater decentralisation in some systems, while elsewhere control of the curriculum has been moved to the centre and responsibility for resources delegated to schools. In summary, the chapter examines how the language of decentralised management has been applied and sets a context for interpreting and understanding it as a national and international phenomenon.

Chapter 3, 'Markets, collectivities and decentralisation', is intended to provide a conceptual framework for understanding the diversity of forms of decentralised management. Where Chapter 2 shows how the language of decentralised management is applied to a wide range of educational phenomena, Chapter 3 proposes a conceptual framework for analysing and understanding these phenomena. It is not sufficient to describe decentralisation; we also need to understand the contexts underpinning the specification of policies in any one country. Centred upon the concepts of *interest* and *decision*, our framework identifies four *ideal* forms of school-system management. We then consider how, in practice, actual cases of decentralised management might be 'mapped' onto the framework. The chapter is central in developing our argument on the need to understand systems of decentralised management in some detail if we are to understand and predict some of their outcomes.

The focus on decentralisation is altered in Chapter 4. It begins by recognising that decentralisation is not necessarily good in itself. The virtues and otherwise of specific schemes of decentralisation – and centralisation – are contingent upon the wider educational purposes they are intended to support. In Chapter 4, therefore, we examine wider issues of educational purpose and derive from that discussion four concepts – autonomy, accountability, efficiency and equity – which, we argue, are central to analysis of the achievements of schools and educational systems. Taken together, the descriptive framework of Chapter 2, the analytical framework of Chapter 3 and the four criteria for evaluating decentralisation in Chapter 4 provide the foundation for the remainder of the book.

Part II, 'Decentralised management in practice', begins with Chapter 5 in which we examine decentralisation as an international phenomenon. The chapter applies the frameworks of the earlier chapters and reports the diversity of policies of decentralised management in eleven[1] countries: England and Wales, New Zealand, Australia, USA, Germany, Chile, Russia, China, Poland, Uganda and Zimbabwe. In addition to examining published literature, we draw upon papers available to us through our contributions to OECD projects as well as our wider research network. Countries are grouped in ways which reflect the *orientation* of various national initiatives and, in so far as it is possible, we assess the impact of these changes in terms of our evaluative concepts of autonomy, accountability, efficiency and equity.

Chapters 6 to 9 examine one of the more radical versions of decentralised management, namely the local management of schools (LMS) reforms in England and Wales. The nature of local management (LM) and the scale of the reported data, drawing upon information from over 800 schools, makes the study of interest to other countries, and its location within the conceptual framework set out earlier provides a basis for a comparative analysis of particular value. Each chapter is organised to reflect our four evaluation concepts so that Chapter 6, for example, reviews the changes in the autonomy of these schools. After summarising the scope of delegation in England and Wales, Chapter 6 shows the use made of financial delegation in terms of priorities for the budget. The chapter also examines the impact of changes on staffing, including changes in employment contracts and the number of teaching and non-teaching staff. Views upon the continuing role of local government in the provision of certain services are described and analysed. In this way, the chapter provides a means for examining the nature of institutional autonomy over human and physical resources. In its concluding discussion it considers the way in which LMS has increased some forms of autonomy while limiting others.

The restructuring of responsibilities has had a major effect upon the second of our evaluative criteria, accountabilities within the school system. In Chapter 7, a range of these accountabilities are discussed, but particular attention is given to data on the role of the governing bodies of each school. Since these bodies represent the principal forum for formal accountability in the new system in England and Wales, evidence of their impact is of major importance in assessing how the new accountabilities are working. We explore the implications of these data on practice against the intentions of national policy.

Chapter 8 examines the crucial area of how decentralised management in England and Wales is affecting the quality and standards of learning in schools, which we summarise as an efficiency criterion. Whether LMS is contributing to improved efficiency must be a key test of the changes, and we draw upon evidence from our studies as well as on the findings from other studies. Evidence of the effects of the changes on the nature and quality of planning and management in schools, on levels of participation in decision-making and how the changes are affecting pupil learning are the key components of the chapter. With respect to the latter, we report evidence on relationships between changes in resource levels and the reported effect on learning.

While Chapter 8 is largely concerned with an overall assessment – what is being achieved as a result of decentralised management – Chapter 9 examines the distribution of those benefits in terms of our fourth evaluative criterion: what are the equity consequences of the changes? The chapter draws evidence from a second study undertaken by the authors on the funding of pupils, the funding of schools of different types and the funding of schools with different intakes. This enables us to consider the effect of the changes on different *groups* of pupils and upon the capacity of the school system to serve pupils with *individual* needs. Data are also included on how changes in pupil enrolment to particular schools, as well as the degree of competition for pupils, are affecting schools. Set against our information on competition, we provide evidence on reported initiatives of inter-school collaboration, entered into as a means of limiting the effects of competition.

Part III, 'Schools at the centre?' contains our final chapter in which we review the evidence we have drawn together on decentralisation in England and Wales and as an international phenomenon. We consider the diversity of approaches to decentralised management in terms both of differences in the distribution of responsibilities between countries and in the diverse orientations and directions of change. The chapter shows how an analysis of difference and diversity requires a sound understanding of the nature of specific schemes if we are reliably to comment upon their effect on autonomy, accountability, efficiency and equity. The chapter concludes by asking what these changes mean for the outcomes of schooling and, in terms of our views about educational purposes, the direction in which schools and school systems must develop. Above all, the chapter asks, if schools are primarily concerned with learning, how do we ensure that decentralised management places that at the centre?

Taken as a whole, the book combines a number of aspects which are complementary to each other. We believe the theoretical treatment is a means for deepening our initial understanding of decentralised management as a national and international phenomenon. Drawing upon this material for our comparative analysis is intended to assist discussion in an area where overgeneralised comparisons of national reform can be misleading. The analysis of evidence from the national case study, itself rooted in accounts drawn from over 800 schools, provides further illumination of the importance of a theoretical framework to guide our analysis, and the need for a cautionary approach to such an analysis if we are to properly understand these phenomena. Finally, theory and the empirical account combine to inform our assessment of what is taking place and how we can learn from it, not only to develop policies for school systems or to improve the practice of school management, but to secure improvements in the quality of teaching and learning in schools – our intention is that this focus *adds value*.

Part I

Understanding decentralisation

Chapter 2

The scope of decentralisation

WHAT CAN BE DECENTRALISED?

In the opening chapter of their book, *The Self-Managing School*, Caldwell and Spinks discuss the nature of the resources that are increasingly being delegated to schools. Their definition is broad and worth quoting in full:

> knowledge (decentralisation of decisions related to curriculum, including decisions related to the goals or ends of schooling); technology (decentralisation of decisions related to the means of teaching and learning); power (decentralisation of authority to make decisions); material (decentralisation of decisions related to the use of facilities, supplies and equipment); people (decentralisation of decisions related to the allocation of people in matters related to teaching and learning); time (decentralisation of decisions related to the allocation of time); and finance (decentralisation of decisions related to the allocation of money).
>
> (1988: 5)

Their inclusion of *knowledge* and *technology* in the list gives resources a broader definition than might be expected. More conventionally, resources are defined as the human and physical resources which are transformed into the learning and curriculum experiences of children. However, for the purpose of discussing the nature of self-management – or decentralisation in the language we shall use – there are considerable advantages in building upon this broader usage because it provides a starting point for devising a framework which allows us to review all the responsibilities which might be delegated to a school. Such a list requires some additional items to those suggested by Caldwell and Spinks. We suggest the inclusion of four further items, all of which have a crucial bearing on the nature of schools and the resources which are theirs to manage. These are: (i) admissions: decentralisation of decisions over which pupils are to be admitted to the school; (ii) assessment: decentralisation of decisions over how pupils are to be assessed; (iii) information: decentralisation of decisions over the selection of data to be published about the school's performance; (iv) funding: decentralisation of decisions over the setting of fees for the admission of pupils.

Schools meeting these additional criteria most clearly are independent non-government schools and, in fairness to Caldwell and Spinks, their definition and discussion of decentralised school management is confined to publicly funded schools. That said, the decentralisation of responsibility for these four additional functions does not apply exclusively to the non-government sector and different types of publicly funded schools exercise varying levels of control over admissions, assessment and information. There is also sufficient diversity in the funding arrangements of different types of government schools to require its inclusion as a distinguishing characteristic when defining decentralised management. Not only does this diversity apply to publicly funded schools in different countries but it can also apply to schools of different types within the same country. In England and Wales, for example, each of the main types of publicly funded schools differ in some degree in their funding and their delegated responsibilities.

Completing the list of criteria also requires a broader definition of *power*. As used by Caldwell and Spinks the term is a general statement ('authority to make decisions'), presumably over those resources which are then specifically defined. To whom power is delegated, however, is not always clear, as in the case of the distribution of responsibility between the head teacher and the governing body of a school in England and Wales. How power over one type of resource interacts with another, such as staffing and pupil admissions, is also sufficiently complex and dynamic to make the *sum* of delegated power difficult to predict. In some degree we recognise these complexities in Chapter 3 in which we set out a framework for analysing the various ways in which societies decide who gets what in the distribution of educational resources and opportunities. Deferring that discussion to a later chapter allows us here to focus on a description and analysis of the other ten defining characteristics of decentralisation.

In the remainder of this chapter, we organise these ten characteristics into four larger sets: *curriculum and assessment* includes knowledge, technology and assessment; *human and physical resources* includes material, people and time; *finance* includes sources of finance and funding mechanisms; *access* includes admissions and information. We will review these in the context of the seven main types of publicly funded schools in England and Wales. Four of these – county, voluntary aided, voluntary controlled and special agreement – are also known as locally managed (LM) schools, leaving the fifth category as grant maintained (GM) schools. A sixth category are GM schools known as Technology Schools, a status which arises from special sponsorship from industry and requires the sponsors to have a place on a school's governing body. The seventh category are City Technology Colleges (CTCs). Fewer than twenty in number, these are independent – private – schools in terms of legislation but receive all funds for their day-to-day costs from public funds.

CURRICULUM AND ASSESSMENT

All LM and GM schools are required to provide the national *curriculum*, as specified in the 1988 Education Reform Act and subsequent Orders. They are also subject to the national *assessment* arrangements arising from the legislation. These requirements do not apply to CTCs. The delegated management of an LM school is further constrained, however, by the policies of its Local Education Authority (LEA) because the school is required to develop its curriculum policy within the general guidelines of the LEA policy. Having 'opted-out' of the LEA, no GM school is subject to the policies of the LEA which it has left. Voluntary aided and voluntary controlled LM schools and those GM schools which were aided or controlled decide their own syllabus for religious education.

On curriculum and assessment, then, LM and GM schools and CTCs comprise a hierarchy of self-management with the greatest amount of formal discretion available to CTCs and least to county LM schools. None of these schools are wholly decentralised in terms of their curriculum. In their original conception, CTCs were expected to provide a curriculum that had a distinctively technological bias and it might be expected, therefore, that their curriculum proposals would be scrutinised by the Department for Education and Employment (DfEE) and the Office for Standards in Education (Ofsted) to see if they meet these requirements. In practice, there has been such difficulty in launching a sufficient number of these colleges that the DfEE has been flexible in judging whether proposed colleges meet its specification of institutions with a particular emphasis on technology and science (DfE/WO, 1992).

The methods of teaching and learning adopted by schools – the *technology* – cannot be wholly independent of their curriculum and assessment arrangements. If programmes of study and their related assessment arrangements place emphasis on testing the acquisition of skills as against knowledge, for example, there are inevitably implications for the way learning can be organised. As the traditional autonomy over curriculum and assessment enjoyed by schools in England and Wales is reduced, therefore, it may be that their flexibility in the selection of methods of teaching and learning is reduced. In statutory terms, the government has no right to make directions on methods of teaching and learning, although the processes of school inspection we discuss later in the chapter can be expected to affect choices. For the technology of learning, as with curriculum and assessment, the new types of schools in England and Wales can be ranked in the same hierarchy of self-management, the CTCs with the greatest level of discretion and locally managed county schools with least.

What is notable about curriculum and assessment in England and Wales is the evidence it provides for centralisation as against decentralisation. While much is made of the decentralisation introduced in England and Wales, with the exception of CTCs, all schools now have much less authority over curriculum and assessment than before 1988. It shows how decentralisation can proceed simultaneously with centralisation and, moreover, that the net change may be to increase the degree of centralisation.

HUMAN AND PHYSICAL RESOURCES

Decisions over the appointment, suspension and dismissal of teaching and non-teaching staff – *people* – are delegated to all types of publicly funded schools in England and Wales, in changes which generally extend levels of decentralised management. In making staffing appointments and deciding upon the complement of staff, schools can make their own decisions provided they work within the limits of their financial budgets. Unlike CTCs, LM and GM schools share a statutory duty to work within nationally specified terms and conditions, although, since these allow increasing levels of delegation to the LEA and each school, we might expect diversity to emerge between LEAs on the one hand and between them and GM schools on the other.

While GM schools and CTCs are the employers of their staff, this is not so with all LM schools. The staff of county LM schools remain the employees of the LEA but for voluntary schools, it is the governing body which is the employer. In the event of disputes over grievance and/or dismissal the difference between LM schools and the others has particular significance. Provided an LM school – county and voluntary – acts within the guidelines laid down by its LEA, it is the LEA which is treated by the courts as the responsible body.

The schools are also differentiated with respect to their responsibilities over the allocation of *time*. Unlike CTCs, national curriculum and assessment requirements place boundaries on the freedom of action of LM and GM schools, although neither the DfEE or local authorities have the power to specify precise allocations of time to subjects. However, the DfEE has given directions to LM and GM schools on the total amount of time spent by children in attending the formal curriculum. As to the conditions of service of staff, only CTCs have the degree of decentralised management which allows them to negotiate the contracted hours of teaching staff, LM and GM schools both having to observe hours defined in nationally determined conditions of service. All schools have the authority to decide which teachers should be allocated to specific programmes and to make decisions, within their budget, as to how many staff to employ. It is a matter for each school, for example, to decide on its complement of teaching and non-teaching staff. There are no regulations on maximum size of class, about the overall pupil–teacher ratio or the mix of teaching and non-teaching staff employed at the school site.

The proportion of an LEA's general schools' budget which is actually delegated to LM schools is another facet of the decentralised management of people. Some LEAs retain more services at the centre, decisions which clearly limit the choices of an LM school. There are, however, nationally specified limits on the minimum that must be delegated to schools.

Decentralisation of decisions on the use of *material* (facilities [premises], supplies and equipment) varies between LEAs as well as with type of school. CTCs and GM are both highly decentralised in respect of decisions over the use, maintenance and development of their facilities and their choice of supplies, suppliers and equipment. They differ with respect to the home-to-school transport arrangements for their children where, for GM schools, the responsibility still lies with the LEA. The extent of decentralised management of facilities for LM schools will depend upon its LEA and whether or not the school is voluntary aided. LEAs differ in their view of which parts of the premises can safely be delegated to schools and this will affect the definition of schemes and, therefore, the extent of decentralised management. Voluntary aided schools already have responsibility for much of the structural maintenance of their premises and this distinguishes these schools – a quarter of all schools – from others. They also have more flexibility than non-aided LM schools on the allocation of contracts for services such as grounds maintenance and school meals.

All publicly funded schools in England and Wales make their own spending decisions on learning materials, such as books and other equipment. There are no government-produced textbooks which schools must purchase and, for the most part, schools make their own decisions on the purchase of texts. The introduction of the national curriculum and, more particularly the system of national assessment, has constrained some choices; for example, secondary schools now have to ensure that their students are familiar with some key Shakespeare texts.

The delegation of responsibility for human and physical resources to the school site is the most radical component of decentralisation in England and Wales. Even within this area of delegation, however, the national government has added to its authority in terms of specifying the length of the school year and the number of hours of formal teaching which students of different ages must receive.

FINANCE

Since LM schools are the most common form of school in England and Wales, we will begin by summarising their funding arrangements. This is all the more appropriate, in view of the fact that the funding of GM schools is derived from the rules for funding LM schools.

The Government's framework for LEA schemes of decentralisation is outlined in Figure 2.1: The structure of LEA budgets. This establishes a minimum proportion of overall budget (the General Schools' Budget, as defined in national guidelines [DfE, 1994]) that should be delegated to schools, having excluded large and uneven items: capital, specific grants, home-to-school transport and school meals. What remains is known as the Potential Schools' Budget (PSB) and 85 per cent of this must be delegated to LM schools (DES: 1991).

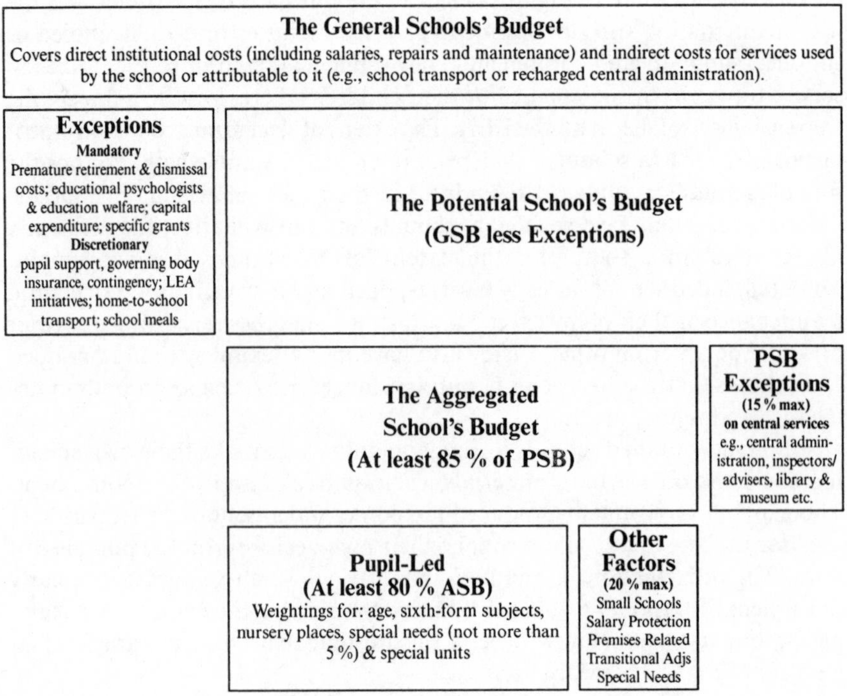

The General Schools' Budget

Covers direct institutional costs (including salaries, repairs and maintenance) and indirect costs for services used by the school or attributable to it (e.g., school transport or recharged central administration).

Exceptions
Mandatory
Premature retirement & dismissal costs; educational psychologists & education welfare; capital expenditure; specific grants
Discretionary
pupil support, governing body insurance, contingency; LEA initiatives; home-to-school transport; school meals

The Potential School's Budget
(GSB less Exceptions)

The Aggregated
School's Budget
(At least 85 % of PSB)

PSB Exceptions
(15 % max)
on central services e.g., central administration, inspectors/ advisers, library & museum etc.

Pupil-Led
(At least 80 % ASB)
Weightings for: age, sixth-form subjects, nursery places, special needs (not more than 5 %) & special units

Other Factors
(20 % max)
Small Schools
Salary Protection
Premises Related
Transitional Adjs
Special Needs

Figure 2.1 The structure of LEA budgets

LEAs may exercise some discretion within this framework. It allows them to determine the total resources available to schools, the specific scope of delegation and decisions on the precise basis for allocating resources. For example, the funds allocated for the running costs of each school are determined on the basis of a formula and the allocation to each school is known as its budget share. Working within the national guidelines an LEA defines its own formula, although each must also be approved by the DfEE. In delegating the 'large majority' of expenditure, schools become responsible for salary costs, day-to-day premises costs, books, equipment and other goods and services. Capital expenditure is not delegated to schools.

Although allocated by a formula, a school receives its funds as a lump sum and it determines allocations to different budget heads. This also applies to GM schools, their funding being largely shaped by the funding arrangements of the local authority in which they are located and of which they were previously a part. Whilst GM schools have received additional funds from the

DfEE, their basic allocation is the local LM formula allocation plus an amount that represents the money retained by the LEA from the PSB to provide common services for its schools. The basic funding of CTCs is linked to the average level of school funding among LEAs in the local area.

For LM schools, decentralised financial control gives them power to authorise spending; the schools do not actually receive money to be placed in school bank accounts, although more recently some schools have been authorised to use cheque books. GM schools and CTCs, however, receive a monthly cash transfer from the government and manage their own bank accounts.

In addition to this basic funding, all these schools receive some funding which is earmarked for specific purposes. Funds for the professional development of teachers, for example, must be spent on that activity and cannot be spent on other needs. Schools periodically receive funds for capital programmes, although these vary enormously from one school to another. Allocations are for specific projects and reflect needs and priorities. It is an area of spending where GM schools have been favoured by comparison with their LM counterparts.

All these schools are required to provide free education and cannot demand financial contributions from the families and households who use the schools. It is legal for schools to invite voluntary contributions to support activities, such as special visits to museums, and it is recognised that these can be cancelled if insufficient contributions are received. Clearly, this places some pressure on households to make the contributions requested.

ACCESS

Regulating the *admissions* of pupils to a school is an aspect of decentralisation which can have a critical effect on the quality of its pupil intake and on the differentiation of the school system. With respect to this criterion, schools fall into three broad categories and for none is responsibility entirely delegated. CTCs are required to manage their admissions so that their pupils, drawn from a large catchment area, are intended to be broadly representative of that catchment. They can, however, interview parents and pupils enabling the school to evaluate commitments to the college curriculum and to progression beyond the compulsory phase of schooling. Even with an intake which may be comprehensive in their measured ability at eleven years old, these processes can mean that, on aspects of attitude and aspiration, the intake may be far from representative of its catchment. In summary, therefore, a CTC is subject to external control in specifying its admissions regulations but has some discretion in determining how that policy is applied.

It might also be argued that denominational LM and denominational GM schools could be in a very similar position. The 1988 Act allows the governing bodies of denominational schools to insist that a specified proportion of their intake be members of their denomination and if it is necessary to preserve the school's character they have the power to restrict admissions below the school's capacity (DES, 1988). There are parallels here with the admissions arrangements for selective schools which can choose to limit admissions below the school's capacity if a higher intake will alter the character of their traditional intake. For church and selective schools, these are arrangements which mean some external control of the admissions regulations but a good deal of decentralised management in their application.

For a minimum of two years after leaving their LEA, all GM schools are expected to continue taking an intake of the same character as when the school was within the LEA. Applied rigorously – retaining and applying the earlier arrangements – this could mean that the profile of pupils admitted to the school might not change. Whether or not this occurs, or is subject to change, such as the introduction of interviewing arrangements, is a key aspect of the differentiating effect of those schools. After two years, however, GM schools can apply to alter their admissions procedures. This has mainly been used to extend admissions to include 16-18 year olds, a change which is perceived as making schools more attractive to those who wish to proceed to higher education.

The position of non-denominational and non-selective LM schools appears to be more clear-cut. They share with similar GM schools a requirement to admit pupils to the level of the school's *standard number*. The criteria determining admissions if a school is over-subscribed are set by the LEA. Typically, these include attendance of siblings and geographical proximity of a child's home to the school, regulations which can be checked relatively easily for fair practice. With respect to admissions policies, therefore, these schools do not appear to have decentralised responsibilities. It is possible, however, for a school to claim that its curriculum has special features, for example in the Arts, which can allow it to give preference to students with special aptitudes in that area. Even for these schools, therefore, there is some scope for decentralised management. This is consistent with the government's expressed preference for greater diversity between schools, shaped by parental preferences. It is for these reasons that national policy is permissive, encourages diversity and is moving to increase the discretion of all schools with respect to admissions.

The range of delegated responsibilities over admissions is related to issues of student and parent choice which, in turn, are shaped by the *information* published about schools. There are national regulations specifying the information which must be published and distributed to parents of children attending the school and to those parents with children due to enter the school system or transferring to another school. At the stage of entry, schools are required to prepare a prospectus that must contain information on, for example, levels of pupil attendance. When pupils transfer from primary to secondary schools all parents receive information showing the examination performance and attendance rates for all secondary schools in the LEA.

All publicly funded schools are also subject to a regular inspection, undertaken using detailed guidelines prepared by the government's Office for Standards in Education (Ofsted, 1995). The inspections themselves are allocated, on the basis of competitive tender, to teams led by inspectors trained and certified by Ofsted. The inspection report is a public document and the summary report, prepared by the inspection team, must be distributed to parents. All parents receive an annual report on the financial and academic performance of the school their child attends and schools must arrange a meeting at which this report is the principal item of business. Schools are also required to provide an annual written report to parents on the progress of their child and this must set out achievements on the national assessments.

THE DISTRIBUTION OF RESPONSIBILITIES

Figure 2.2 is an attempt at summarising the distribution of responsibilities for locally managed county schools in England and Wales. Along the top we have set out the four main sets of responsibilities which could be delegated to schools, although we recognise that each of these sets contains items which can be treated differently. On the side, we have shown the four tiers of responsibility: the national central authority, the regional authority, the school site and the family. The arrows indicate direction of contemporary change.

	CURRICULUM & ASSESSMENT	HUMAN & PHYSICAL RESOURCES	FINANCE	ACCESS	
CENTRE (DfEE)	specifies curriculum and national assessment ↑	framework for employment; standards of premises ↑	guidelines for spending and formula ↑	specifies information to be published and approves admissions policy changes ↑	
REGION (LEA)	advice and guidance	premises	specifies total and formula ↓	sets admissions policy and administers process ↓	
SCHOOL	methods	primary responsibility	spend within budget; no fees	distributes specified information ↓	
FAMILY	withdrawal from sex education	no role	small voluntary contributions	choice of school subject to space and entry criteria	

Figure 2.2 The distribution of responsibilities for locally managed county schools in England and Wales

The presentation is schematic and not a detailed statement of responsibility. It applies only to locally managed county schools and it would have been possible to prepare a somewhat different statement for other school types in England and Wales. In preparing the Figure, our intention is to illustrate the scope for different schemes of decentralised management and the framework will be used again in our comparative review in Chapter 5. Regarding the general direction of change, on curriculum and assessment, the principal movement has been one of centralisation. As to human and physical resources, there has been centralisation to the national ministry in terms of the power to define rules, and decentralisation of the day-to-day exercise of power to the school site. The regional authority has clearly lost power. The changes in finance are comparable, the national ministry taking powers to set guidelines on finance, the school having power to set priorities within its budget and the region losing power to both. Finally, there have been some changes to access and this has given greater power to the national ministry and to some families; schools have also gained power in certain circumstances.

Clearly, it is open to governments with a sovereign Parliament to define schemes which centralise or decentralise control of the curriculum – or staffing or premises or finance or access – or any such combination as they believe appropriate. The specific distribution of responsibilities within an education system – the overall balance of centralisation and decentralisation – is a choice for each national system and, observing the system in England and Wales alone, it is clear that there can be variety in forms of decentralisation even within national systems. The specific forms of decentralisation will not be an accident but, on the one side, represent assumptions about how schools and school systems function and, on the other, the kinds of changes in schools which governments believe are necessary.

If we are to predict possible outcomes from the changes, it is necessary to examine them in some detail so that possible interactions between components of the reforms can be understood. For example, by making governing bodies the agencies that make decisions on the recruitment and dismissal of staff *and* tying funding largely to pupil numbers *and* requiring pupils to be admitted to a school's capacity, a *pupil-as-voucher* system has been created. This puts pressure on schools to compete for pupils in order to attract the funds needed to employ their staff. It is but one example, albeit an important one, of the means by which the systemic and organisational context of schools has been altered. The introduction of greater competition through the *pupil-as-voucher* system is not neutral in its effect, and can be expected to influence who gets what in terms of access to resources and educational opportunities. If we are to understand and predict these and other changes, a conceptual framework is needed for an analysis that goes further than the descriptive mapping of responsibilities contained in this chapter. Chapter 3 is intended to provide such a framework. In providing an overview of how education services are provided and distributed, it enables us to describe, analyse and explain different approaches to decentralisation.

Chapter 3

Markets, collectivities and decentralisation

DECISION AND INTEREST

For the contemporary school system in England and Wales, explanations of how education is provided by schools are now couched in the language of 'markets'. This is well illustrated by an extract from the *Times Educational Supplement*, which described the purpose of the 1988 reforms as the creation of a

> consumer-driven market in which schools compete for pupils by trying to offer the best goods and a greater variety of choice. Under this market mechanism, schools which fail will go to the wall. But for those schools which remain, this new system will increase their power and enhance their status.
>
> (1991: 11)

Through this 'market', it will be those schools which are able to attract pupils who decide what is to be provided, by whom and to whom. Whilst this is a description which has verisimilitude – the 'air of being true, the semblance of actuality' – it is, none the less, only a partial view of the contemporary school system. The 'market' in the curriculum, for example, is constrained almost to the point of non-existence. Its absence was summed up by Sir Keith Joseph:

> The best 'national curriculum' is that resulting from the exercise of true parental choice by parents and children acting collectively, and being provided collectively by governors and teachers in response to that choice. The substitution of a government-imposed curriculum is poor second best
>
> (cited in Chitty, 1989: 217)

On the formal curriculum, then, the 1988 changes were in the opposite direction to the 'market'. Indeed, what can better illustrate more hierarchic control than a circumstance where it is the Secretary of State who now decides when history ends?

'Markets' and 'hierarchies', however, are not the only means by which society decides how much education it requires, what is to be provided, who is to provide it and to whom. In setting out their views of the alternatives, Thompson *et al.* (1991: 3) propose a three-way classification: markets, hierarchies and networks. Markets, their proponents would claim, co-ordinate automatically:

> The pursuit of self-interest by individually motivated and welfare-maximising individuals leads to the best outcome not just for them but also for society as a whole.

In the circumstances where the market 'fails', co-ordination:

> needs to be consciously organised in the form of a hierarchy. Administrative means need to be brought to bear if co-ordination is to be effectively achieved. Control must be overtly exercised.

They go on to suggest, however, that:

> neither the market nor hierarchy will lead to proper co-ordination because both neglect the informal mechanisms that typify a network of relatively independent social elements. It is only by emphasising the cross-cutting chains of social, political and economic relationships that constitute networks that co-ordination will be, and is, achieved.

This differs from the three-way classification provided by Barry (1987). He identifies altruism as one option in his three-fold classification of 'ways of organising a society for the production of *wanted* goods and services: altruism, central command and the market'. He is, however, sceptical of altruism:

> Altruism presupposes that individuals, without either the incentives of personal gain or fear of punishment, will satisfy the wants of others in a system of generalised reciprocity. It is now generally agreed that this places impossible burdens on a fragile human nature and human knowledge.
>
> (1987: 161)

Writing of ways in which industry is organised, Bradach and Eccles (1989: 277) refer to 'the existence of stable long-term relationships between independent exchange partners' described variously as 'co-operative arrangements, relational contracting, joint ventures, quasi firms, global coalitions and dynamic networks'. Unlike Thompson *et al.* (1991), they do not see these arrangements as a third model to be set alongside markets and hierarchies. They advance three arguments for this. The first is that what are often presented as polarities – markets and hierarchies – are often found mixed together empirically. Second, markets, hierarchies and their 'combinations' lead to the formation of 'collateral social structures' and third, the trust arising from these collateral social structures more often complements rather than replaces markets and hierarchies. The remainder of their paper is then organised around what they call the three control mechanisms that govern economic transactions between actors: 'price, authority and trust – which map roughly on to market, hierarchy and relational contracting' (1991: 279). They conclude with an argument that:

> in some cases the overall *structure of transactions* can affect the management of each transaction. Specifically, we examine *Plural Forms*, where distinct and different control mechanisms in the same organisational structure are operated simultaneously by a company to perform the same function.
>
> (1991: 278)

From these different sources we are now presented with three sets of allocative mechanisms: markets, hierarchies and altruism; markets, hierarchies and networks; and a third which stresses plural forms that combine markets and hierarchies.

If we are to reconcile these separate but overlapping classifications, we might begin by noting the use of altruism in Barry's classification. Altruism is a noun, the definition of which, as having 'regard for others as a principle of action', embodies a statement of belief about the motive underlying behaviour. This principle of action is the opposite to the founding principle of the market system, which relies on self-interest as its behavioural or motivational foundation. These opposing motivational principles, however, provide the first step in developing a framework for reconciling *and* elaborating these overlapping sets of allocative mechanisms. By asking the question, *in whose interests are decisions made?*, it is possible to conceive of a range of replies which are rooted in opposing motivations. These could range from an assumption that people always make decisions which reflect their self-interest to an assumption that people are so altruistic that their decisions always reflect the interests of others. We have no need, at this stage in the discussion, to form any judgement as to whether one type of motivation is more commonplace or more powerful than another.

A second step in reconciling these overlapping classifications involves asking a more obviously empirical question: *who decides?* In the market, for example, decisions are decentralised to the individual, who is theoretically free to choose whether or not to engage in the exchange process which the market provides. Such decentralisation is a necessary organisational consequence of the assumption of self-interest. Only when people are free to choose whether or not they wish to enter an exchange relationship – the basis of co-ordination in the market – can they act on the basis of their self-interest. By contrast, such freedom is not an option in an hierarchical form of co-ordination where, once decisions are made, individuals are obliged to act upon them or be subject to penalties for non-compliance. Thus, parents and guardians in the UK cannot choose whether or not they want their children educated between the ages of five and sixteen, although there is choice – more for some than others – as to the type and location of that education.

Figure 3.1 is the result of bringing together these questions and their associated principles of organisation. The horizontal axis is labelled the *locus of
interest* and represents the motives underlying decision, ranging from self-
interest to altruism (self/other). The vertical axis represents the source of
decision, ranging from individuals in highly decentralised arrangements to
centralised systems where decisions are made by some appointed or elected
leader or executive group (decentralised/centralised). In each corner of the
quadrant we have named four *ideal type* forms of allocative mechanisms:
'market', 'command', 'college' and 'collective'. These ideal types form the
basis of the discussion in the next section which both clarifies their characteristics as ideal types and matches each with illustrative forms based upon
practice.

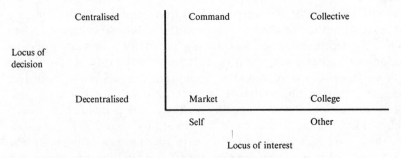

Figure 3.1 Allocative mechanisms as ideal types

Absent from these ideal types are networks. That this should be so is a consequence of their plural form. By definition, they would appear to have
characteristics that borrow from the ideal types. Their significance, particularly for management and change, however, is of considerable interest but
they are excluded from this discussion since its main purpose is to outline
allocative mechanisms as ideal types. In terms of our later discussion these
plural forms appear to represent what we call mixed economies of provision,
a practice when provision is through mixed modes of market, command,
college and collective.

ALLOCATIVE MECHANISMS AS IDEAL TYPES

In this section, an account of each ideal type is provided together with examples of actual circumstances which approximate to each. Some attempt will
be made to recognise the strengths and limitations of the four mechanisms
and, *inter alia*, the virtues of a mixed economy of allocative mechanisms.

The market

Le Grand *et al.* describe markets as:

a form of economic organisation in which the majority of allocation decisions are made through the ostensibly uncoordinated actions of large
numbers of individuals and private firms. The co-ordination of activities . . . comes about because each factor of production (land, labour and
capital) and each commodity has a price to which diverse groups respond
in a way that reconciles their separate actions.

(1992: 21)

They go on to stress the role of the price mechanism in reconciling the actions
of consumers and producers and in determining market output. Shackle
summarises the duties fulfilled by price:

It must gather information, distil it into knowledge, and deliver that knowledge to every person in the market. These three duties are all done at one
stroke, by means of one notion, that of the *price* expressed in terms of a
single good.

(1973: 4)

A number of demanding conditions must be met if markets are efficiently to
co-ordinate the production of goods and services. The market must be competitive, allowing providers and consumers freely to enter or leave. They must
also have information on all the available choices. Without such knowledge
there is the risk that choices will not be as efficient as they could be. The costs
of engaging in an exchange – contract or transaction costs – must be low relative to price. Self-interested behaviour is necessary for market success:
altruists do not respond to price signals and, therefore, convey imperfect
information. Finally, there must be an opportunity for profit-taking.
Standard economic textbooks use the term *perfect market* to describe these
conditions and it is recognised as an ideal type. In real markets, imperfections
exist – limited information, barriers to entry and exit, and so forth – and there
are circumstances where these become so severe that they require regulatory
intervention. What these and more grievous faults may be are considered
below but, first, what virtues are claimed for the market?

By placing the individual at the centre, markets recognise and harness self-
interest as a motive force in human behaviour. This is taken into account
through a decentralised system of decision-making which allows people
voluntarily to enter exchange relations. Miller notes the link made by
liberals between the market and the associated argument about individual
diversity:

liberalism begins from a premise of individual diversity: each person has
his own unique conception of what it is that makes life worth living, and
therefore is entitled to pursue that conception to the best of his ability. A
natural corollary is that social institutions should form a neutral arena in
which each conception is given an equal chance of success.

(1989: 72)

The virtues of the market are stated much more strongly by others. Thus, Novak argues that an emphasis upon individual diversity, expressed through market forms of organisation, is the basis of

> efficiency, productivity, inventiveness, and prosperity. It is also a defence of the free conscience – free not only in the economic decisions of everyday life. It is, thirdly, a defence of the pluralist order of democratic capitalism against the unitary and commanded order of socialism.
>
> (1991: 112)

While many will disagree with this degree of enthusiasm, it is likely that market forms have an appeal which is probably wider than is sometimes suggested by its critics – more especially when viewed against alternative arrangements. How many teachers in Britain, for example, would express a preference for a system of employment where, at the end of their training period, they were directed to teach in a specific school 'somewhere in Britain' (a not uncommon feature of teacher employment in many other systems)? What enthusiasm would there be for a system which abolished the market in book publishing and produced only the texts which were to be used in teaching? How extensive would be the support for a housing policy which directed where we lived as a means of ensuring that the neighbourhood of each school contained a distribution of social groups which reflected the national pattern? Certain equity benefits attach to each of these three options but they compete with other compelling human rights. If these examples illustrate that the market has more virtues than are sometimes recognised, it also has defects.

Proponents of markets recognise market failure and market imperfection. Market failure refers to public goods, examples of which are policing and national defence. While no individual has a direct interest in personally purchasing a national defence force, it is in each individual's interest to have such a force: the market mechanism's reliance upon self-interest fails to produce a wanted service and State provision is required. In addition to these, Glennerster (1992: 17) mentions environmental issues, public health and sanitation. As to 'the common education of all children in a nation', he recognises this as another example 'if viewed as a good thing'. In some ways, this is a curious observation because education fails Glennerster's own definition of the properties of public goods which include non-excludability and non-rivalry, definitions of which can be obtained from Glennerster (1992: 17). There is also clear evidence of a willingness by families to purchase education for their children.

If education fails the test of what constitutes a pure public good it may, none the less, be regarded as a quasi-public good. This would be the case if there were substantial externalities associated with its production and consumption. Externalities are benefits which are associated with a good or service but are not directly obtained by the individual consumer. Thus, if we all benefit from the qualities associated with living in a more educated society, there is a case for subsidising the cost of education to individuals so that demand increases, although Blaug (1970) provides a good critique of a number of taken-for-granted assumptions about the nature and extent of externalities in education.

In addition to the market failure associated with public goods and externalities, there are market imperfections associated with monopoly and imperfect competition. Glennerster (1992: 19–25) provides a useful explanation of these in the context of welfare services. These imperfections prevent the market from allocating resources efficiently and provide a case for non-market intervention. These criticism provide, however, an agenda for only limited intervention.

There are more fundamental critiques of the market. One is rooted in the argument that the neo-liberal view of liberty is defective because it excludes the right to resources. Another challenges the neo-liberal view that the market, as such, cannot be unjust because 'there can only be distributive injustice where there is a distributor' (Plant, 1990: 10). In addition to this critique, Plant presents the case for positive rights in terms of an entitlement to resources and uses education as an example.

These critiques of the market and the case for education as a positive right leads to the position that the State should finance these entitlements. As to the formal means of providing them, however, this could be through competition by institutions in the public and private sector, although Plant (1990: 29) envisages State provision for services such as education with rights guaranteed through citizen empowerment. This is seen as a 'counterpart to the power which the consumer has in the market' (1990: 29):

> One clear example is in education where the provision of the national curriculum could then be seen as an entitlement, with redress if the school fails to provide it. If entitlement is combined with limited-term contracts for producers, it could be a powerful mechanism for ensuring that some performance indicators are adhered to
>
> (Plant, 1990: 21)

Plant suggests that this approach is a more plausible means of citizen empowerment than 'the usual solution to the same problem proposed on the Left: that bureaucracies and professionals should in some way be made more democratically accountable'. The latter has a place at the 'macro level' but, he suggests, means very little to the individual consumer of State services (p. 30). His subsequent references to the literature on Public Choice and the weaknesses of professional accountability suggest that Plant is quite sympathetic to the view that individuals are motivated more by self-interest than altruism. In terms of Figure 3.1, it would seem that his analysis is rooted in the relationship between 'market' and 'command' as ideal types.

Command

The limitations of the market we have discussed so far provide a rationale for intervention and the need for some non-individualised decision-making. It brings us to 'command' as an ideal type. This refers to a condition where decisions are highly centralised and where we assume decision-makers choose on the basis of self-interest. It should be emphasised, however, that although 'command' is often identified with the State-owned organisations and is typically presented as the opposite of the 'market', this is not the usage here. The distinction between 'markets' and 'hierarchies' presented by Berger is relevant:

> By 'market' is usually meant an allocative and distributive mechanism, the counterpart of which is not the State but 'hierarchy' and 'planning'. Whereas the 'unit act' of markets is voluntary exchange, the 'unit act' of hierarchies is 'command'.
>
> (1990: 104)

Use of the term 'hierarchy' ('command' in our usage) as against the 'State' has at least two important benefits. First, it almost certainly has greater empirical validity. Within what is often classified as the market sector (firms in the private sector) there are organisations whose operations – at least in part – may be better understood through the language of hierarchy and command rather than market and voluntary exchange. The work of Leibenstein (1966) on X-efficiency theory, for example, represents a view of market-based organisations where the command systems are able to impose organisational goals other than the profit-maximisation which traditional economic theory predicts. Equally, the State sector has never been isolated from the market: chronic difficulties in the supply of maths teachers, for example, owe much to conditions in the wider labour market (Zabalza *et al.*, 1979). Second, in challenging the implied identity of markets with the non-State sector and hierarchy with the non-market sector, it facilitates greater flexibility in the application of words and ideas between the 'market' and the 'State'. This is already well-established in terms of the literature on Public Choice. Theorists such as Buchanan (1969, 1978) reject 'any kind of organic theory of the state which superimposes higher "values" on those of individuals' (Wiseman, 1978: 79). The public servant, for example, is viewed as one concerned with goals such as high salary, perquisites of office, power and patronage rather than efficiency (Mueller, 1979: 158). This perspective represents what Miller (1989: 43) describes as the 'underlying libertarian assumption that our moral responsibilities are entirely negative in character'; 'market' and 'command' represent this assumption about our moral character.

'Command' as an ideal type can co-exist with political processes for making decisions on the allocation of resources. In effect, the political process at a system level could provide a means by which the economically disadvantaged can use their voice to claim resources which they would not be able to obtain through the market. In an idealised form, this political process responds to the commands of the electorate and allocates resources in ways which reflect the preferences of dominant groups. If political groups do not respond to these preferences they can expect to be punished by loss of power at the subsequent election. Given the assumption of self-interest, it might be expected, none the less, that public servants will use their discretionary authority between elections in ways which reflect their self-interest – perquisites of office, a minimal commitment to their employment contract, and so on.

An approximation to the ideal type of 'command' is the national curriculum, a policy based on the premise of self-interest in at least two ways. First, to the extent that education was seen as failing to meet the needs of the economy, reforming education was necessary in order to fulfil the electoral imperative of improved economic performance. Second, the policy clearly views teachers as a group whose actions are shaped by their own self-interest. Control of the curriculum had to be taken away from this producer group whose own curriculum preferences would, otherwise, predominate.

Plant's (1990: 21) acceptance of 'limited-term contracts for producers [as] a powerful mechanism for ensuring that some performance indicators are adhered to' is an interesting statement of the inter-relationship in practice between the ideal types of 'command' and 'markets'. Whilst his view of positive rights means that he supports the need for decisions on levels of resources to be centralised and resolved through the political process, his comments on teacher tenure suggest approval for the *pupil-as-voucher* attributes of LMS, where tenure is dependent recruitment of pupils.

Thus far, it can be argued that the greater the weight we choose to attach to self-interest as a motivator of decision and choice, the more circumspect we must be of 'command' systems. Such systems are necessary, however, the more we are persuaded that 'markets' have unwelcome distributive outcomes. There would seem to be no easy resolution to that conundrum and one consequence must be eternal vigilance! An important part of such vigilance would involve a democratically accountable command system. It also requires regulations, however, which limit the discretion of providers and enhance the knowledge and powers of service users. Many of the quasi-market forms described by economists writing on contemporary changes in the public sector fall within these frameworks (see Glennerster, 1992; Le Grand *et al.*, 1992; Saltman and von Otter, 1992). In the education system as changed by the 1988 Act, for example, the co-existence of changes which approximate to 'command' and 'market' are reconcilable if their purpose is taken to be reductions in the discretionary authority of professional groups, whose self-interested behaviour was viewed as inimical to the interests of others.

What if it is the case, however, that decision-making is not reducible to self-interest? What happens if we relax the assumption of self-interest?

Collective

The idea of individuals acting outside their self-interest is developed by Sen (1977a), who introduces concepts which take us towards altruistic forms of behaviour. Sen's concept of 'commitment', for example, cannot be incorporated into a standard self-interest-based model. An example of commitment would be where the thought of torture to someone else does not make you feel sick but you believe it is wrong and are prepared to do something to stop it. 'One way of defining commitment is in terms of a person choosing an act that he believes will yield a lower level of personal welfare to him than an alternative that is also available to him' (Sen, 1977a: 92). Commitment is a case of 'counter-preferential choice' and is closely connected with an individual's moral code.

Miller's (1989) examination of altruism provides a more extensive typology than Sen's concept of 'commitment' and counter-preferential choice. He identifies six types of altruists: from 'needs altruists' who want to know how their money is spent to 'superconscientious altruists' who will do their duty *and* that of others if they fail to contribute. The six categories are: (i) needs altruists who want to know how their money is spent; (ii) preference altruists who give because they believe it is right to do so and would, therefore, be content with cash distribution; (iii) calculating altruists whose behaviour in giving will depend upon calculations on how others will behave; (iv) reciprocal altruists who will contribute on condition that others will; (v) conscientious altruists who acts on the assumption that others will act similarly; (vi) superconscientious altruists who will do their duty and that of others if they fail to contribute. Miller argues that whilst some types of altruists would give under any circumstance, others are likely to give only within the framework of a welfare state. This issue is important as it affects the welfare consequences of a taxation-based welfare system. 'Calculating' and 'reciprocal' altruists, for example, might be expected to give only if they were confident that others would also do so. A society of superconscientious altruists, on the other hand, would not require a system of compulsory taxation and such a system diminishes the welfare obtained from the act of giving. If we were to conclude that more altruists are of the calculating and reciprocal variety rather than the conscientious and superconscientious types, the argument that social welfare is increased through a compulsory welfare state would be stronger. Contrary to the arguments of neo-liberals, therefore, it would be contended that enforceable agreements add more to welfare than a system based upon a voluntary principle.

Concepts such as Sen's counter-preferential choice and Miller's calculating and reciprocal altruists are important in making judgements about the means of paying for welfare in general and for education in particular. The greater our recognition of humanity as social animals who have altruistic tendencies the more we can conceive a society which owes some of its decision-making to normative considerations of what is right for people other than themselves. To conclude, further, that these altruists were of the calculating or reciprocal type, would be a more compelling reason for incorporating altruism into welfare provision through the system of general taxation. It then follows that allocative mechanisms which have a family likeness with the 'collective' in Figure 3.1 are not unlikely.

The 'collective' as an ideal type, therefore, represents conditions where decisions are taken centrally by altruists, in a society peopled principally by calculating and reciprocal altruists. It contrasts sharply with 'command' where decisions are made at the centre only because self-interested individuals recognise that their self-interest will be better served by some decisions being centralised. The social order of the 'collective', on the other hand, is one where its members draw satisfaction from an increase in the goods available to others *and* where there is general agreement that the efficient production of these goods and services requires complex organisations and centralised decision-making. These decision-makers would also make (altruistic) decisions on which goods and services should be produced. Such decisions – at a societal level – might well be shaped by electoral processes which, in terms of the ideal type, would be characterised by voting behaviour which reflected a concern for the welfare of others rather than self.

To what extent, in practice, can we identify forms of resource allocation which approximate with the 'collective'? Consider these comments by Titmuss (1970) on the creation of the Health Service:

> The most unsordid act of British social policy in the twentieth century has allowed and encouraged sentiments of altruism, reciprocity and social duty to express themselves; to be made explicit and identifiable in measurable patterns of behaviour by all social groups and classes.
>
> (1970: 225)

Far from being an unlikely form of social organisation, therefore, many of the creations of the Welfare State have a resemblance to the 'collective' as an ideal type. This resemblance is based, to an extent, on the proposition that the electoral support for the main structures of the Welfare State, not least a State-financed education system, is based upon a degree of altruism, grounded perhaps in an elemental principle of natural justice. We are suggesting that State finance of schools does not arise solely from the politics of self-interest – 'command' – but from the belief that it is right. Moreover, we are not aware of any compelling evidence which suggests that popular support is declining for continued state finance of schools. There is also evidence that some local authorities, in devising their local management funding formula, were able to allocate more money to schools serving disadvantaged communities than had been the case earlier (Thomas and Bullock, 1994).

The resemblance of the 'collective' to the creations of the Welfare State is also based on the degree of autonomy allowed to workers in the welfare services. For many years, arrangements for their management and accountability appear to have owed much to the view that staff were working on behalf of their clients. The supervisory regime was minimal. In education, for example, a survey undertaken by the DES in the mid-1970s on local authority arrangements for monitoring the curriculum showed few procedures in place. Moreover, some authorities replied that it was not their business to monitor the curriculum (DES, 1977). Such limited arrangements for central monitoring would be consistent with a society where choices are shaped by codes of altruistic behaviour; resources spent on monitoring the curriculum would simply be unnecessary. Unlike continued public support for the provision of education, it is less obvious that the public now view teachers as sufficiently altruistic to continue their work with the minimal supervision typical of the past.

College

In 'collective' forms of resource allocation, welfare is derived impersonally from the act of giving. In the 'college', by contrast, there is more likely to be a personal connection between the provider and the recipient. Indeed, the title of this ideal type was chosen because it has the merit of creating an image of relatively small groups, where the consequences of an individual's actions upon others can be anticipated. This addresses some of Barry's (1987: 161) scepticism about altruism, which is based not only on his views about a 'fragile human nature' but on how information on needs would be transmitted in a large society. His scepticism notwithstanding, he concludes by suggesting that 'altruism is only conceivable in very small communities where there is broad agreement about ends and purposes'. Whilst we might not, in practice, expect such organisational structures to exist in a pure form – any more than any of these ideal types – they may well provide conditions which might be approximated.

In the case of the school system, for example, the motivation of many of our 300,000 governors may well be some form of altruism. Indeed, it is one of the paradoxes of the 1988 legislation that the implementation of the market-like LMS involved giving formal powers over resources to governing bodies, many of whom may have taken on the post as an expression of social commitment – although probably expressed for many as a concern for the welfare of 'their' school.

Where ideal types give way to a more complex social reality of mixed motivation, it is appropriate to recognise some form of altruistic behaviour as a component of the commitment of some working groups. The self-image and rhetoric of professional groups, for example, often lay claim to modes of behaviour which place the interests of clients ahead of those of the service provider. We do not need to accept such a rhetoric uncritically – and we must also recognise the self-interest which underlies paid employment – but we should not also dismiss the readiness of some to work long hours in demanding environments because of moral codes which include principles of service to others. Indeed, in terms of the stronger market orientation of LMS, an important empirical issue is the extent to which altruistic decisions will confound *some* of the anticipated outcomes of the market; in Chapter 8, we examine evidence of inter-school co-operation introduced to counter the pressure on schools to compete against each other.

We might also note Titmuss' proposition that altruism draws forth acts of reciprocity. One of the benefits he associated with the collective provision of welfare services was that it recognised and encouraged altruistic behaviour. If this reasoning is correct, it might equally be asserted that more emphasis upon self-interest will draw forth reciprocity in its kind. However, this is to anticipate some of the issues which arise if we begin to consider a practice where allocative mechanisms are mixed models of the *ideal types* and where the emphasis as between *types* is changing.

MANAGING SCHOOL SYSTEMS

In moving away from a consideration of ideal types, we might consider our choices. Do we accept a model of humanity which assumes counter-preferential choices and certain forms of altruistic behaviour, believing that some decisions are taken for reasons of duty and others on the basis of some concept of human rights? If so, are we required to reject the view of humanity driven by the motive of self-interest and its manifestation as the 'economic man' of Public Choice theorists with their abiding concern for developing rules for coping with the 'free-rider' problem? Or is this choice a false prospectus and instead we have to make sense of a world where forms of self-interest and forms of altruism not only co-exist in a society but are also embodied in each individual in that society? We do well to recognise, for example, that protagonists of the market do not reject the existence of altruism but argue that it is not a reliable basis on which to ensure the production and distribution of goods and services. We might also note that Miller was reluctant to assume a society of superconscientious altruists and was inclined to rely upon a compulsory taxation system as a means of ensuring the continuing contributions of calculating and reciprocal altruists.

Making sense of a society where, for the most part, elements of self-interest and altruism are contained in all its members suggests that we might expect the production and distribution of goods and services to occur through a variety of allocative mechanisms. Since these would not be *ideal types*, we would expect an incidence of *mixed models*. Indeed, it is a central argument of this chapter that we cannot choose – absolutely – between market and non-market forms of producing and distributing educational services; not only do our examples suggest forms of allocation which *approximate* to each of the ideal types but we suggest that *all* are necessary for the working of our school system, if we are to accommodate their failings and take advantage of their strengths. We hope it is also clear that in an activity as large and extensive as a school system, there is no single allocative mechanism but very large numbers of them. The co-existence of 'command' for the curriculum, the 'market' of LMS and the 'college' of professional commitment are merely illustrative of the complex mix of allocative mechanisms which mean we necessarily occupy a mixed economy.

Two fundamental issues are consequent on our proposition that we necessarily occupy a *mixed economy* of allocative mechanisms for providing education. The first of these is the premium it places on empiricism so that, as we argued on p. 16 possible inter-actions between components of a reform can be understood: an example illustrates the significance of empiricism.

The need for empiricism

Work we have done on the funding of schools shows that some LEAs used the change to formula funding to increase their support to schools with a high proportion of pupils with additional educational needs (Bullock and Thomas, 1993a). In terms of the typology in Figure 3.1, such LEAs would be using their discretionary powers in ways which approximate to the 'collective'. How might such decisions inter-relate with the 'market'-centred changes which have altered schools into cash-limited cost centres with jobs dependent upon pupil recruitment? If the level of support for a pupil with additional educational needs is very high, some schools may be quite keen to recruit them – targeting pupils who bring in high revenue. The extent to which this is (legally) possible, however, will depend upon another allocative mechanism – the rules on admission arrangements. These rules are often defined in terms of distance from school but, in some LEAs, are more complex and include factors like the curriculum orientation of the school. Differences between LEAs in these rules will affect the discretionary power of schools in any competition for pupils and in the differentiation which may occur in patterns of recruitment. It will also be affected by ethical judgements, whereby some head teachers may refuse to employ 'marketing' strategies.

What we are suggesting is that different configurations of the formula, admissions rules and the ethical position of head teachers may have quite different effects in terms patterns of pupil admissions and, therefore, who gets what, where and from whom. More importantly, however, it was ever thus. Before LMS was introduced, there were rules governing admissions which, in some LEAs, gave schools more discretionary power than schools elsewhere. On funding, we ought not to conclude too hastily that arrangements before 1988 were necessarily more equitable than new procedures. The old system was subject to political manipulation which did not necessarily favour pupils and schools with additional needs, and there were opportunities for head teachers to take advantage of local rules, procedures and practices to the benefit of their school. Among the important findings of an early study of schools costs by Hough (1981) was not only the lack of information on costs but the difficulty the researchers had in providing explanations for significant differences in spending levels on comparable schools in the same LEAs. Moreover, where the complement of teachers was determined on the basis of a formula, such as the pupil–teacher ratio, the inter-action with the labour market for teachers may well have meant that the more socially advantaged schools had more highly paid teachers (Zabalza *et al.*, 1979; Smithers and Robinson, 1991). In effect, whilst policies may have been pursued which ignored the workings of the teacher labour market, they did not prevent the labour market having an effect.

We hope we are not being misunderstood. In setting out some merits of the new forms of allocative mechanisms and some de-merits of older forms, it should not be thought that we are offering a defence of the new regime. Our argument is that we must try and understand the empirical complexity of these allocative mechanisms if we are to manage them purposefully. This brings us to the second issue consequent on managing a mixed economy – a need for clarity of purpose.

In rejecting as over-simplistic any choice which juxtaposes 'markets' against some alternative(s), the need becomes more urgent for clarity about the purposes of education and the wider social principles it is expected to meet.

Purposeful decentralisation

We reject the view that either centralisation or decentralisation is good in itself. We also reject any simple choice between one allocative mechanism as against others. The case for or against decentralisation and for or against markets is subject to the larger test of how they contribute to achieving the purposes of education and the individual, social and economic principles subsumed within them. Only if we are clear about these purposes and principles can we begin to assess the 'rightness' or suitability of a particular combination of centralisation and decentralisation and the desirable mix of allocative mechanisms. Clarity about purposes and principles then provides a basis against which we can interrogate evidence on the effect of specific forms of decentralisation and the impact of changes in the mix of allocative mechanisms. Such clarity is a precondition for the purposeful design both of the mix of centralisation and decentralisation and the mix of allocative mechanisms through which we provide educational opportunities. It means we cannot express a view on whether or not decentralisation is a 'good thing' without assessing its effects against a conception of wider principles and purposes. These provide the theme of the next chapter.

Chapter 4

Purpose and principles in decentralisation

Decentralisation is not an end in itself but a means for achieving other ends or purposes, some of which are by no means always educational in their orientation or emphasis. In some systems decentralising the responsibility for meeting some of the costs of education to families is primarily motivated by a concern for controlling and reducing the charge of education on the public sector. Whether or not the size of the public education budget is a concern for a government and a reason for decentralising, however, the case may none the less have an explicitly educational rationale. In England and Wales, for example, that part of decentralisation which has given schools control over spending priorities was presented as an opportunity for schools to match resources to their own assessment of educational needs and priorities – in this sense enhancing their role as educationists. Elsewhere, educational ends are obvious and direct, as in North Rhine Westphalia where the intention was to enhance the quality of the curriculum by giving teachers greater control over teaching programmes (Haenisch and Schuldt, 1994).

This diversity creates dilemmas for identifying criteria by which we assess the impact and success of decentralisation. One option is to apply criteria which are consistent with the declared goals of policy; if this is cost reduction, we can verify whether this has occurred. If, on the other hand, a declared aim is the democratisation of school governance it would seem both appropriate and essential to assess whether that is being achieved. The advantage of such an approach is that by using criteria which are consistent with declared policies, outcomes can be evaluated in their own terms. We suggest, however, that such an approach has limited merit for assessing the impact of decentralisation: a policy which decentralises some of the costs of education from the public budget to the family budget can certainly be evaluated in terms of its effect on the public budget but not to ask wider questions as to its consequences would be regarded by many as an unacceptable omission. We would, therefore, expect widespread agreement for a view that policies should be evaluated in ways which are wider than their publicly stated purpose. Identifying the framework for such an evaluation is the principal purpose of this chapter and we do so in the two stages represented by the two main sections of the chapter.

In the first section we introduce three distinct descriptions of the nature and purpose of education. A full and adequate treatment of each of these is not within the scope of this book but we include them in order to recognise the diversity of views and the nature of the debates arising from them. Not to do so is to risk adopting a *taken for granted* view that education is defined by what schools or school systems do – or claim that they do. We conclude the section with some discussion of whether it is legitimate to give primacy to one set of purposes as against others. In this respect, the discussion engages with the much larger controversy in philosophy and in social science about the nature of knowledge. This leads into the second section where we derive and identify four principles which, we argue, provide the basis for evaluating the impact of decentralisation. These are autonomy, accountability, efficiency and equity and we consider why each is a legitimate principle for evaluating reforms in any system. They are drawn upon subsequently for the comparative survey of decentralisation in Chapter 5 as well as providing the organising principles for the four-chapter case study of decentralisation in England and Wales.

THE NATURE AND PURPOSE OF EDUCATION

The nature and purpose of education is itself a matter of controversy. It is not surprising, therefore, that the criteria by which we assess the performance of students, schools and school systems are themselves matters of dispute. Their nature and extent would be the basis of a study in itself and our purpose is more limited, concerned to signal the depth and extent of controversy by reference to different views. We provide two brief vignettes and one slightly longer, all three hopefully sufficient to illuminate the larger debate.

Vignette 4.1: Education as an end in itself

It is more than a quarter of a century since Peters published *The Concept of Education* (1967) and with Hirst *The Logic of Education* (1970), yet their analysis remains a powerful statement of education as a concept and process. In his examination of educational process, Peters emphasises the moral dimension of the activity. This applies to content and procedures:

> if something is to count as 'education', what is learnt must be regarded as worthwhile just as the manner in which it is learnt must be regarded as morally unobjectionable; for not all learning is 'educational' in relation to the content of what is learnt.
>
> (Peters, 1967: 12)

He goes on to argue that this moral dimension implies no commitment to content, such content being contingent upon the standards of valuation within any particular social system. He also argues that the procedures of education must be 'morally legitimate'. Given that what counts as 'morally legitimate' is based on values which are by no means universal, this position has some resonance with relativist arguments in social science. Upon further reading of Peters' work, however, it becomes less certain that the position he is adopting is relativist. He is, for example, able to identify attitudes 'implicit in the practice of the teacher':

> desirable things such as a passion for poetry, nuances of style and argument, objectivity towards facts, respect for persons; undesirable things such as partisan allegiances, contempt for people of different persuasions, bad manners, and class-consciousness.
>
> (Peters, 1967: 18)

He argues that education requires an ability to grasp underlying principles and not 'mere knowledge' as well as an 'all-round type of development'. On the latter, he poses a problem:

> is the saying 'Education is of the whole man' a conceptual truth in that 'education' rules out one-sided development? Or is it an expression of our moral valuations about what is worthwhile?
>
> (Peters, 1967: 15)

Despite this caution, however, he later emphasises the importance of critical thought as a key educational process:

> Societies can persist in which bodies of knowledge with principles immanent in them can be handed on without any systematic attempt to explain and justify them or to deal honestly with phenomena that do not fit. Fixed beliefs are thus perpetuated. When this is done we are presumably confronted with what is called indoctrination; for indoctrination is incompatible with the development of critical thought.
>
> (Peters, 1967: 23)

He suggests that this is not easily developed because of our tendency 'to believe what we want to believe', and he cites Plato's idea of 'thought as the soul's dialogue with itself' as a metaphor expressing the inter-play of reason and belief which is necessary for developing our capacity of critical thought (p. 25). It is a concept of education which contrasts vividly with the statement of aims and objectives of the Department for Education and Employment.

Vignette 4.2: Education for work

The DfEE's (1996: 6) current statement of aims and objectives provides a view of the present governments sense of the nature and purpose of education. We cite it in full:

THE AIM
To increase the nation's competitiveness and quality of life by:

- raising the levels of educational achievement and skill for all through initial and lifetime learning;
- the advancement of understanding and knowledge; and
- promoting a flexible and efficient labour market.

THE OBJECTIVES

- To raise general standards of educational and skills achievement and ensure progress towards the National Targets for Education and Training.
- To help unemployed and other disadvantaged people into work.
- To encourage employment patterns, practices and attitudes which promote individual choice and enterprise and remove barriers which prevent entry into the market.
- To equip young people for the responsibilities of adult life and the world of work.
- To enable individuals to realise their full potential by achieving skills and qualifications at the highest level of which they are capable.
- To encourage people to take greater responsibility for their own development.
- To encourage lifetime learning so that people can keep their skills and knowledge up to date and respond flexibly to the changing demands of the labour market.
- To enhance choice and diversity in education and training.
- To provide a framework to encourage employers to invest in the skills needed for competitive business and a successful economy.
- To promote women's interests in education, training and employment; and to promote effective equality of opportunity for people from ethnic minorities, people with disabilities and older workers.

While we recognise that the statement of aim includes reference to 'quality of life', the objectives clearly indicate that this is to be increased by improving the skills and achievements of people in work. What is pervasive is a concept of education which values the contribution it can make to the economic capacity of people. Entirely missing, for example, is a view of education as contributing to the development of an individual in ways which might contribute to the quality of their life outside work or the role of education as an end in itself. Thus, the position seems to be that what schools or colleges do should be judged in terms of functional employment. We find it extraordinary that the test which the DfEE applies to the achievements of the education system of one of the richest countries is whether it makes us better workers! This elision of quality of life with conventional economic measures of standards of living stands in marked contrast to critiques and practical alternatives being developed by philosophers such as Nussbaum and economists such as Sen (Nussbaum and Sen, 1993). Such an alternative is illustrated in the UN Development Programme's *Human Development Report 1990*:

Human development has two sides: the formation of human capabilities – such as improved health, knowledge and skills – and the use people make of their acquired capabilities – for leisure, productive purposes or being active in cultural, social and political affairs . . . According to this concept of human development, income is clearly only one option that people would like to have, albeit an important one. Development must, therefore, be more than just the expansion of income and wealth. Its focus must be people.

(1990: 10)

Here we have a view of human development which challenges the traditional practice of relying on national income statistics as a proxy for social welfare – standard of living – comparisons. Alongside the measure of GNP, the UNDP report produces indices of human development which incorporate data on items such as life expectancy at birth and adult literacy rates. The resulting human development index (HDI) is none the less an instrument which focuses on measurable attributes rather than more complex notions of human fulfilment and quality of life. The point of the HDI here is the contrast it provides with the DfEE: although both focus on 'measurables', it is possible to have a breadth of measures which challenge the dominance of GNP. The resulting Human Development Index (HDI) produce some significant changes in rankings: the USA drops seventeen places (129 on GNP to 112 on HDI) whilst Sri Lanka rises 45 places (38 on GNP to 83 on HDI). In essence it is an approach which takes the view that, of two States with comparable levels of GNP, the one with a better distribution of key attributes of life – such as life expectancy or higher levels of literacy – has the higher level of human development.

The implications for education of this approach have been explored by Doyal and Gough (1991) and, together with some observations based upon Peters' work, provides the basis for the third vignette.

Vignette 4.3: Education for development

In an examination of 'universal' human needs, Doyal and Gough identify education as integral to the development of the capacity to participate properly in social life. As to their definition of education, they use UNESCO's definition of learning, which is more general and, therefore, less demanding than Peters' concept of education:

any change in behaviour, information, knowledge, understanding, attitudes, skill or capacity which can be retained and cannot be ascribed to physical growth or to the development of inherited (instinctive) behaviour patterns.

(1991: 214)

As compared with Peters, this definition seems to us to lack a 'morally unobjectionable' feature and allows, for example the skill of breaking into and driving away cars to count as 'learning'. The definition leads them to refer to 'the linguistic, numerical and scientific skills to prepare them for the employment tasks available' (1991: 182) which may be closer to a concept of training as against

Peters' of education. Their general concern, however, is the development of those capacities which 'enable members to understand and interpret the rules of that culture', a position which bears some similarity to Peters' emphasis on critical thought and they summarise the capacities which need to be developed in an individual as *autonomy of agency* and *critical autonomy*. Contained within *autonomy of agency* are notions of *understanding* and a *psychological capacity* to act:

> individuals express their autonomy with reference to their capacity to formulate consistent aims and strategies which they believe to be in their interests and their attempts to put them into practice in the activities in which they engage . . . Three key variables affect levels of individual autonomy: the level of *understanding* a person has about herself, her culture and what is expected of her as an individual within it; the *psychological capacity* she has to formulate options for herself; and the objective *opportunities* enabling her to act accordingly.
>
> (1991: 59–60)

They go on to consider the implications of this concept of autonomy for the *provision* of education which should be made, and suggest that it means:

> a core curriculum of subjects, more or less the same for all cultures, including basic numeracy, general social skills, physical and biological processes, general and local history and vocational abilities which are relevant to further employment. Ideally, learning of this kind readies students for active participation in the entire spectrum of practices/choices on which the continuation and, hopefully, the improvement of their well-being depend.
>
> (1991: 215)

This statement includes a clear message about part of what education-as-schooling does in terms of contributing to an individual's economic well-being, by inculcating skills and capacities which enhance employability and, in doing so, the authors make assumptions about continuing labour patterns. In terms of a more fundamental analysis of education, however, the absence of clarity about the process of education makes this a more limited concept than that proposed by Peters. It may be that more is intended than is stated and, in an earlier chapter, they do suggest that *autonomy of agency* is 'compatible with relatively high levels of critical reflection' (1991: 68). None the less, it is in their second concept of *critical autonomy* that we find an implication of process which is closer to that required by Peters' definition of education:

> To criticise and to make choices *between* the current rules of one's own culture and the rules of others requires a broader transcultural knowledge. However proficient someone is in knowledge of her own culture she will be unable to subject it to searching scrutiny without a knowledge of other social systems and an understanding of the rules of comparative method . . . a curriculum . . . must include the teaching of *different* cultural traditions and provide a forum for these to be discussed and debated openly.
>
> (1991: 216)

The achievement of *critical autonomy* is contingent, however, upon political free-dom: 'For critical autonomy to be a real possibility, individuals must have the opportunity to express both *freedom of agency* and *political freedom*' (1991: 68). It should be noted, Doyal and Gough argue that further and higher education are the means for developing this wider consciousness, and access to higher educa-tion is suggested as a proxy indicator of critical autonomy. That critical autonomy must await further and higher education is, we would argue, unnecessarily cau-tious about the capacities of younger learners and, limited in the sense that it seems to assume that this wider consciousness should be developed – or is most appropriately developed – in educational institutions. It also appears to neglect the multi-cultural nature of most societies and, indeed, of the ways in which, in many countries, the media bring information about other cultures into homes. These are circumstances which require schools to work with young people in developing frameworks for understanding the rules of different cultures and to be able to use 'comparative method' to discuss and openly debate 'other social systems'. Such approaches to the curriculum would, moreover, contribute to an understanding of their own culture and its rules for participation.

In terms of our own position, it is our view that education implies a concept of the curriculum which assumes learning to be a participatory activity and, in this respect, has clear implications for pedagogy. It is unlikely, for example, that effec-tive preparation for active participation in society will be facilitated by a pedagogy which relies on passive learning. The principle of participation can also be inter-preted as requiring some discretion over what is taught, a core curriculum being complemented by local choice over the remainder. The degree of curriculum cen-tralisation might be assessed against this model, examining the size of the core and the degree of discretion. In this respect, it becomes apparent that in defining purpose, it is impossible to ignore issues of educational organisation, including the distribution of responsibilities between the centre, the region, the school and the family. In other words, the 'mapping' of responsibilities shown in Figure 2.1 (p. 15) begins to provide some evidence on the extent to which a system represents conceptions of *autonomy of agency*: a wholly centralised curriculum, for example, may be inimical to an adequate manifestation of autonomy.

Each of these vignettes puts forward somewhat conflicting notions of the nature and purposes of education. They also illustrate both the way in which education is an essentially contested concept and how its organisation is con-sequent upon purpose. The nature of these contests manifests the continuing debate about the status of knowledge in the social sciences.

Defining educational needs

Doyal and Gough directly tackle the nature of the relativist debate in social science and its impact upon the idea of human needs represented in the *Human Development Report*. They begin by rejecting the view that 'only

individuals can decide goals to which they are going to attach enough priority to deem them needs' (1991: 9). Integral to their thesis is the proposition
that implicit in the position of several schools of thought in the social sciences is an appeal to some external and objective concept of human need.
This proposition is argued in and through their critiques of orthodox economics, the New Right, Marxism, cultural imperialism, radical democrats
and phenomenological arguments. Each, they argue, makes some appeal to
an external and objective conception of human need and brief reference to
their analysis of the New Right's position illustrates their argument:

> When we consider the New Right we are confronted with the problem of
> implicit non-preferential standards – the belief that some preferences are
> objectively more important than others. For adherents are not morally
> neutral about capitalism. They believe that it is a *good thing* – that the pro-
> ductivity and freedom which they claim it engenders is worth encouraging
> and defending.
>
> (1991: 24–5)

In commenting on some critiques of cultural imperialism, they observe a 'frag-
mented relativism' which has 'proved to be both incoherent and politically
destructive' (1991: 29):

> relativism in the name of attacks on cultural imperialism, racism or sexism
> only sounds plausible when agreement already exists about who and what
> is to be regarded as good or bad. It backfires, however, when it is realised
> that cultures of oppression are still cultures with their own internally con-
> sistent moralities . . . British imperialism constituted a coherent culture.
> Why then do radical pluralists believe it to have been morally wrong unless
> they believe that there are some things that are just not morally acceptable
> whatever the culture?
>
> (1991: 30)

In their own challenge to relativism, Doyal and Gough argue:

> All of the examples of relativism which we have examined thus far have
> attempted both to denounce universal standards of evaluation with one
> hand only to employ them to endorse some favoured view of the world
> with the other.
>
> (1991: 33)

By contrast, they argue that the consistent relativist:

> must not chop and change in this way. But the consistent relativist – one
> who regards the whole of social life as a 'construction', each aspect of
> which has no more or less veracity than any other – enters a moral waste-
> land into which few have feared to tread.
>
> (1991: 33)

In such a wasteland, '"objectively", there is not much to choose between anti-Semitism and humanitarianism. Racism will appear vicious to a humanitarian while humanitarianism will appear vapid to a racist' (Feyerabend, 1978: 8–9). In rejecting this wasteland position and in arguing for the existence of an implied concept of need in a wide range of social science thought, Doyal and Gough go on to argue that we are able objectively to choose between alternative social conditions:

> A wide range of concepts concerning the evaluation of the human condition seems inextricably linked to the view that universal and objective human needs do exist . . . Human needs, we argue, are neither subjective preferences best understood by each individual, nor static essences best understood by planners or party officials. They are universal and knowable, but our knowledge of them, and of the satisfiers necessary to meet them, is dynamic and open-ended.
>
> (1991: 2–4)

This is a view which suggests that it is possible to identify educational needs in ways that are valid and allow inter-personal comparisons. It is an approach which also seems to be consistent with the views of Evers and Lakomski who propose a relationship between moral reasoning and our social theories: 'moral reasoning is embedded in theory laden reasoning in general, and develops most readily along with our overall theory of the world' (1991: 189). They go further and argue that

> maintaining the social relations of inquiry is as relevant to moral theory as it is to empirical theory . . . The common theoretical virtues of problem solving and promoting the growth of knowledge are used to adjudicate rules or principles of social and administrative practice.
>
> (1989: 186)

In this way, the openness of theories to a continual process of testing for consistency, simplicity and comprehensiveness also becomes a defence of the 'open organisation and community' (1989: 186–7).

Evers and Lakomski's proposition that the social relations of inquiry can be used to adjudicate rules of social and administrative practice have a particular relevance for us in focusing our analysis on decentralisation. While we have set out three perspectives on the nature and purpose of education, it remains for us to consider how decentralisation might contribute to achieving purposes arising from those perspectives and the general principles we can use in assessing its impact.

ASSESSING THE IMPACT OF DECENTRALISATION

We indicated at the beginning of this chapter that we propose to use four concepts in our analysis of the nature and impact of educational decentralisation.

These four – autonomy, accountability, efficiency and equity – raise central questions against which systems can be assessed and compared. We introduce them here and apply them as part of a framework for the comparative analysis in Chapter 5 and the structure of Chapters 6, 7, 8 and 9 on the case study of England and Wales.

Exploration of the way in which decentralisation has changed autonomy addresses the question *who is taking more control and/or less control over decision-making?* Greater centralisation of the curriculum, for instance, lessens the autonomy of educators in schools while delegation of responsibility over resources strengthens it.

Accountability is concerned with studying the question *has the dialogue of accountability improved or worsened?* The choice of the word 'dialogue' signals our concern that performance is not easy to measure and what is required is dialogue of accountability between providers of educational services, their funders and 'clients'. If education were to be provided in a perfect market, marketeers would argue that accountability would happen automatically in the sense that unwanted services would not be bought. Given the mixed economy of exchange, however, it is vital to assess the impact of decentralisation upon dialogues of accountability.

In the definition of efficiency that we apply, equal status is attached to 'what is got out' as well as to 'what is put in'. 'What is got out' of a system can clearly be related to educational values and purposes and, in assessing and comparing the impact of decentralisation, the question it raises is, *in the context of educational purposes, has the match between resources and needs been improved or worsened?*

The fourth evaluative concept we apply is equity and its concern with who benefits. In effect we pose the question of *has decentralisation made the system more or less fair?* We examine these concepts below.

Autonomy

In a comparative analysis of how decentralisation has affected autonomy, we apply this concept at three levels: the autonomy of the individual learner; the autonomy of the educator; and the autonomy of the institution.

A common theme of each of our vignettes of education is the contribution they make to individual autonomy. Doyal and Gough place the concepts of autonomy of agency and critical autonomy at the core of human development. The former is concerned with an ability to formalise consistent aims and objectives and to put these into practice while the latter involves an ability to make choices between the rules of one's own culture and another. This has echoes with Peters' view that a concept of education must include an ability, among other things, to challenge fixed beliefs. Developing within an individual the capacities to think critically in these ways and to be able to act out those beliefs we regard as central to a concept of education and, therefore, a prime test of decentralisation. A reading of the DfEE's statement of objectives also shows some concern for an individual to be able to make choices in relation to employment, although they are significantly narrower in scope than that of Peters or Doyal and Gough. In criticising the DfEE's public position, we might observe that the national curriculum is more broadly based, although significantly it has almost no space for some critical features of human development. This includes giving attention to the idea of citizenship and, with reservation (the definition is culture-specific and assumes a democratic society) we share the view of the National Commission on Education:

> It is clear that children at school should learn about the society in which they live and how they can contribute to it. They should come to understand how decisions are made in a democratic society and how they can learn to take part in them through discussion and the ballot box. They need to know how Parliament and other democratic institutions work, and the place of the law in safeguarding our rights and freedoms. They need to understand how wealth is created. They need also to learn how they themselves can become active members of society. They must know what rights they have, but also what responsibilities they must bear as good citizens.
>
> (1993: 39)

Although it is not entirely apparent what is meant by a 'good citizen', these would seem to be essential characteristics in developing an individual's critical autonomy. Yet, unless a school in England and Wales is particularly alert to non-statutory guidance on cross-curricular themes it could easily fail to address several of these, despite a general statutory requirement to do so.

These comments indicate the importance of the nature of the formal curriculum as being one source of information for testing the nature of autonomy being 'taught' in an educational system. Another will be concerned with who makes decisions about that curriculum. In the discussion of Doyal and Gough we expressed concern about the comparative absence of statements on the nature of pedagogy, as we take learning as a participatory activity to be another test of autonomy. We would expect this to mean, normally, scope for some discretion about content, methods of teaching and learning, as well as a recognition of a need to support the learner as an active participant in the process. Educator autonomy, however, can be expected to mean more than discretion over the curriculum and how it is taught. The decentralisation of responsibility over resources is another way in which autonomy can manifest itself in a system. The ability for educators to decide the match between resources and needs is *one* of the ways by which autonomy over the curriculum is given meaning.

As with the curriculum and pedagogy, understanding the nature of autonomy over resources must include examining what it means in practice. Decentralising powers over people and physical resources to a school principal is very different from decentralising to a governing body representing a

wider community; and the quasi-market decentralisation of local management of schools, with its consequences for competition and job insecurity
also differs from earlier forms of financial delegation. These observations are
part of wider issues about the way in which teachers are organised and work
together in schools; these also need to be consistent with the concept of
autonomy of agency and critical autonomy. Failure to organise work to support autonomy would exclude a major part of their life experience from the
day-to-day practice of the freedoms, obligations and responsibilities embedded in a concept of education. An autonomy-based approach is consistent
with Evers and Lakomski's (1991) argument about the logic of an open
organisation: how we manage education should reflect the nature of the
educational purposes we have set ourselves.

We need to recognise, however, that the test of an appropriate level of
autonomy will need to take account of the practical conditions of an education system. In some parts of the developing world, for example, the extent of
the 'modern-industrial' cultural capital upon which an educational system
can draw may be very limited, such that the school system may not have the
capacity currently to sustain extensive institutional autonomy without causing damage to other objectives. There is clearly great variation in the level and
quality of the social capital invested in schooling, not least in terms of the
quality of the teaching force in different societies, and this must be a factor in
the extent of autonomy given to schools. It may be, for example, that the
degree of curriculum decentralisation needs to be a function of the capacities
of the teaching force to define their own curriculum. The less developed a
teaching force, the more likely the need for a central specification of the curriculum which offers clear guidance and materials to teachers. Set against
that, the general case for extending curriculum autonomy is strong, as is that
for pedagogy and resources. In our subsequent application of autonomy as an
evaluative criterion, we shall endeavour to take account of learner, educator
and institutional autonomy. Such an analysis, however, must be consistent
with an appropriate recognition of accountabilities.

Accountability

The autonomy we have set out above is not an unfettered licence for learners,
educators and institutions to do as they please. In its broadest sense, social
order is sustained by individuals accepting limits to their behaviour and,
indeed, part of a concept of education is about recognising and accepting the
obligations of mutuality entailed in membership of a society. Our focus here
is narrower, however, and is concerned with the accountabilities and mutual
obligations owed by stakeholders within educational systems. This includes a
recognition that in a government-financed education system there are
accountabilities by which those employed in the public sector are accountable
for the resources made available to them. There are also accountabilities to

parents and pupils and to members of the wider community. Such account-abilities, primarily between professional educators and others, must also be conducted in ways which recognise the distinctive role of educators as specialists in this activity. We do not see this accountability as a simple answerability to external diktat, whereby the what and how of teaching and learning are decided by external agencies. If that were the case, we would find it difficult to conceive how the critical autonomy of educators – to which we have referred above – could be sustained in the work setting. Rather, we envisage processes of accountability more akin to a dialogue and debate between interested parties.

Decisions on what schools do and how they do it is not an area which is the exclusive domain of any group, although different groups will have a greater voice in some areas as against others. We argue this position for two principal reasons. The first of these is the recognition that educators owe an account to a range of stakeholders for what they do: how well accountabilities work is an expression of the vitality of that society. The stronger the dialogue among groups constituting a society, the more likely that the relationships within that society are understood and shared. The second reason is the contribution which a good dialogue of accountability can make to the quality of schooling. Teaching is characterised by uncertainty and the need to make judgements in conditions of uncertainty. There is no wholly reliable guide to the best course of action in all the circumstances faced by teachers and principals. In the quintessential human activity of teaching, a method which works once with one group does not always work at other times – and seldom in the same way. For these reasons, dialogue among teachers on approaches to teaching and the support of learning can improve quality. In the same way, the management of schools can be improved through dialogue and, at a minimum, a principal giving an account to others, such as governors, can enhance critical reflection about circumstances and choices. As we argue below, accountability has a place in contributing to the efficiency of schools.

Efficiency

Efficiency is one of the more abused words from the lexicon of economics, having often been used by governments in the last decade as a code for cheapness. It is not our usage: efficiency is not to be equated with parsimony. A concern with efficiency demands that as much attention is given to what is obtained from resources as the resources themselves – 'what is got out' is at least as important as 'what is put in'. In this way, efficiency is part of a conceptual framework which, while giving attention to the resources devoted to education, gives equal status both to educational purposes and how well those are being achieved. To claim this for efficiency, however, will not dispel an anxiety associated with its application; there is a real concern that, in practice, there is a tendency to concentrate on easily measured educational outcomes at the expense of those which are no less important but for which 'objective' measures are not available. As to this concern, we take the view that, generally, efficiency in education is not amenable to being measured on some calibrated scale but will normally be an outcome of informed judgement based upon a range of information.

Central to our approach, therefore, is the view that applying efficiency to education represents *a way of thinking* which asks questions about resources in schools, for what purposes they are used and to what extent these correspond with intended purposes. It means that our concern is not only whether schools are *effective* in meeting the purposes or objectives they set themselves, but whether they are *cost-effective*, ensuring that their human and physical resources are well-matched to those purposes. While there are some differences between the strict definitions of *efficiency* and *cost-effectiveness*, they do not affect the argument put forward here and the concepts can be treated as having the same meaning. A clarification of the differences between them is given in Thomas and Martin (1996: 22–4). An earlier study notes the distinction between the effective and the cost-effective school:

> effective schools are those in which pupils of all abilities achieve to their full potential. Whether that performance is achieved using more rather than fewer resources is not, strictly, a part of the assessment of effectiveness. On the other hand, the amount of resources is an essential component of the assessment of cost-effectiveness. Thus, if two schools which are comparable in every respect are equally effective in terms of performance, the one that uses the smaller amount of resources is the more cost-effective. A school that uses its resources more cost-effectively, moreover, releases resources which can be used to promote further development. Cost-effectiveness, in this sense of the term, is highly desirable.
>
> (Mortimore and Mortimore with Thomas, 1994: 20–1)

The opportunities created for releasing resources for further development are the fundamental reason for our concern with efficiency. We take resources for education to be scarce – to an appalling degree in some societies – and with many educational needs unmet, the case for efficiency has a strong moral force. We recognise that this moral force is problematic because the more efficient school does not necessarily release resources to the less efficient, leading to the possibility of increased inequalities. Translating a *way of thinking* into an operational concern with cost-effectiveness in schools is a separate problem and one where we cannot ignore the problems of measurement. Assessing efficiency or cost-effectiveness will require qualitative judgements about schools based upon a range of information; such information, moreover, will typically be incomplete because uncertainty and limited knowledge are endemic conditions of schools as organisations. In our application of the concept to the case study of England and Wales it means relying, in large part, on the evidence of teachers, head teachers and governors and their judgement of the performance of their school. What we do not do in this book is seek to report on judgements of efficiency linked to a clear concept of education. Such a study would be timely, fascinating and difficult.

Equity

If efficiency emphasises 'what is got out' as much as 'what is put in', equity is concerned with 'who benefits?'. It is a wide ranging and fundamental question which must be alert to a range of circumstances and needs. In the first of these, we recognise and accept that equity means asking questions about the distribution of education and its benefits *between* social groups which include, among others: ethnic and income groups. Our concern about these disparities is linked to a clear value position, such that we can incorporate in our definition of equity a view provided by Secada (1989: 3) who argued that, as a position, disparities between social groups in society are 'an injustice in the educational system's distribution of its goods and that affirmative steps should be taken to remedy those injustices.' A focus upon differences between social groups is, however, too limited and fails to address circumstances *within* social groups. In England and Wales, for example, it might be argued that the national curriculum provides a statement of educational entitlement. This statement of entitlement is linked, however, to disparities in the funding of schools in different parts of the country, and between young people of different ages, which raise pertinent questions about the distribution of opportunities to which access is being gained, even within social groups. If our fundamental concern is with disparities in educational opportunities, therefore, it must extend to differences such as these, as much as between social groups.

Concern with disparities within and between social groups must not overlook the needs of *individuals*. In defining equity and giving it meaning in practice, we believe it is necessary to review the distribution and benefits of education as obtained by individuals with specific educational needs and which are not associated with conventional definitions of social groups. These might include, for example, young people with hearing and visual impairments and a whole range of other specific learning difficulties. We recognise that in the case of some individuals with specific learning difficulties there can be overlap with their social circumstances, as in those 'labelled' as having emotional and behavioural difficulties; this does not mean we can use membership of social groups as a substitute for recognising individuals' needs.

CONCLUSION

The four evaluative concepts we distil – autonomy, accountability, efficiency and equity – raise central questions: who is taking more and less control over decision-making? Has the dialogue of accountability improved or worsened? Has the match between resources and needs been improved or worsened? Is the system more or less fair? Together, they provide a means of engaging in a comparative assessment of forms of decentralisation in different education systems. Chapter 5 provides such a comparison in eleven countries.

Part II

Decentralised management in practice

Chapter 5

International perspectives on decentralisation in education

While decentralisation is recognised as a taken-for-granted international trend, its uncritical acceptance as a concept can fail to appreciate its distinctive focus in different educational systems. By drawing upon descriptions of reforms in the compulsory school sector in a wide range of national settings, this chapter illustrates this variation. Using ideas about allocations, mechanisms and mixed economies discussed in Chapter 3, the first section argues that moves towards decentralisation in different countries can be grouped into two sets, one of which has a principal focus on professionalism and the other on regional decentralisation. The second main section uses the matrix on distribution of responsibilities from Chapter 2 to describe change in each of the countries under the four headings: curriculum and assessment, human and physical resources, finance and access. The ideal types – command, market, college and collective – explored in Chapter 3 are then used in an analysis of the direction of change. For each country we also discuss the reforms in terms of our evaluation criterion of autonomy, accountability, efficiency and equity.

COUNTRY GROUPINGS

Decentralisation has had important consequences for teacher professionalism. The more market-like reforms in some systems, may in part be characterised by a tendency towards this deprofessionalisation of teachers, in some cases by enhancing the role of non-professional groups. In other systems, a set of features including, for example, the delegation of responsibility over resources to school principals and greater centralisation of the curriculum, have consequences for professionalism which result in its redefinition – increased professionalism in one area and limited in another. Other systems are experiencing a form of decentralisation which seems to be leading to an enhanced notion of professionalism. A report of five national systems demonstrates this variety.

The other set – of six systems – represents a form of decentralisation to regions or municipalities. Characteristics of these systems include a concern to shift funding responsibilities from the centre to more local levels and less well developed notions of professionalism. This set consists of six less developed countries which we sub-divide into those introducing a form of education vouchers and increasing municipal funding; those increasing both municipal and non-government funding; and those increasing contributions from non-government funds and parents.

CHANGING PROFESSIONALISM

Deprofessionalisation

England and Wales

In terms of *curriculum* and *assessment* the reforms in England and Wales have resulted in centralisation of the curriculum whereby the government specifies the curriculum and national assessment; the regional level has responsibility for advice and guidance; the school for the teaching methods and, at the family level, there is discretion to withdraw pupils from sex education. At the centre, the responsibility for *human and physical resources* is in terms of a framework for employment and standards for premises. There is some responsibility for premises at the regional level but the primary responsibility for human and physical resources rests with the school. Guidelines for the distribution of *finance* are produced by the centre; the regional level is responsible for setting total spend and the funding formula; the school is able to determine spending within the limits of its budget and may not charge fees; and the family may be invited to make small voluntary contributions. In terms of *access*, the centre specifies information to be published and approves admissions policy changes; the region sets admissions policy and administers the process; the school is responsible for the distribution of information and the family may choose schools subject to space and admissions criteria.

In terms of the direction of change, pupil-led funding and competition for pupils are just two indicators which suggest a move towards a 'market'-based system. This is coupled with greater 'command' with more power at the centre over the curriculum and the funding framework.

The reforms in England and Wales may be characterised by deprofessionalisation and loss of trust in the profession indicated by concerns about producer capture and a perceived need for greater consumer control. With respect to the ideal types in Figure 3.1 (p. 20), it amounts to a move away from 'college' towards 'market' and 'command'.

In terms of our evaluation criteria, decentralisation has been complex in its effect. The autonomy of schools has been enhanced in the area of control over human and physical resources but control over deciding what is taught has been reduced by the national curriculum. Accountability has been altered and the role of the professionals challenged – the market-like features have meant the producers have become accountable to the consumers. The impact on efficiency depends on the ability of competition and markets to improve provision. This is a theme we consider more fully in the later case study. The impact of the reforms on equity is also complex; although education remains free at the point of consumption, there is concern that competition for pupils is likely to be unequal in its effect and that this will disadvantage less privileged members of society.

New Zealand

In 1988 the *Picot Report* recommended radical devolution of power, resources and responsibilities to schools and their communities (Macpherson, 1993). The Government released a white paper, *Tomorrow's Schools*, accepting most of Picot's recommendations and the implementation process was set in train. The role of the State government has become one of regulator, funder, owner and purchaser: it reviews and audits the school system (Rae, 1994).

Responsibility for *curriculum and assessment* lies with the centre and the school. The centre is responsible for setting the framework, approving school charters, monitoring performance and providing specialist support services. Trustees at the school level are responsible for performance and establishing the school charter. Approaches to pedagogy are determined by the principal and teachers. Much of the responsibility for *human and physical resources* rests with the trustees, majority membership of the board being held by parents. Trustees' responsibilities include the appointment and dismissal of staff and the maintenance of buildings and grounds; day-to-day management responsibility rests with the principal. The centre issues guidelines for personnel, administration and governance and the national review agency assesses a school's use of funds against charter objectives. The Ministry is responsible for teachers' salaries, and salary and conditions are negotiated nationally. In terms of *finance*, the central government distributes funds and trustees allocate and manage the school's operational grant and locally raised funds. Schools can vire operational grant to teaching salaries. *Access* is to school capacity within a system of open enrolment. School boards determine admissions criteria.

The direction of change resembles that occurring in England and Wales: movement towards the 'market' is indicated by open enrolment and towards 'command' by a national curriculum and examinations framework. In terms of the analysis of Chapter 3, this appears to represent a move away from a reliance upon the professional modes of behaviour characterised as the 'college', appealing to the self-interest of the 'market'. It appears to limit the scope and authority of professional educators.

Applying our evaluation criteria then, autonomy of schools has been enhanced in terms of the management of a school's operational grant but the ring-fencing of staffing salaries makes it more limited than the system in England and Wales. Greater central control of the curriculum and assessment also limits autonomy. Accountability has been strengthened by performance monitoring against charter objectives established by the school and the government. The efficiency of the change depends upon 'market' benefits being generated. The impact of the reforms may threaten equity: the details of enrolment schemes are currently left to the discretion of individual oversubscribed schools although they must not breach the requirements of the Race Relations Act (1971), the Human Rights Commission Act (1977) and the Bill of Rights Act (1990) (Wylie, 1995).

Redefining professionalism

Australia

This description focuses on government schools in Australia. Between a quarter and one third of Australia's schools are non-government schools and include independent schools and the Catholic school system, the latter charging only minimal fees and receiving some support in the form of Federal grants. Non-government low-fee schools can receive up to 75 per cent of the costs of schooling a pupil in a government school (Louden and Browne, 1993).

Schools have formally constituted decision-making groups – known as school councils or boards – containing staff and community representatives. The role of these bodies varies across States as does the degree of control the school has over the curriculum and physical and human resources. Typically their role is one of endorsing plans and authorising budgets.

Each of the states has responsibility for its own system of education. There is, however, a similar direction of movement across States. Sharpe (1995: 12) identifies some of the key characteristics of the Australian system:

- While all states and territories are engaged in devolution, the speed of change, the aspects of management chosen for devolution, and the change processes utilised have varied markedly from system to system.
- The prime focus for change is in the areas of utilities, buildings, flexible staff establishment, local selection of executive and teaching staff, the development and strengthening of school councils and the establishment of school charters.
- Control over curriculum has tended to become more centralised in most systems.
- The most devolved systems are currently Victoria, NSW and the Northern Territory, while the least devolved is Queensland.
- The current lighthouse for devolution is the Victorian Schools of the Future project.

Reforms in Australia have led to greater centralisation of *curriculum and assessment* in terms of national competencies and consistent forms of assessment and reporting. The Australian Education Council sets national goals for schooling, a framework within which each State provides a curriculum reflecting local needs. Within State-wide policy guidelines, schools develop their own curriculum suited to needs, although autonomy is limited in the secondary sector by the Secondary Education Authority. The centre is primarily responsible for *human and physical resources*, setting the number, use and mix of staff. Responsibility over teaching staff is not delegated to schools. The delegation of resources to the school is limited to grants for items such as teaching aids, equipment, consumables and minor buildings work. However, some States such as Victoria, have recently extended delegation. In terms of *finance*, responsibility for these operational and related costs rests with the principal, in consultation with school decision-making groups. Schools may make charges and request voluntary contributions from parents for things like textbooks, student consumables, excursions and activities. *Access* is governed by a community expectation of equity and access.

The direction of change in Australia is something of a mixture: towards 'command' in terms of curriculum and staffing; 'college' and the local 'collective' with respect to the management of utilities and the degree of choice of staff because of the shared decision-making of principals with school councils.

This mix of directions suggests a redefinition of professionalism whereby the role of professionals has been altered with a diminished role in relation to the curriculum, but enhanced on human and physical resources, decisions on the latter being in partnership with schools councils. We certainly do not detect the same pressures to use 'markets' as used in England and Wales and New Zealand in order to control teachers.

The reforms in Australia suggest that professional autonomy still exists in terms of the ability to develop curricular to suit needs, albeit limited by State-wide policy. In terms of the devolution of control over operating and related costs, much of this is to the principal. Accountability has been altered, however, by the enhanced role of school decision-making groups. The potential for efficiency gains will depend in part on whether school principals use their authority effectively in matching resources to needs. Our level of information is too limited to say much about impact on equity other than to reiterate the community expectation that it should be protected.

The United States of America

Mapping the education system in the USA is complicated by the existence of States within a federal system. There is no centralised Ministry of Education and 'the real control of elementary and secondary education and hence its change or reform, still resides in the states' (Steffy and English, 1995: 28). In a break with tradition, however, national educational goals and standards

('Goals 2000') have been set at the federal level. Commenting on the system, Koppich and Guthrie state:

> the provision of public education is the responsibility of each of the 50 states, though much of the actual policy-making authority resides with the governing boards of the 15,200 local school districts . . . Because each state maintains substantial government, autonomy over education matters, the kinds of schooling reforms enacted and the rates at which they have been adapted have varied greatly.
>
> (1993: 55)

The three waves of reform (Jacobson and Berne, 1993) in the USA have primarily been driven by the perceived need to improve economic competitiveness. The first wave was initiated by *A Nation at Risk* in 1983 (NCEE) and resulted in 'more of the same', for example, longer school days and years; increased graduation requirements, increased teacher salaries. The second wave, associated with such documents as *Tomorrow's Teachers* prepared by the Holmes Group in 1986 and the Carnegie Forum's *A Nation Prepared* (1986) recognised that 'more' was not enough; rather, the teaching profession and the schools needed restructuring. This related to teacher preparation, roles and responsibilities and site-based management. The third wave, after 1990, is a drive for systematic reform, for State and national curriculum frameworks and standards and increased parental choice (Boyd, 1994). Integral to this approach to reform is the argument that it is the responsibility of schools to educate thoughtful, competent, and responsible citizens and the State to define what this means (Smith and O'Day, 1991).

An important feature of the restructuring of school systems in the United States is the inclusion of reforms alternatively referred to as school-based management, shared decision-making and decentralised management. Some form of school-based management is now widespread in America (Drury and Levin, 1993). Although the practice of school-based management varies from State to State, it can include increased responsibility for budgeting, curriculum and staffing to principals, teachers, parents and the community. In their analysis, Drury and Levin (1993) suggest three models of control with respect to school-based management: principal-control, teacher-control and community-control. Although these models do not exist in a pure form, they serve to illustrate important differences between States in their systems of decentralisation. For example, the school-based management model in Chicago is one of the most radical: decision-making powers rest with principal and parents through local school councils. The school-based management model in Monroe County is one in which decision-making rests with the principal.

The freedom of schools to determine *curriculum and assessment* is limited by federal, State and district level responsibilities. At the federal level, 'Goals 2000' set educational standards and the National Education Standards and Improvement Council has developed a voluntary national curriculum.

Graduation requirements and testing in basic skills are set by the States and district curriculum guidelines are produced at the regional level. The responsibility of the school is to modify, supplement and deliver the curriculum with the emphasis on determining the *how* rather than the *what* to teach.

Typically within school-based management, the school site governance body (school-site council, local school council, planning team, advisory team) has considerable responsibility for *human and physical resources*. School-based management usually allows the school to select the mix of staff within a State and district regulated system which sets class size, tenure and collective bargaining agreements. Areas of responsibility not typically delegated include insurance, legal fees, major repairs, custodial services, taxation, transportation and food services (Drury and Levin, 1993). In terms of *finance*, schools typically receive either a lump sum budget based on pupil numbers or a portion of the total budget, for equipment, materials, supplies and services. In addition, schools may receive direct funding from the State or federal level for particular programmes. In some systems there is total freedom to vire funds, carry forward underspend and overspend; in others the practice is restricted. *Access* is limited in some areas of the country by the bussing-in of students as a means of ensuring racial mix.

In considering the direction of change, what emerges here is an emphasis on decentralisation, notably with respect to resource choices and much less so on the curriculum. The decentralisation is more like financial delegation rather than a pupil-as-voucher market economy, although funding levels are largely based on pupil numbers. In many States the responsibilities over resources are to the principal. In this respect we observe a redefinition of professionalism, where the latter has additional power over resources but is subject to greater external influence over the curriculum.

School-based management in the USA enhances the role of the principal and, in this sense, suggests that professional autonomy has been enhanced. The system also allows some degree of curriculum modification and the degree of State specification remains low. There has clearly been some strengthening of accountability, which arises in terms of greater State influence on the curriculum and the role of schools' councils in those States which involve them in the management of resources. Whether greater efficiency arises from this will depend on how well principals assess needs and match resources to the task. Our level of information is too limited to comment on the impact on equity.

Enhanced professionalism

Germany

The unification of Germany after the destruction of the Berlin Wall at the end of 1989 has resulted in widespread policy upheaval and reform. Of prime concern is the need to 'equalise the living and working conditions in the two parts of the country' (Lehmann, 1994: 2470). Germany is divided into Länder (States), each with its own government and Ministry of Culture. Within each Land, the Ministry of Culture has overall responsibility for the education system. Aspects of responsibility in some of the larger Länder are also held at Regional and Education Authority level.

Recent reforms in some German Länder have focused on curriculum and assessment. In the Land of North Rhine-Westphalia for example, guidelines and syllabuses were issued in 1985. Welcomed by teachers, these have changed the approach to teaching. The reform, argue Haenisch and Schuldt:

> is designed to give the individual school the maximum possible scope to interpret the agreed educational principles and methodological fundamentals in its own way. Accordingly the guidelines and syllabuses are formulated briefly and on a level of abstraction allowing a wide potential for practical application.
>
> (1994: 22)

The general aim is to provide a basic framework within which teachers can develop work best suited to their own students. Within this framework, schools are required to develop their own 'school programme'. Land Ministries, however, set the number of sessions per week, authorise school textbooks (teachers select from an approved list) and establish curricular guidelines (including syllabuses and recommended teaching methods). Schools are free to determine the content of their project topics. The centre remains primarily responsible for *human and physical resources*. Most costs, particularly personnel, are fixed and met by the Länder, and little flexibility remains over the spending of the small budget for teaching and learning materials and equipment provided by the school authority. *Finance* for schooling is the responsibility of the Länder. State schools do not charge fees. The data available to us do not enable us to comment on changes in *access*.

The striking feature of the direction of change here is the relative absence of a search for various mechanisms of strong control, whether this is undertaken through the 'market' or by 'command'. In that respect, there seems to be a powerful assumption that decisions are shaped by the needs of collectivities and there is less apparent concern about self-interest – trust between groups seems to have been sustained. It is a system which remains professional in orientation with limited apparent concerns about producer capture.

Although there has been little decentralisation of responsibility for human and physical resources, curriculum reforms provide a basis for an enhanced professionalism. Trust in the professionals is illustrated by school governors having the power of inspiration and influence rather than control.

In terms of our four evaluation criteria, autonomy has been enhanced with more decisions made at the school level, particularly over approaches to teaching. There has also been an increase in the power of parents, a change which, in principle, adds to their capacity as autonomous agents to act on the basis of their preference. There has been a move away from viewing schools as governmental institutions to seeing them as service agencies. There seem to have been only modest changes with respect to accountabilities. The enhanced role of educators places reliance on the accountability to clients traditionally associated with professional roles. The efficiency of the changes will depend on how educators use their new autonomy. As to equity, the unification process is creating demands for greater equality in living and working conditions.

REGIONAL DECENTRALISATION

The second set of six national systems is drawn from less developed countries which have in common decentralisation to regional or municipality levels. Our set includes countries such as Uganda and Zimbabwe which have comparatively low levels of income but it also includes countries such as Poland, Chile and Russia where education systems are well developed and where economic capacity places the country close to the richer countries of the North. The economic development of China places it close to this group.

The context for educational reform in less developed countries requires outlining in order to appreciate their specific circumstances. In particular, issues concern access, resources and autonomy. In terms of *access*, some countries face difficulties in providing universal primary education. Lockheed (1995: 3) reports that 'according to UNESCO data, in 1990, only 76 per cent of children of primary school age were enrolled in school in developing countries'. Of those who do start school, fewer than 70 per cent reach the final year of the primary cycle. Lockheed notes that in most countries the drop-out rates are greatest for girls and for students in rural areas. Social and cultural norms in some of these countries suggest that parents place lower importance on the education of girls. A number of developing countries such as Sudan, Ethiopia, Mali and Somalia, are also afflicted by poverty, drought and war, all factors which affect access to school. While these are issues for Uganda and Zimbabwe, they are less pertinent for the more developed societies in Poland, China, Chile and Russia.

Insufficient *resources* for education is the major impediment to education in all these countries. Colclough (1993: 6) observes that 'poor countries have higher rates of population growth, and thus proportionately larger school-age populations . . . the size of the educational task facing them is greater than for the richer countries'. The costs of schooling exceed national resources in many developing countries. Lockheed (1995: 5) comments that 'according to the World Bank, between 1980 and 1990, real spending per student at both primary and secondary level fell in developing countries in Latin America, Africa and the Middle East'. Recent reforms in some of these countries focus in part on ways to diversify sources of funding for education in an effort to increase resources for education. The purpose of decentralisation of basic education in many developing countries includes diversification of revenue sources, increased accountability and greater efficiency. Even in the more developed systems of Poland, China, Chile and Russia, these are problem areas.

In terms of *autonomy*, Lockheed (1995: 18) notes that schools in many developing countries have the decision-making responsibility over the selection of textbooks but 'only in a few cases do school-level personnel have full autonomy with authority over all critical aspects of school management: budget, curriculum and personnel'. She also notes, however, teachers working in isolation and in small communities in remote areas often have autonomy over teaching methods. A consequence of this is that curriculum implementation plans are sometimes impeded. No central plan, however, is free from teacher distortion, although accountability procedures impact on implementation.

In the following discussion the six systems have been divided into three groups. The first has introduced a form of education vouchers and increased municipal funding; the second group is increasing both municipal and non-government funding; and the third group includes those increasing contributions from non-government funds and parents.

Vouchers and municipal contributions to funding

Chile

A geography of isolated and mountainous regions makes the administration of the education system in Chile difficult, although it does not prevent strong central influence. Chile has twelve autonomous regions and a metropolitan area each with their own administrative system.

Responsibility for *curriculum and assessment* is shared. The Ministry of Education sets a national curriculum for primary and secondary schools and administers national tests. Within this teachers have comparative freedom to adapt the curriculum to suit the needs and characteristics of their school. The planning of the school curriculum is the responsibility of the Centre for In-service Training, Experimentation and Educational Research, a section of the Ministry of Education. As Rodríguez (1994: 744) explains:

> the schools are free to define the curricula and syllabuses they consider adequate to comply with the objectives and content determined by the Ministry. The Ministry then has to accept these curricula, proposing changes if necessary.
>
> (1994: 744)

The Ministry distributes textbooks but schools can choose those they prefer.

Municipalities are primarily responsible for *human and physical* resources.

Reforms since 1981 have shifted responsibility for the delivery of services from the centre to the municipalities and to non-profit private schools. School premises were transferred from the Ministry to the municipality in 1980 (the Decentralisation Act) and teachers became the employees of the municipality rather than the government. Much responsibility over *finance*, however, remains with the Ministry of Education. The central government school attendance grant – a kind of government voucher – distributes funds to municipalities on the basis of the number of pupils attending school each month. The results of national tests and other social indicators are used by the national ministry of education to target additional support to the poorest schools (Lockheed, 1995). Schools are categorised as high, medium and low risk and compete for improvement funds within each category. The Ministry also provides textbooks and school meals for poor children. The Regional Development Fund makes capital grants to municipalities. With a decline in the real value of the voucher, municipality funding has increased since the reforms were introduced (to the level of 10 per cent in 1991), although their contributions are not compulsory.

Educational vouchers can be used in any non-profit-making school which, typically, are those with some religious affiliation and providing free schooling. A consequence of this has been the increase in enrolment at these private schools which, by 1990, catered for about one third of the school population. These schools also receive textbooks and free school meals but not capital grants. Additional resources brought in by more pupils in a municipal school have the effect of reducing municipal contributions. In the private sector, however, these additional funds can be used to increase the salaries of the school managers.

In terms of *access*, 80 per cent of the school population is enrolled in school and most complete the eight years of primary schooling. About 20 per cent of these repeat one or more years. The educational voucher encourages schools to compete for pupils though many parents have no real choice, more especially those in rural areas. The Ministry collects and publishes data on indicators of performance, including school retentivity, attendance, achievement of academic objectives, enrolments, and human and financial resources.

The focus of decentralisation here is from the centre to the regional level with the municipality having an increased responsibility for funding schools. The level of school funding is determined by the number of pupils – a kind of voucher – which may be used in non-profit-making private schools. This gives the system market-like features and encourages competition for pupils. These are changes which were to have echoes of those in England and Wales and in New Zealand.

In terms of our evaluation criteria, *autonomy* has been increased at the regional level with little going to schools. Formal accountability has been strengthened through national assessment. The prospect of *efficiency* gains will depend on the 'market' feature of the changes leading to better decisions on resources. As to *equity*, the reforms have impacted in terms of funding: non-compulsory contributions from municipalities favour private schools because they are able to use the resources brought in by more pupils to the benefit of the school whereas they simply reduce the municipal contribution in municipal schools.

Russia

For the proposes of this description, 'Russia' refers to the Russian Federation, one of the fifteen former republics of the Soviet Union. The system of education in Russia, like much else, is in a state of flux, as the country moves away from its communist foundations and takes on features of a market economy. In terms of education, there has been a shift from a highly centralised system in which the State determined society's needs, to a more decentralised system. Progress, however, has been hampered by insufficient funding for the implementation of reform. Nikandrov comments:

> The very important transition from authoritarian to democratic schooling (and management of it), and from strictly imposed unity to diversity will certainly be slow in most educational institutions.
>
> (1994: 5106)

A much greater proportion of the content of the *curriculum* may now be determined at school level. The system has moved from one in which the core curriculum was determined by the Soviet Union, to one which has a much smaller nationally determined framework. The Russian Federation component has been replaced by a greater regional component including native language and literature, history and geography. There is also a school-determined component based on pupil choice and optional studies. The 'educational standard' introduced by the 1992 Law on Education defines a mandatory content – the basic core curriculum – and standards within subject domains. This State standard regulates the total length of school education and academic workload per week (Lednev *et al.*, 1995: 20–1).

There has been little decentralisation of responsibility to the school level for *human and physical* resources. School councils, composed of the teaching body, elected representatives of senior pupils, and parents, were established and intended to have considerable power in the selection of staff. Because of certain problems, however, including powerlessness in practice or abuse of power, there has been a move towards the return of some powers to local government such as selection and appointment of the school head teacher.

Since 1988 the *financing* of education has shifted from the Union to the republican level. Nikandrov (1994: 5103) comments that 'attempts are being made in Russia in the early 1990s to establish a reasonable distribution of educational financing between the state, the city, and the district levels'. As in other countries facing intense financial crises, the move to decentralise to more local authorities is motivated in part by the opportunity this gives to make those authorities responsible for aspects of the funding of education. There is not yet a uniform system, however: in some centres, funding for education is directed through taxation while in others it is through a system of central allocation. Private sponsors are also being encouraged to contribute to the funding of education.

The 1992 Law on Education introduced a type of education voucher:

> In practice it means that if a student prefers a private school charging fees, the student (or his or her parents) receives a cheque for the sum that would have been spent on the student in a state-run free-of-charge institution; this cheque should in law be accepted by any private school, with the rest of the money being supplied by the student.
>
> (Nikandrov, 1994: 5103)

On *access* we have little evidence of change, although the growth of a private sector clearly re-structures the choices available to some parents.

The focus of decentralisation here involves movement from the federal level to lower levels of government which are taking greater responsibility for funding schools. The introduction of vouchers – which may be used in fee-charging private schools gives the system market-like features. A movement towards collectivities is also suggested however, by the democratisation of education and the shift in power to more local levels. In summary, the old 'command' system is being re-structured by a 'mixed economy' which retains some 'command' but appeals to concepts of 'collective' and 'college' commitment in defining the curriculum while opening the choice of school to more 'market' principles.

In terms of our evaluation criteria, the weakening of the centrally determined curriculum improves professional autonomy. Accountability has altered with a shift away from the inspection of whole regions or cities by the ministry, to greater use of inspections *by* region and city level authorities. Whether efficiency is increased will depend upon the response of the new 'mixed economy' of provision. The reliance on 'command' in the old system placed great emphasis on the centre always making the correct decisions and, in this respect, the prospect of change must be good. With respect to equity, however, the introduction of a voucher and the private sector suggests it is of low priority.

Increasing municipal and non-government funding

Poland

Poland has a population of about 40 million and is currently undergoing political and economic transformation as it moves from a communist to a market economy. It is a time of financial stringency and in the early 1990s this was reflected in a decline in educational expenditure as a proportion of GNP.

In Poland there are forty-nine *voivodeships* each supervised by a *kurator*. Each *kuratorium* is divided into a number of municipalities, or *gminas*, which range in size from those serving a population of 500 to those with more than one million.

The Ministry of Education provides *curriculum* guidelines for every grade in every subject. There is, however, no national curriculum and schools can devise their own curricula if permission is granted from their kuratorium. A core curriculum for primary and secondary schools is under development with greater emphasis on applied knowledge, foreign languages (especially English) and IT. Textbooks require Ministry approval although the monopoly of the Publishing House for Schools and Pedagogical Books is now broken. Kuratoria inspectors supervise the implementation of the curriculum and regional methodological centres train teachers in syllabus implementation, although there is growing teacher autonomy over teaching methods (Komorowsta and Janowski, 1994). Kuratoria also specify the school structure document (containing information on the organisation of teaching, number of employees etc.). Head teachers draft the document which receives approval from their gminy.

Recent reforms have led to changes in the distribution of responsibilities for *human and physical resources*. School superintendents in kuratoria are consulted in the establishment of schools; influence kindergarten and primary school systems, including the setting of area boundaries; consent to school closures and evaluate headteachers. Responsibility for the operation of some secondary schools rests with kuratoria, which also set budget and safety and hygiene regulations. Gminas have recently gained responsibility for the operation of kindergarten and primary schools (and some secondary schools), including premises and equipment. They establish systems of public primary schools, including boundaries (in consultation with school superintendents) and provide free transport for students who have to travel beyond the prescribed distance. The school director (the gminy official with chief responsibility for municipal primary schools) is responsible for hiring school principals and kindergarten managers. They evaluate head teachers in co-operation with school superintendents and consider appeals concerning the evaluation of teachers' work. School principals hire teachers and keep administrative and finance records.

As regards *finance*, the State provides subsidies for school buildings and maintenance, and teachers' salaries. The Ministry of Finance sets a formula for the distribution of these subsidies to municipalities. Kuratoria finance post-primary schools. Where gminas have responsibility for secondary schools, the superintendent makes a specific grant for the operation of these schools. All gminas have responsibility for the finance of kindergartens and primary schools, the latter since 1996. Expenses for the operation of public kindergartens are covered from municipalities' own incomes and from general subsidies. Funds for the maintenance of public primaries and municipality secondaries are met by State subsidies (in theory). These funds are meant to meet the operational costs of schools. Schools have responsibility for keeping finance records. The cost of maintaining a child in kindergarten is met by parents.

In terms of *access*, all children have the right to one year of pre-school education. Movement to the next grade in primary school is dependent on assessment and those students not promoted must repeat whole grades. Around 15 per cent of students do not complete post-primary education.

The State has been insufficiently financing the maintenance of school buildings. Transferring responsibility to the municipalities for primary school buildings is resulting in greater local investment in education although it should be recognised that gminas have a history of contributing to the costs of schooling. Greater reliance on community funding is suggestive of a move towards the 'collective'. Movement away from 'command' is also evidenced by growing teacher autonomy over approaches to teaching. This suggests a greater belief in the principles of the 'college', as described in Chapter 3.

There is evidence of enhanced professional autonomy over teaching methods. It may be conjectured that the accountability of schools to their local community has been enhanced by more local funding of schools. In addition, local communities typically hold head teachers in high regard, viewing them as community leaders. It remains to be seen, therefore, how these new local accountabilities develop in practice. Decentralisation of responsibility of funding school maintenance may attract more resources and a local concern for their efficient use. Given considerable variation in the resource base of gminas, there is a threat to equity: there have been significant differences within Poland over the extent of own-source revenues for education. (Thurmaier and Swianiewicz, 1995).

China

On the basis of enrolment, China has the largest education system in the world with 161 million pupils in compulsory schooling. The central committee of the Chinese Communist Party (CCP) instigated educational reforms in 1985 focusing on the structure, financing and administration of the education system. With the leadership of Deng Xiaoping in 1978, a 'modernising' policy within the CCP may be discerned. The principles of this policy are a move away from a centralised planned economy to a 'socialist market economy' based on public ownership. Within this context, the purpose of education shifts from the ideological promotion of communism to the need to meet the skills requirements of the 'socialist market economy'.

The State Education Commission, through expert groups, formulates *curricular* guidelines for primary and secondary schools. Within this framework, school curricula are developed to suit local needs and approved by the Primary and Secondary School Teaching Materials Board of the State Education Commission. The 1985 reforms shifted responsibility for the provision of *human and physical resources* to lower levels of government. Figure 5.1 sets out the layers of government and responsibilities for education.

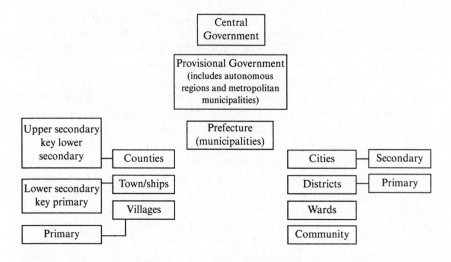

Figure 5.1 Layers of government and responsibilities for education

Thus, secondary schools are the responsibility of cities and, in rural areas, the responsibility is divided between counties and townships. In urban settings, districts are responsible for primary schools; in rural areas this falls to the villages.

The reforms addressing the *financing* of education represent a shift from a centralised system of financing with its contingent narrow revenue base to a decentralised system with a diversified base (Tsang, 1993). In the old centralised system, lower level governments gave all tax revenues to the high level government and then received all expenditures from the higher level. Since 1982, a multi-level public financing system has been in operation whereby each level of government is responsible for its own finances.

Not all educational provision is funded from taxation. Rural primary schools are financed primarily by the community. For other sectors, the relevant level of government is responsible for the provision, funding, and administration of the schools. The funds raised at these levels meet the costs of personnel and, typically, little else. Higher levels of government distribute additional funds via categorical grants for specific purposes. These grants constitute a minor fraction of the total expenditure on education. Another source of funding for schools is the social contribution – school-generated funds including those from 'school-run factories'; external resources such as loans from contractors for the school buildings, donations from industries and overseas Chinese and other compatriots (Yeung and Bannister, 1995: 60); and school fees. Tsang (1993: 10) reports that students in basic schooling do not pay tuition fees but they do 'pay nominal amounts of other school fees to support non-personnel school expenditures'. These non-government funds for education have a long history, particularly for the funding of basic education, but the amounts collected from these sources are increasing.

In terms of *access*, the enrolment of primary aged children reached 98 per cent in 1990, of which 78 per cent continued on to lower secondary school (Teng Teng, 1994).

An underlying purpose behind the reforms is a shift from the promotion of communism to a 'socialist market economy'. This shift is significant but the centre still retains control over purpose. In effect 'command' over the general direction of the system is retained while the message about purpose has been altered. However, the system is decentralising from the centre to lower levels of government to some degree. Lower levels are becoming more responsible for the funding of schools as well as for some aspects of the curriculum, suggestive of a move towards 'collectivities'. Greater reliance on local communities for funding and increasing non-governmental funding appeals to local self-interest.

In terms of our evaluation criteria, the weakening of the centrally determined curriculum improves professional autonomy and represents a greater reliance on the judgement of professional educators. This has consequences for accountability, in that there is greater reliance on the professional commitment to the pupil-as-client. The shift of financial responsibility to localities and communities may increase demands for more accountability of educators to those levels. We do need to recognise, however, that the whole concept of accountability may be viewed quite differently within the norms of the culture. As to efficiency, the move from a highly centralised 'command' system reduces the risk of mistakes being compounded across provinces and the nation as a whole. On equity, the appeal to local finance and community support might be expected to favour more advantaged groups but that will very much depend on cultural norms and attitudes. Equity, however, is threatened by reliance upon local government and community funding which may result in variation in the quality of facilities and teaching. Richer local communities can provide more resources. Further, key (or centre) schools are more favourably resourced in comparison with regular schools

Increasing contributions from non-government funds and parents

Uganda

Located in the centre of Africa, Uganda gained independence from Britain in 1962. Since that time the country has experienced the liberation war of 1979 with peace and political stability not being restored until 1986. The great majority of people live in rural areas. Population growth between 1980 and 1991 was at the rate of 2½ per cent, a decline on the earlier decade, due in part to a rise in mortality and decline in the standard of living. A little under half of the population is aged four and under.

Uganda has a centrally determined core *curriculum*. Odaet (1994) explains that the National Curriculum Development Centre is responsible for developing the national school curriculum. The syllabus for each subject at each grade, the writing of textbooks and materials, including teachers' guides, are developed by subject panels. These panels include teachers, inspectors, members of examining boards and teacher training institutions. The resulting curriculum is implemented and progress monitored, at least in theory, by the schools Inspectorate.

The Ministry of Education and Sports is officially responsible for the management and administration of *human and physical resources*, headed by the Commissioner for Education (Administration). However, a form of *de facto* decentralisation is taking place, as Odaet explains:

> Despite the historically strong central role of the Ministry of Education and Sports, finances, communication, and staffing have reduced the effectiveness of headquarters in exercising control over the district- and school-level operations. This 'de facto' decentralisation is particularly prominent in the primary education subsector where the operation of the school is the responsibility of the headteacher and the School Management Committee in which the Ministry of Education and Sports exercises influence in a limited way by nominating their representatives. The School Management Committee, with the headteacher as the secretary, oversees school policy formulation and implementation. Its activities include supervising school budgets, reviewing educational performance, overseeing student and staff discipline, and making plans for school facilities expansion and repair.
>
> (1994: 6498–99)

Education is part-*financed* by the government but money from parents is used to pay for teaching and learning materials, to supplement teachers' salaries and for capital works. Large numbers of the population do not have *access* to education. The main long-term educational priority is for universal primary education. About half of the school age population was not in primary school in 1989; the drop-out rate is high with about one third starting primary grade one completing primary or basic education. Just a quarter of those completing primary schooling continue onto some form of secondary education and, of those completing primary school, only one in four successfully complete lower secondary schools; just 5 per cent of the population gain 'O' levels.

The direction of change is towards *de facto* decentralisation enhancing the role of the head teacher and school management committee. The system, however, retains command over the curriculum. The use of money from parents to pay for teaching and learning materials, supplements to teachers' salaries and capital work is suggestive of appeals to the principles of the 'collective' and of the 'market'. The direction of change here again brings to the fore the significance of cultural norms when interpreting change. The decentralisation of greater enforceability over resources can be viewed as appealing to local self-interest or to altruism, 'market' or 'college'/'collective' or some combination. How it is judged can only properly be understood through empirical enquiry.

The autonomy of the head teacher and school management committee in the area of school policy, budgets, performance review, expansion and repair has been enhanced but is limited in terms of the curriculum. As a whole, however, the autonomy of the principal and the school has been increased. How accountability has been altered will depend on how stakeholders interpret this role in Uganda. The structural change with its reliance on community and family finance points to an expectation of greater demands on educators to be more accountable. Efficiency effects are very difficult to assess in a context where policy on finance depends so much on the basic task of finding resources. This makes equity a lower order priority, as those with resources are more likely to secure the benefits of the system. Equity is also an issue in other respects. A greater proportion of boys than girls continue on to secondary schooling and gain 'O' levels. This is explained by social and cultural attitudes, which place greater importance on the education of boys. Access to school has also become increasingly unequal as parents who cannot afford to contribute have to withdraw their children from school.

Zimbabwe

Zimbabwe did not gain independence from the United Kingdom until 1980. During colonial rule, much of the education for the indigenous Zimbabweans was organised by churches. Since liberation, in contrast to the general trend in Africa, Zimbabwe has managed to double primary enrolments in the early 1980s. This has been achieved in a country with 40 per cent of the population of school-age (Gatawa, 1994).

Zimbabwe has a national *curriculum* at primary level and core subjects at secondary. The curriculum is set at national level by subject panels, co-ordinated by the Curriculum Development Unit. Membership of these panels includes teachers, education officers, representatives from higher education, churches and teacher associations. The Curriculum Development Unit also approves the list of textbooks and learning materials for use in schools. Schools select from this list. In terms of *human and physical resources*, most schools are owned by church authorities or district councils although the centre is responsible for the appointment of teachers. Much of the responsibility for the *financing* of education rests with the central government which pays teachers, supplies materials and allocates building and tuition grants.

However, a shift towards greater community responsibility for the financing of education may be noted. Colclough (1993: 9) comments on the 'devolution of financial responsibility to communities – for the construction of schools, and to contribute to school expenses'. Until 1992, primary schooling was free but now fees have been introduced as a way of recovering some costs. Grants are available for some socio-economic groups. All pupils pay fees at secondary school. This limits *access* at secondary level. Primary schooling is compulsory and upon completion, all who so wish, and can afford to, can continue onto secondary school.

Community involvement in the construction of schools is suggestive of a movement towards some notion of the 'collective'. Moving onto families a requirement to meet some of the costs of schooling indicates an appeal to 'market' principles.

The autonomy of schools in Zimbabwe is limited by the centrally determined curriculum including an approved list of textbooks and learning materials. More local autonomy occurs in terms of school premises given that they tend to be owned and constructed by local communities. There may be moves to greater accountability in view of contributions from parents and communities. The nature of this can be expected to be culture specific and influenced by traditional relationships between teachers and their communities. Assessing the efficiency effect of these changes is very difficult and it is impossible to set aside the pressures for cost transfers to families as a way of reducing the public cost of schools. As to equity, a significant drawback of these reforms has been the growing differentiation in the quality of the provision provided by schools with those serving more affluent communities being better resourced.

CONCLUSION

Commenting on international educational reform, Fowler, Boyd and Plank observe the influence of the political and economic climate:

> The English-speaking countries, for example, have adopted market-oriented reforms to a greater extent than have the developed nations of Western Europe. These differences can be explained in terms of distinctive political traditions and varying degrees of economic crisis. Similarly, differences exist among the less developed countries. Some of them are pursuing aggressive policies of economic development, while others are experiencing mass starvation or civil war and must accord education reform a relatively low priority. The countries of Eastern Europe represent a special case. They have highly educated populations, but with the collapse of their communist regimes and command economies, they may lack the resources to maintain the educational systems that they have inherited.
>
> (1993: 154–5)

In England and Wales there has clearly been more emphasis on the operation of quasi markets than has been the case elsewhere in Europe. New Zealand has also been driven by a more explicit theoretical agenda than most other countries. This is much less obvious in Australia and the USA where the challenge to the 'producer interest' of teachers has, so far, been markedly less significant. In developing countries the agenda of restructuring has involved a focus on the realignment of the relationship between the State and the economy. In Eastern Europe much of the initial attention has been devoted to institution building. The agenda has depended, to a considerable extent, upon the initial starting point, for example with more concern for privatisation where there has been extensive public ownership. The motivations for and consequences of decentralisation depend on a range of associated factors including, as identified by Sharpe (1995), a country's political and economic climate, the change processes adopted and other concomitant changes such as cuts in funding.

These observations indicate the diversity of decentralisation and the direction of change across the eleven countries. Indeed, the organisation of the chapter is intended to represent this diversity. What is also apparent, however, is that there are limits to what we can say about these countries without more detailed information. This becomes all the more apparent when we examine in more detail the changes in England and Wales in the next four chapters. The source of this material is a three-year study of the impact of LM. Undertaken by the authors for the National Association of Head Teachers (NAHT), the LMS 'Impact' Project initially analysed information from over 800 schools and followed up 169 schools in the years 1992 and 1993. A set of thirty-eight schools was visited. What emerges from a more intensive empirical inquiry are the complexities and unpredictabilities that become apparent as we move from accounts of policy to evidence of practice.

Chapter 6

Managing autonomy
Delegation in practice

THE COMPONENTS OF DELEGATED MANAGEMENT

The decentralisation of responsibilities in England and Wales is largely about finance and human and physical resources. It is also about decentralisation to schools with head teacher and governing bodies being given the powers to make decisions. In the context of our earlier discussion of autonomy, therefore, the changes relate to two levels of autonomy – the principal and the institution – and make no direct reference to learners. In this chapter, then, our intention is to examine how the autonomy of head teachers and governing bodies has been used. Decentralisation of responsibility for finance has given schools the autonomy to make their own judgements on spending priorities from their delegated budget: it is for schools to assess needs and match resources to them. Evidence on how schools have responded to these new administrative and managerial responsibilities provides the basis for the first section of this chapter.

Delegation of responsibility over staffing has given schools the status of quasi-employer of staff; the head teacher and the governing body have the authority to decide, within the limits of their budget, how many and which staff to employ. Unlike the circumstances in most school systems, schools in England and Wales cannot now be required to accept teaching and non-teaching staff at the direction of administrative officers from a regional office. This change in the relationship of staff with their employers provides the basis for three sections in this chapter. In these we examine evidence of changes in the contractual position of teaching staff and changes in their number and distribution. It is followed by an examination of the impact of local management on the range of non-teaching staff employed in schools. The final section on staffing contains three *vignettes* on how schools have dealt with different aspects of their new staffing responsibilities.

The fifth section of the chapter recognises that, even with the degree of decentralisation that has occurred in England and Wales, there remain resources which are managed by the LEA. What these are, how head teachers and others assess their value, as well as other forms of support provided by the LEA are the main themes examined. Taken together, our focus in this chapter is both descriptive and evaluative, seeking to understand how schools have responded to the new responsibilities over resources.

MANAGING THE BUDGET

The scope of delegation

How schools spend their delegated budget is one important test of the value of local management. The case for the change would be weak, for example, if it became apparent that schools spent money in much the same way as LEAs did before the change, as it would suggest that schools are no better placed to assess needs and match resources. The absence of reliable information on school expenditure before local management was introduced makes this an impossible question to answer directly but, as an alternative, we can examine evidence on reported change provided by head teachers over the three years of survey data available to us. We set this in the context of Table 6.1 which provides some data to illustrate approximate size of budgets for smaller and larger primary and secondary schools in the survey period.

Table 6.1 Illustrative formula budgets

School	Roll	£ 1991	£ 1992	£ 1993
smaller primary	150	177,300	195,750	203,250
larger primary	250	295,500	338,750	362,250
smaller secondary	650	1,140,100	1,213,550	£1,231,100
larger secondary	1000	1,754,000	1,867,000	£1,894,000

In spending from these budgets, each school is required to work within its limit and to meet all main direct costs, including the actual salary levels of teaching and non-teaching staff working on the school site. The emphasis on meeting actual salary costs has been a matter of contention and differs, for example, from practice in Scotland; the government has remained determined, however, that schools must meet actual costs.

Budgeting and virement

Setting spending priorities

Schools and their governing bodies are able 'to vire between all expenditure heads in the delegated budget including between teaching and non-teaching staff' (DES, 1988: para. 109). Such freedom, however, is subject to various standards of financial administration (Audit Commission/Ofsted, 1993): One standard specifies that:

The budget should reflect the school's prioritised educational objectives, seek to achieve value for money and be subject to regular, effective monitoring.

(1993: 3)

The flexibility of setting priorities and being able to vire in mid-year is clearly welcomed by head teachers and is seen as one of the major advantages of LM. On the second and third questionnaire, heads responded to an attitude statement: *I welcome the ability to vire between budget headings.* Comparing the responses of 123 primary and 40 secondary heads to this statement in 1992 and 1993, the vast majority agreed or agreed strongly with the statement: 94 per cent in 1992 and 95 per cent in 1993. Similar responses were found when the set was divided into heads of larger and smaller primary schools.[2] Virement was welcomed by 90 per cent of heads of smaller primary schools (29) in 1992 and 93 per cent the following year. Of the larger schools in this sector, 95 per cent of the heads (91) in 1992 and 96 per cent in 1993 welcomed the ability to vire. *All* the heads of the secondary schools agreed or agreed strongly with the statement.

Given these freedoms, in the first survey we asked about changes in spending on books and educational equipment. These have a particular significance for schools in England and Wales because they represent those areas – traditionally known as capitation – where spending has long been delegated to schools and which are the learning resources used in classrooms. Prior to LM, schools had resources for capitation items delegated but could not determine the size of this budget. LMS allows them to determine the size of the capitation budget within their overall budget. Head teachers were asked to indicate whether, since the introduction of LM and taking account of inflation, the amount spent on books and equipment had increased, decreased or remained the same: 50 per cent of schools with LM had increased spending on both items whilst 16 per cent indicated that the amount had declined.

In the third survey, undertaken in 1993, head teachers were asked to specify the amount made available for capitation items (including money for books, materials and equipment) for the financial years April 1992/3 and 1993/4. A set of seventy primary and seventeen secondary schools provided us with sufficient data to calculate both these amounts as a percentage of their annual formula allocation. In the primary sector, the average capitation budget in 1992 amounted to 3.4 per cent of the formula allocation, declining to 3.1 per cent for 1993. We also calculated the *difference* in the amounts allocated for capitation items in this period, the mean difference being a reduction of £244. As a set of seventy schools, thirty-one had reduced capitation spending, ten had kept the amount the same and twenty-nine had increased spending.

In the secondary sector the proportion of formula budget allocated to capitation items is similar to that in the primary sector, although here there is evidence of a small increase. In 1992, spending on capitation items accounted for 3.3 per cent of the formula budget, increasing to 3.5 per cent in 1993. The average increase in cash terms amounted to £3,358. Eleven schools in the set increased spending, five decreased capitation and one did not change.

In summary, despite comparable proportions being spent on capitation items, there is some evidence of difference between the sectors. In the secondary sector the trend is towards an increase in spending whereas the reverse is evident in the primary sector. Since these data cover only two years, and the number of secondary schools is small, we draw conclusions with caution.

Reductions to budget heads

In the 1993 survey, head teachers were asked whether, in setting the budget for the year, expenditure in any area had been reduced. One hundred and nineteen primary and forty-one secondary schools responded to this question. More than half of these (62 per cent primary; 54 per cent secondary) indicated that some expenditure had been reduced. We asked heads to give information on cuts in five areas: teaching staff, non-teaching staff, premises, capitation items and other. The most common area for budget reduction in the primary sector was capitation, 77 per cent indicating cuts. The next most likely area for reduction was premises at 62 per cent; 39 per cent made cuts to teaching staff and 32 per cent to non-teaching staff; 22 per cent indicated 'other' areas of cuts. This contrasts with the choices of heads of secondary schools. In this sector, the most common area to suffer a budget reduction was teaching staff, 77 per cent. Cuts to budgets for premises and capitation were also common at 62 per cent and 57 per cent. Twenty-three per cent had made cuts to non-teaching staff and 19 per cent to other areas.

There is a noticeable difference between the sectors in the protection of the teaching staff budget, secondary head teachers being more likely to select teaching staff as an area for cuts. This may be explained by the relatively limited flexibility in primary schools in terms of staff commitments.

Contingency funds

Many schools have set aside funds into contingency reserves, the scale of which we have examined. In 1991, 479 schools had created a contingency fund, representing 77 per cent of those replying to the question on the first survey.

Head teachers were asked about amounts held for contingencies. For a small set of schools – thirty-one primary and twelve secondary – we have been able to calculate and compare the size of the contingency budget as a percentage of formula allocation for each of the four years from 1 April 1990 to 1993. In the primary sector, the average proportion of formula budget reserved for contingencies increased from 1.5 per cent in the first year to 2 per cent in 1991, stabilising at 1.8 per cent in 1992 and 1993. For each year, this set includes at least one school with nothing in the contingency budget and others with a contingency of 5.2 per cent of the formula budget in 1990, 1992 and 1993; in 1991, one school held 10.7 per cent of its formula budget for contingencies.

The average proportion of formula budget held for contingencies in the small set of twelve secondary schools increased over the period, although the percentages are lower than in the primary sector. In 1990, 0.8 per cent was held for contingencies, increasing to 1.6 per cent in 1991, 1.7 per cent in 1992 and 1.8 per cent in 1993. As in the set of primary schools, for each of these years, at least one had nothing in this fund. The maximum proportion of formula budget held increased in this period, from 3.4 per cent in 1990 to 4 per cent in 1991 and 10.2 per cent in 1992; one secondary school held 14.8 per cent of its formula allocation for contingencies in 1993. In addition to these planned contingencies, set at the beginning of the year, schools have also underspent on their budgets, a matter which has created difficulties when the schools sector argues that it is not adequately funded. We also recognise the ambiguity of this term and the possibility that whilst some schools will differentiate between underspend and contingency reserves, others will not.

Underspends

Schools and their governing bodies are not able to plan to overspend: expenditure in a year must not 'exceed the available budget, as adjusted for surpluses from previous years, income receivable, provisions for pay or price increases and other contingencies' (Audit Commission/Ofsted, 1993).

Eighty-eight per cent of LM schools replying to the first survey, reported that their budget to April 1991 was underspent, a finding which confirms much comment at the time. It should not be a surprising outcome since we might expect caution from schools managing budgets for the first time, in a system which allows carry-over to another financial year and requires them to keep their spending within cash limits.

We also have data from one hundred and seventeen primary and thirty-eight secondary schools on the incidence of underspending in the years to April 1992 and 1993. In the primary sector, 90 per cent of schools underspent in 1992 and 78 per cent in 1993. In the secondary sector, 90 per cent underspent in 1992, declining to 79 per cent the following year in both sectors, a small but increasing number of schools reporting overspending in 1993.

In the primary sector, the average underspend represented 6 per cent of the school's formula allocation in 1992, falling to 4 per cent in 1993; the average size of the underspend in the secondary sector also decreased, from 4 per cent to 3 per cent. This is comparable with data and observations made by the Audit Commission:

[schools] usually hold unspent balances of funds at the end of the year, amounting to 5% of the school budget on average for primary schools and 3.5% for secondary schools . . . Whilst excessive balances are undesirable, progressive unjustified growth in balances is even less attractive . . . If a balance of funds continues to be held for no particular purpose, then it would be understandable if local authorities take this into account when setting the general schools budget even though the extent of surpluses may not be evenly spread amongst schools.

(1993: 1, 32)

The HMI report on the implementation of LMS commented on underspend and possible reasons for it:

many schools are not spending their full budgets . . . (I)n most schools the level of underspend exceeds any income which they are generating. This appears to be happening for a number of reasons. Schools tended to be extremely cautious in the early phases. Early budget statements from LEAs were not always accurate . . . caution has been increased by the fear that LEAs may reduce planned budgets to avoid charge-capping.

(1992: 19)

We invited head teachers to comment on their over/underspend and perhaps the most important feature of many of the earliest replies is that the final underspend does not appear to have been planned; only 17 per cent of heads planned the underspend in the year to April 1991. In subsequent years, underspends were more often planned. In the primary sector the main reasons for underspending in 1992 were given as planned, caution and savings on staffing. In the following year the more common reasons cited included planned, staff savings, caution and good management. In the secondary sector, in 1992, explanations included planned, caution and good management and these were also the main reasons given in 1993.

Marren and Levacic (1992) report the spending decisions of a set of schools in their first year of LM. They note the cautious approach and comment that the 'vast majority of schools' in the LEA studied 'finished 1990/1 with a comfortably, if not embarrassingly, large surplus'. Of this underspend they write:

A large carry-forward is a double-edged sword. The schools may well have insured themselves against future deficits but it has caused some councillors to question the level of funding to schools if such savings were possible. It also calls into question whether such saving is an efficient use of the budget and could not have been better used in serving a school's particular needs. In the schools' defence it has to be remarked that they were operating under the threat of impending cuts and a lack of clear financial information about such things as energy expenditure.

(1992: 148)

Certainly previous underspends in schools in our sample proved invaluable, supporting schools through difficult years, as the head of one school explained:

> We benefited initially with a £27,000 carry over. That has virtually gone this coming year as we had a £10,000 over-spend on budget (new heating system in nursery class, over-spend on ancillary staffing and IT equipment). Our budget for this year has been drastically cut by the LEA. Outline budget £10,000 over the actual budget we receive.

Underspends have not prevented schools seeking other sources of financial support.

Supplementing the budget

Our 1991 data show that 79 per cent of schools supplemented their budget share in some way, the sources principally being parental and general fund-raising activities. On our visits to schools a number of interviewees spoke of a greater reliance on parental financial support. The deputy at one school told us that parents were asked to make greater contributions. The clerical assistant at another thought that parents were asked too often for help. The chair of governors at this school commented that 'the last two years in ...shire have been blighted with budget cuts – thank goodness for a helpful PTA!' One head teacher reported that without parents' support 'we'd be lost', and one of the teachers spoke of parents fund-raising for essentials.

Greater reliance on parental contributions for essentials, particularly to support the capitation budget, was evident. A teacher at one such school commented that PTA funds were now being used for more every day items, such as glue, rather than 'extras'. The general agreement at this school was to maintain staffing levels above the LEA recommendation, although the amount available for the capitation budget was directly affected by this. One teacher commented: 'would like to see more expendable equipment . . . but not at the expense of removing our present teacher/child ratio'.

The total amount added by parents and fund-raising activities remains small, however, HMI observing that the total 'represented less than one percent of the total budget share':

> Among primary schools some generated only tiny amounts, while the most in the study was £2,500. In the secondary schools of the study the range was from £6,000 to £28,000 in a school which had let its facilities during vacation time to a language school . . . . Similarly, parents vary in their ability to contribute to school funds. The generation of income produced between 0.1% and 1.7% of the budget share of the schools in the study.
>
> (1992: 18)

Some head teachers are particularly successful in attracting supplementary funds; one head in our sample gained funds from a number of sources, including the PTA, church funds, the village trust, letting the school house, bank investments and the use of parents. The PTA raised £10,000 in ten months to help pay for a mini-bus with the head teacher writing to forty trusts.

We complement these general data on spending priorities and budget supplements with vignettes of budgeting from a primary school and a secondary school.

Two years budgeting: two vignettes

Both schools have been fully locally managed since April 1990 and for each we give budget plans for two consecutive years. From the summary data provided the extent to which budget plans reflect Development Plans is not clear. It is the view of the Audit Commission/Ofsted (1993: 4) that 'The process of allocating the budget should not simply be an incremental process from one year to the next but should reflect, in monetary terms, the school's aims and objectives within the available resources'.

Vignette 6.1: A secondary school budget

In 1993 this school had 1025 secondary age pupils on roll, a decline of 45 pupils on the previous year, although the LEA was seen as having a dampening effect on competition for pupils in the area. The number of full-time teaching staff has fluctuated, from 67.2 in 1991 to 72.4 in 1992 and falling to 70 in 1993. Staff have been lost through natural wastage and compulsory redundancy. The head teacher indicated that the budget to the year ending April 1993 had been overspent, because 'salary increases were under-funded by Government'. In budget planning the school never had sufficient resources to allocate to a contingency fund; spending on capitation items had increased from £59,000 in 1992/93 to £81,487 for 1993/94. The budget plans for these years are detailed overleaf.

Substantially less (a reduction of £135,252) was allocated to teaching staff costs in 1993/94 compared with the previous year. The school made such reductions by staff cuts. More was spent on premises related costs, specifically 'other' costs, and supplies and services, most notably in the area of capitation and general supplies and services and £53,000 for 'deficit balance brought forward'. The school experienced a reduction in income and no surplus to carry forward into the 1993/94 budget plan.

	Budget 92/93	% tot exp	Budget 93/94	% tot exp
Employee Costs	1792837	90	1671821	82.7
Teaching Staff	1662987		1527735	
Non-teaching Staff	128850		141106	
Indirect Employer Costs	1000		2980	
Premises Related	92000	4.6	164206	8.1
Repairs and Maintenance	24000		38616	
Energy	50000		54000	
Water Services	15000		19640	
Rent and Rates	-		-	
Other	3000		51950	
Transport Related	7000	0.4	6990	0.3
Supplies and Services	101750	5.1	177823	8.8
Capitation and General	59000		81487	
Communications	9000		8950	
Catering	3200		4116	
Miscellaneous	1550		1670	
Exams	29000		28600	
Deficit Balance brought forward	-		53000	
Income	141111		34800	
Surplus	66000		0	
Use of Premises	15000		17000	
Phone	100		200	
Other	60011		17600	
Total Expenditure:	1993587		2020840	
Less Income:	141111		34800	
	1852476		1986040	

Vignette 6.2: A primary school budget

These budget plans are for a junior and infant primary school with 400 pupils on roll in 1993, compared with 401 in 1991 and 382 in 1992. The head teacher reported that competition is 'low-key but exists'. The number of full-time equivalent teaching staff has increased from 15.5 in 1991 to 17 in 1992 and 1993. In the year to April 1992 the budget was underspent by £21,000 because of 'prudent/cautious budgeting' and the underspend the following year was £18,000 through 'prudent housekeeping with a view to countering expected cuts for 1993/94'. From 1992/93 to 1993/94 contingencies were reduced from £10,000 to £2,000 and capitation declined from £15,000 to £10,500.

	Budget 91/92	% tot exp	Budget 92/93	% tot exp
Total Employee Costs	**440999**	**87.6**	**482057**	**83**
Teaching Costs	335801		382373	
Non-teaching Costs	104223		96554	
Indirect Employer Costs	975		3130	
Premises Related	**39000**	**7.7**	**45493**	**7.8**
Repairs and Maintenance	15050		15400	
Energy	13000		13655	
Cleaning/Domestic supplies	650		800	
Water Services	1500		1800	
Rent and rates	8800		13838	
Transport Related	**1620**	**0.3**	**2250**	**0.4**
Supplies and Services	**21850**	**4.3**	**50190**	**8.7**
Supplies & services general	2500		3600	
Capitation	15000		15350	
Communications	1350		1800	
Catering	2310		2810	
Clothing/laundry	-		200	
Miscellaneous	690		3532	
Contract cleaners	-		22898	
Income	**125**		**4000**	
Use of premises	100		40	
Phone	25		10	
Clerical costs recharge	-		3950	
Total Expenditure:	**503469**		**579990**	
Less Income:	**125**		**4000**	
	503344		**575990**	

Comparing the budget plans for 1991/92 and 1992/93, it is evident that spending has been increased in most areas – especially teaching costs (although non-teaching staff costs have been reduced and the percentage of total expenditure on employee costs has reduced from 87.6 per cent to 83 per cent). More has been spent under the supplies and services heading (4.3 per cent of total expenditure in 1991/92; 8.7 per cent in 1992/93, most of the increase being accounted for by the apparent delegation of contract cleaning costs in 1992/93. A clerical costs recharge explains most of the increased income.

For both years the school planned to spend more than its formula allocation by drawing on the previous year's carry forward, its small additional income and the previous year's contingency.

Budget administration

In this section we consider the roles of the head teacher, governing body, school administrator and staff in the administration of the budget. Other aspects of their roles are considered elsewhere.

The head teacher

According to the Audit Commission/Ofsted (1993) the duties of the head teacher regarding the management and administration of the budget include: profiling the budget and forecasting cash flow to take account of likely spending patterns; ensuring accountability where budgets are delegated within school (for example, to heads of departments, curriculum-leaders); and providing regular reports to the governing body on spending, including sums committed but not yet paid, against the approved budget. In summary, the head teacher's role should be more one of 'managing' than 'administering'.

Practice varies. At one secondary school a new part-time post of school manager facilitated the head teacher's role; he believed he uses his time better with the support of the school manager. Setting up the system had taken time, he commented, but now 'things were running well'. The deputy head was less happy: he was responsible for the day-to-day management of buildings and maintenance and would be glad to be rid of these responsibilities. At an infant school, the head teacher and a teacher with a B allowance administer the budget, protecting the secretary who felt unable to cope with the changes. Here, the head teacher did many duties carried out by administrative assistants elsewhere, such as making out orders, processing invoices and checking the LEA's printout. The deputy commented that the head was involved in 'too much administration, not enough managing'.

Administrative/clerical staff

> The proper administration of bank accounts is a fundamental financial control. In particular, regular bank reconciliations are essential.
> (Audit Commission/Ofsted 1993: 15)

Typically, these duties are carried out by clerical/administrative staff who are responsible for the preparation of reports comparing the amount spent or committed to date against their budgets (Audit Commission/Ofsted, 1993). As HMI (1992: 17) report, 'initially all LEAs managed the money and paid all bills centrally' but an increasing number are allowing their schools to have independent banking and cheque books. Some head teachers reported the frustrations in the procedure of passing bills for payment via the LEA. Three write:

In this school LMS gives more flexibility but generates more admin. work which is hampered by an inefficient central paying procedure and the SIMS package – both should be scrapped!

I would like to be a cheque book school and be able to pay bills ourselves and on time, rather than making payment through County Hall.

Deficiencies in system: SIMS has limitations, reconciliation is time-consuming and difficult to administer. Cheque-book management would be much more efficient and satisfying.

On the benefits of administrative decentralisation, two administrators made the following comments:

Much more efficiency and quickness regarding ordering materials/repairs etc. and dealing with payments – can now order direct – choice of from whom.

Since April 1992 we have had our own bank account which has benefited the school even more. Dealing with suppliers on a personal basis, instead of through the Authority, has improved these relationships.

The governing body

The role of the governing body is intended to be one of oversight: the Audit Commission/Ofsted (1993: 5, 7) state that they should ensure 'that virements assist in achieving the school's overall aims and objectives' and

that the duties of staff concerned with financial transactions are, as far as is practicable, distributed so that at least two people are involved with both receipts and payments. The work of one person should act as a check on the work of the other.

This is essentially a responsibility for accountability and will be examined in the next chapter.

Budget delegation and staff perceptions

In their replies to the first survey, 88 per cent of heads with LM expressed the view that staff are now more aware of the financial implications of decisions. Certainly, discussions with teachers and others on our school visits indicated that LM had created a heightened awareness of costs. A teacher at one school, for example, felt 'more aware of the cost of things and economy'; at another, a teacher thought that 'it has made staff far more aware of the mechanics, costs etc. of running an organisation'.

This greater awareness of costs was viewed positively in some schools. The head teacher at one school spoke of teachers being 'more aware of budget decisions and the value of good house-keeping'. Teachers felt that items were chosen with more care; the increased awareness of resources and how long they lasted, had led to more care being taken in their selection. One teacher commented:

> More care taken in choosing items that will benefit the majority . . . We are more aware of the cost of articles . . . If we think of the budget as 'our' money then it becomes more relevant how we spend it.

On the third questionnaire, heads commented: 'staff are more aware of what things cost – they are happy to save energy etc. if they know the money can be spent elsewhere'; 'it has made teachers, parents and governors more aware of the financial situation and made us all less prepared to accept second best'.

In the first survey, head teachers were also asked to respond to a statement on whether budget decisions had caused deep divisions among the staff. While 66 per cent of heads disagreed or strongly disagreed with this statement, there must, none the less, be concern for the 13 per cent of head teachers who agreed or strongly agreed with the statement. Tensions were certainly in evidence at one school we visited where teachers were very unhappy that money was being spent on an extension to the administration area and not on much needed curriculum resources. They thought that money tended to be spent on more 'showy' things such as the refurbished library and the offices. The chair of governors was aware of this tension and spoke of some staff wanting more books rather than extended office space.

These concerns reflect the negative attitude in some schools to a greater awareness of costs. For example, a deputy commented: 'Everything is short! Staff are more aware that it is short and of the onus on them to "make do"! Distracting from more important issues'. A teacher felt that staff were 'more aware of financial tightening up . . . Aware of lack of resources . . . Feel uneasy when asking for new materials'. Another commented: 'We have suffered with a lack of resources. I often have to finance things myself. I even bought writing paper last year'.

At one of the primary schools we visited, it became clear in a teacher interview that she saw classroom decoration as her responsibility and was reluctant to draw on school funds – she talked of carefully peeling off blue-tac in an effort to preserve the decor and that she was 'more aware of the need to look after resources and environment; for example, lights, marking walls with displays, considering a bit of DIY in the classroom . . . You think twice before complaining/commenting about the state of decor in the classroom or school generally, unless you're prepared to don an overall'.

There was widespread concern about lack of money, falling rolls and the danger of losing staff at another of the schools visited. The head commented: 'there is insufficient money to consider buying large items of furniture'. The deputy spoke of the 'greater need to conserve power and water . . . The finances available have necessitated choices to be made between paints, exercise books or copy paper', and that 'LM could become divisive as there is an increasing need for senior management to take unpopular decisions'. One of the teachers said 'I feel that there is a tendency to defer spending on anything other than essentials'.

LM has led to staff awareness of the cost of things, *including themselves*. They had concerns about the cost of illness, their job security and the threat of 'cheaper' staff. On absence, we heard comments such as 'we have to be more aware now of implications of absences due to illnesses etc. in the light of the expense of supply cover'; schools doing 'far more supply teaching to avoid costs accruing to our school budget'. One teacher told us of the heightened awareness of the cost of everything, including illness, and added that since teachers were aware of how much each was paid relative judgements about workload and responsibility were being made.

In terms of job security, we heard anxieties about redundancy and cuts in the hours of non-teaching staff. Staff 'are worried about overstepping the budget which could lead to redundancies'. Other teachers were concerned about 'job security and future prospects'. The approach adopted by the head at one school contributed to teacher anxiety: he claimed to tell the staff that 'kids mean jobs' and that if, through their actions about fourteen pupils leave, then they go too. These issues are considered more fully in the next two sections, the first of which examines the position of teaching staff.

TEACHING STAFF

The funding context

Teaching staff account for the large majority of each school's budget share and schools are required to meet the actual cost of staff from their budget. Unlike delegated management in Scotland, for example, schools in England and Wales are not allocated a budget which reflects the actual cost of staff in their school. As a result, therefore, some schools have salary bills in excess of the average salary costs in their LEA while others gain a financial benefit by having a staffing profile with a lower average cost. This has not been a popular policy for many:

> Average salaries cause great difficulties for schools who have older and more experienced staff. Actual salaries are an absolute necessity or some staff will be made redundant because schools cannot finance them.

> Nationally the average and actual teacher cost is a disaster: (i) younger, cheaper teachers being employed, (ii) undermines morale of experienced teachers; (iii) less job security. *This must be changed.*

Against these views is the argument that funding actual salaries is a means of compensating limited experience with 'extra' cash. It would also go against the cash limited discipline inherent in local management, a view taken by the DfE who see the policy as:

> an incentive to try to save money by employing fewer or cheaper staff. This can happen in a number of ways: not replacing members of staff when they leave; not using available promoted posts or allowances; appointing probationers or younger teachers on the lower points of the pay spine.
>
> (1992: 23)

One head teacher recognised some of the consequences of meeting actual salary costs: 'To award actual salaries . . . will reverse the situation for some schools – they'll attract the most expensive!!!' These effects are explored here in terms of their impact on teacher contracts, the influence of salaries on appointments, number of staff and a set of other issues.

Contracts and appointments

Comparison of the same schools in 1990 and 1991 shows that, whereas in 1990, 78 per cent of schools had no full-time teaching staff on temporary contracts, by 1991 this had declined to 73 per cent of schools. The change is similar in primary and secondary schools. For a sub-group of one hundred and thirty-seven schools, we have data for four years and show this in Table 6.2.

Table 6.2 Teachers on full-time temporary contracts

	1990	1991	1992	1993
percentage of schools with *no* full-time temporary teachers	78	66	56	59
number of full-time teachers on temporary contracts	44	66	85	99

In 1990, 78 per cent of these schools had no full-time temporary teachers, falling to 66 per cent in 1991, 56 per cent in 1992 and 59 per cent in 1993. However, although the *percentage* of schools employing full-time temporary teachers decreased in 1993, the actual *number* of teachers employed on such contracts in these schools has increased: some schools employ more than one full-time teacher on a temporary contract. In 1993, there were ninety-nine teachers on full-time temporary contracts compared with eighty-five in 1992.

If these figures are analysed by sector we find that, in the primary sector (one hundred and four schools), 83 per cent had no teachers on full-time temporary appointments in 1990, falling to 59 per cent in 1992 and rising to 62 per cent in 1993, although the number of teachers employed on these terms rose slightly from sixty-two in 1992 to sixty-four in 1993. The thirty-three secondary schools show a steeper decrease in the number employing no full-time temporary teachers from 64 per cent 1990, 58 per cent in 1991 and 46 per cent in 1992, increasing to 52 per cent in 1993. The number of teachers employed on these terms rose from twenty-three in 1992 to thirty-five in 1993.

Clearly, there has been an increase in the number of schools with temporary full-time teachers in the period 1990 to 1992. In 1993, however, there has been a decrease in the number of schools using fixed term contracts but an increase in the number of teachers on such contracts.

Comparisons of teachers in part-time employment show a similar change. In 1990, 62 per cent of schools had no part-time teachers on temporary contracts, falling to 56 per cent in 1991. Of the one hundred and thirty-two providing figures for four years: 58 per cent of these schools had no part time temporary teachers in 1990, 50 per cent in 1991, 44 per cent in 1992 and 51 per cent in 1993.

The data by sector (one hundred and one primary and thirty-one secondary schools) shows that 68 per cent of primary schools did not have any part-time temporary teachers in 1990, reducing to 53 per cent in 1991 and 49 per cent in 1992 but increasing to 52 per cent in 1993. In the secondary sector 55 per cent of schools had no part-time temporary teaching staff in 1990, 42 per cent in 1991, 29 per cent in 1992 and 48 per cent in 1993. These figures should be viewed with caution because the numbers of schools are comparatively small and we cannot tell where there are instances of two part-timers taking on a post previously held by one part-timer (e.g., a 0.8 being replaced by two 0.4); it may also be that the reduction in part-time temporary staff is an overall reduction in staffing. The response of head teachers to statements on temporary contracts provides some further information.

In 1992 and 1993 head teachers were invited to respond to the statement: *LM has resulted in more teachers on temporary appointments at the school.* In 1992, 42 per cent agreed with the statement, almost as many (37 per cent) disagreed and 21 per cent neither agreed or disagreed. The response in 1993 showed little change. These results are little different when analysed by sector.

Setting aside argument over the value of any change in the proportion of teachers on temporary contracts, there can be little argument that it has implications for the management of schools. Matters of organisational commitment, employment regulations, morale and working relationships *can* all be affected by the nature of the employment contract and this demands different attributes of personnel management. Use of temporary teachers may also impact on pupils. One head teacher wrote:

> I will always be a teacher short as far as I can see into the future. In the summer term I employ a temporary teacher to take the incoming reception class for one term. These Easter entrants then have a change of teacher in September.

If the use of temporary contracts for staff is becoming more widespread, professional development programmes for head teachers need to address the consequences. To complement information on staff on temporary contracts, we collected information on the nature of new appointments. In the year to April 1991, the schools surveyed made 1,099 full-time appointments. 76 per cent of these appointments were permanent contracts and 24 per cent temporary contracts. Primary schools made 717 full-time appointments, 73 per cent on permanent contracts and 27 per cent on temporary contracts. Secondary schools made 382 full-time appointments, 82 per cent on permanent contracts and 18 per cent on temporary contracts. Analysis by school size shows larger schools making greater use of temporary appointments: while 17 per cent of small primary schools made full-time temporary appointments, 30 per cent of larger primary schools did so. In the secondary sector, 37 per cent of small and 45 per cent of larger schools made full-time temporary appointments.

These patterns of permanent and temporary contracts appear to indicate some change in the practice of schools and it is unfortunate that the DfEE does not report on these data annually in order to assess the scale and significance of these employment patterns.

For part-time posts, the pattern of appointment is the opposite to full-time temporary appointments. Data on 420 appointments in 1991 shows 17 per cent on permanent contracts and 83 per cent on temporary contracts with little difference between the sectors. These are similar to an earlier study of secondary schools by Robinson and Smithers (1991) on appointments in 1989.

The influence of salary on appointments

The 1991 survey asked head teachers to comment on the extent to which salary had been a factor in the choice of candidate. Reported by head teachers not to be a factor in 54 per cent (288) of schools, it was a consideration in 18 per cent of schools and 12 per cent expected it to play a part in the future. Comments from three head teachers in the 1992 survey indicate its importance:

> We recruited a 'cheap' standard scale teacher (NQT) to maintain our viability.

> We cannot afford the staff we want.

A third identified it as a problem for teachers:

> Teachers have difficulties understanding/accepting that cost is now a factor when teachers are interviewed for posts.

In the 1992 and 1993 surveys, head teachers were asked to respond to the statement *Because of LM, salary considerations influence selection of teaching staff*. In 1992, 58 per cent agreed with this statement and 27 per cent disagreed with little change the following year, a response which shows head teachers well aware of salary as a factor in the selection of teaching staff. When the data are analysed by sector, salary appears to have a stronger influence on the selection in primary schools where 65 per cent of heads agreed with the statement in both 1992 and 1993; in 1992, 35 per cent of secondary head teachers agreed rising to 48 per cent in 1993. It is a finding which suggests that the greater size of a secondary school budget affords more flexibility in making these decisions.

Number of teaching staff

Changes in the pupil:teacher ratio

Comparing 1990 with 1991, there was an increase in the number of full-time equivalent (FTE) teachers and the number of pupils in the schools, and a deterioration in the pupil–teacher ratio (PTR). For the 409 primary schools which provided data for both years, the PTR for 1990 was 23.0, increasing to 23.2 in 1991. DES data for primary schools in England in 1990 shows a PTR of 22.0 and, for 1991, a PTR of 22.2 (DES, 1992). Both measures show a worsening in the ratios, the more favourable DES measure reflecting the inclusion of teachers – such as advisory teachers – who are not in schools. For the sixty-five secondary schools which provided data for both years, the PTR for 1990 was 15.85, increasing to 16.16 in 1991. DES data for secondary schools in England in 1990 shows a PTR of 15.25 and, for 1991, 15.55. Both measures again show a worsening in the ratios. Separate examination of the ratios for the secondary schools in this set with and without pupils aged sixteen plus show a more favourable PTR in schools with seventeen and eighteen year olds. For the thirty-six schools with pupils up to sixteen years only, the mean PTRs for 1990 and 1991 are 16.21 and 16.70 respectively; for the twenty-nine schools with pupils aged sixteen plus they are 15.41 and 15.48.

For a smaller group of schools we have data on PTR for four years. For nineteen secondary schools, and seventy-one primary schools, we are able to compare the mean PTR for the years 1990 to 1993. For the secondary schools, the PTR has deteriorated, from 15.9 in 1990 to 16.7 in 1993. The PTR in the primary schools deteriorated over the same period from 24.07 to 24.39. These changes have meant cuts in staff in some schools.

Cuts in teaching staff

Some schools are making cuts to the teaching staff and comments illustrate anxieties about job security:

I have had to lose a 0.5 teacher again this year after losing a full-time one last year.

Budgetary considerations are forcing a reduction in staff by two teachers this year with a consequent increase in class sizes. This can only have an adverse effect on pupil recruitment

On a visit to one secondary school, a head of department commented, 'I have grave misgivings about "teacher security" should a school fail to attract sufficient numbers or have a good management team'. By contrast, a head teacher of a primary school saw this teacher vulnerability as a positive change. She recognised that the teaching staff felt unsure about their job security and knew that they no longer had a job for life. This was a good thing according to her, because 'we've carried staff for far too long'.

On our visits to schools, staff were asked to respond to the statement: *I anticipate teacher redundancies at this school as a result of LM*. Among the heads interviewed, 31 per cent agreed with this statement, while teachers were clearly more concerned, 45 per cent agreeing with the statement. Chairs of governors were more confident, only 23 per cent agreeing with the statement. Responding to the same statement in our 1992 and 1993 surveys, 23 per cent of head teachers agreed that redundancies were anticipated.

In 1992 and 1993 head teachers were also asked to report on natural wastage, voluntary redundancy and compulsory redundancy at their school. Twenty-four per cent had lost staff through natural wastage in 1992 and 18 per cent in 1993; 9 per cent of schools lost staff through voluntary redundancy in 1992 and 11 per cent in 1993; 6 per cent lost staff through compulsory redundancy in 1992 and 3 per cent in 1993. In each category, the losses are lower in the primary sector. On staff losses, one head teacher commented: 'We avoided compulsory redundancies by the skin of our teeth but they loom large for next year'. Another wrote:

> For 1993/94 we are reducing staff by 0.5% and will still be in a deficit budget to the tune of £6,400 – this being taken from the 'Contingency Fund'. This is mainly because of the salaries bill (average versus actual). The theory of appointing staff to keep within the budget has not worked here as there have not been any main professional grade vacancies since LMS started and furthermore none of my staff are actively looking for promotion or a move. 'Who would want an expensive teacher?' they say.

A deputy head teacher of a primary school we visited, commenting on a reduction to teaching staff, mentioned the possible consequences of the impact of the formula on the school's popularity:

> The original budget based on average rather than actual costs of staffing resulted in a loss of two teachers: as a result we had to introduce mixed age classes for two years. This was unpopular with the parents and resulted in some children being removed from the school.

A head teacher wrote that 'More teachers are in danger of redundancy. Good experienced professionals will be lost and there will be a chase for cheap novices.'

Given this changing climate, concerns about job security are not surprising. One head teacher wrote: 'Employment rights and job security are destroyed by LMS'. He felt that the latter 'may be necessary to a degree, but not in the "market forces" that operates under LMS'. While some schools made reductions in staff numbers, others were employing additional teachers.

Additional teaching staff

For some schools, LM has heralded a period of prosperity with opportunities to appoint additional staff. Three head teachers report in the second survey:

> (There) have been many advantages – additional teaching and support staff and resources.

> LMS has been a great benefit for this school. We have increased teaching and non-teaching staff.

> This year I am able to fund an additional member of teaching staff which will substantially reduce the overall PTR. I have also been able to fund a full-time ancillary specifically to support rising-fives.

Two others comment:

> We have been able to increase and maintain our staffing . . . and this has had an enormous impact on the delivery of curriculum, particularly in the special needs sector.

> We have been able to improve our staffing provision (special needs 0.4) and additional support assistant hours which has been highly beneficial.

Other schools have been able to maintain an 'over-staffed' position. Comments from one head teacher illustrate this situation and she shows how the decision has affected other areas of expenditure:

> LMS has brought advantages – we have maintained staffing levels (support and teaching) above the level of LEA recommendations but at a cost to capitation expenditure. This means greater dependence on private funds.

Other teaching staff issues

Discretion over salaries and allowances is a key aspect of the new relationship which governors and head teachers have with teachers and this was explored by survey and through interviews during the school visits.

Salary enhancement

The 1992 survey showed that 34 per cent of head teachers had been awarded a salary increase and 17 per cent a year later. The percentages for these two years are higher in the primary sector where 38 per cent of head teachers received a salary enhancement in 1992 and 19 per cent in 1993; in the secondary schools the comparable figures are 24 per cent in 1992 and 10 per cent in 1993. Salary enhancements were similar for deputy heads. Overall, 35 per cent of heads reported salary increases for deputies in the year to April 1992, reducing to 19 per cent in 1993. Fewer schools awarded salary enhancements to members of the teaching staff: 23 per cent in 1992 and 15 per cent the following year.

On the third survey, comments from head teachers included:

> Where's the money for any teacher salary enhancement coming from? Some head teachers appear to have received *large* increases in the last two years – at whose expense?

> Whilst funding is so limited, Governors invariably act cautiously and have not placed staff salary enhancements above capitation.

Allowances

There is some evidence from our school visits to suggest a reduction in the number of allowance posts with schools allocating fewer than recommended. The head teacher at one primary school we visited reported that 'the school cannot fund the incentive allowances for staff which were agreed in the National Condition of Services document'. At another school we visited, allowance B posts had been reduced to A posts. A teacher at a middle school commenting on the consequences of LM at the school wrote:

> Reduction in number of staff ⟶ increased workload ⟶ fewer incentives ⟶ deterioration of career structure.

On the other hand, LM had allowed some schools to increase their allowance posts. The head teacher at one school wrote: 'No real difference in numbers due to overall size of budget but more flexibility in allocating allowances.' At this school there were two Cs, five Bs and five As, one B and part of one C above the LEA allowance quotient.

Use of the supply budget

Although no direct questions are asked on the surveys, there is some evidence to suggest that schools are making savings on the supply budget and that this may be used to enhance staffing levels. Such findings are in line with those of the DfE who write:

> In many primary and secondary schools teaching staff have agreed to cover for one another's absence, so that savings on supply cover can generate extra teaching staff or non-teaching support.

> (1992: 18)

On the other hand, there are examples of schools who are not in such a fortunate position.

One head teacher writes:

> We have had 'first day' cover knocked on the head. This has caused a significant problem for heads like myself who are class based, we now have to double up classes when staff are away. Although the LEA offer an insurance cover for first day, we are not in a financial position to take the offer up.

On a visit to a primary school, one head teacher wrote of the 'serious problem relating to long-term absence or a lot of absence' describing this as a 'financial drain that cannot be budgeted for'. Actively endeavouring to make savings on the supply cover budget can impact on the teaching staff who may feel under pressure not to be absent.

A move towards replacing teachers with non-teaching staff

There is some evidence that money which might in the past have been used to employ teachers is now being used to employ people to support their work.

> We were able to make a part-time teacher redundant and employ a full-time nursery nurse as a result. This has led to us being able to offer a good pupil–teacher ratio in our reception class.

In one of the primary schools we visited the head teacher commented on the 'shift in emphasis from teaching to non-teaching staff'. He had seen it as important to build up the clerical/administrative team so that he could be released to teach. He spoke of having no curriculum involvement (by which he meant teaching) in 1990, 10 per cent in 1991 and 20 per cent in 1992 with plans for 40 per cent in 1993. He planned to increase the number of classroom ancillary hours to free teachers for teaching, reducing the time they spend on activities such as collecting money.

In another school, additional classroom support had been employed for two years: '1.5 additional educational assistants and 0.4 sessional teachers for special needs children'. However, falling rolls had meant 'increased pressure to reduce staffing, that is, ending part-time teacher contract. I think it has encouraged considerations such as replacing teaching staff with educational assistants'. The next section examines the position of non-teaching staff more fully.

NON-TEACHING STAFF

For the purposes of this section, non-teaching staff include non-teaching assistants, administrative staff, caretakers/site managers, cleaners and midday supervisors. We examine how local management has affected them.

Non-teaching assistants

As non-teaching assistants we include teaching assistants, classroom assistants and general assistants, nursery nurses, librarians and technicians. We focus on changes in the number of hours worked by non-teaching assistants in the period 1990 to 1994, drawing on information from seventy-three primary schools and twenty-three secondary schools.

Secondary schools employ more non-teaching assistant hours than primary schools but there is evidence of an increase in both sectors.

We analysed the data in terms of the mean number of hours worked by non-teaching assistants. Table 6.3 shows the average number of hours worked analysed by school size. Interestingly, smaller primary schools now employ more hours of non-teaching assistants than larger schools did in 1990 and all the primary schools have more hours than smaller secondary schools, although there are only ten in the set.

Table 6.3 Average hours per week worked by non-teaching assistants

Sector	1990	1991	1992	1993	No. of schools
Primary	39	42	51	64	70
Large	41	46	53	69	50
Small	31	31	40	45	19
Secondary	138	142	133	116	23
Large	184	191	201	185	12
Small	68	70	65	42	10

The head teacher at one of the primary schools we visited told us that an additional 0.5 nursery nurse had been appointed on a fixed term contract, although the nursery nurse wondered 'why her salary scale is so poor'. The head believed the funding formula to be

> too simplistic with, for example, no provision for nursery nurses (NNEBs) in junior and infant schools . . . Nursery and Infant pupils have additional costs (NNEBs) not accounted for in the formula; these are far greater than technician support recognised as needed for secondary schools.

At another school we visited, the clerical assistant explained that: 'as extra numbers of pupils come to school we employ additional NNEBs to help teachers in the classroom'. Additional non-teaching staff had been appointed at other schools. One head teacher wrote: 'we have been able, for the first time ever, to employ an NNEB, and increase our support staff, using some "social deprivation money"'.

The use of temporary contracts for non-teaching staff is not uncommon. The registrar of a secondary school said: 'we have more part-time support staff . . . library assistant/booking officer, additional secretary. . . . We tend to make temporary appointments initially'. Additional non-teaching assistants have brought benefits to the children, writes a head teacher on the third survey:

> There is no way I would relinquish the flexibility LMS has given me in the running of the school. It has enabled me to employ classroom assistants, improve the environment and be more flexible in the use of supply teachers . . . Although the budget has been tight and the class sizes rather large the children have benefited and their learning opportunities have increased, mainly due to extra adult helpers in school.

Administrative and clerical staff

As administrative and clerical staff we include clerical, secretarial and administrative staff, registrars and bursars. This group have been directly affected by delegated management, in terms of increased hours and by change in duties and responsibilities. In the following paragraphs we provide data on the increase in number of administrative/clerical staff hours, their changing role, re-grades and recognition.

Increased number of administrative/clerical staff hours

Data for the period 1990 to 1993 on the hours per week of secretarial/clerical staff is available for 23 secondary and 103 primary schools. When the number of hours per week worked by secretarial/clerical staff in 1990 is compared with 1993 we can see that the mean has increased from 118 hours to 138 hours in the secondary sector. The primary sector shows a steady increase, from a mean of 28 hours in 1990 to 36 hours in 1993, totals which are in stark contrast to those in the secondary sector.

Analysed by school size, the mean hours in small secondary schools has increased from 82 hours in 1990 to 95 hours in 1993; for the larger secondaries, the increase is from 152 hours per week to 182 hours. In the 22 smaller primary schools weekly hours increased from 18 in 1990 to 23 in 1993; in the 80 larger primary schools, the mean hours increased from 30 in 1990 to 40 in 1993, although, despite such increases, some still felt there were 'insufficient hours to do the work' (senior school secretary).

Additional secretarial time has a cost. In 1992 and 1993, 60 per cent of head teachers agreed with the statement: *As a result of LM, I spend a greater proportion of the budget on support staff.* The pressures to enhance administrative time are clear from the comments of one head teacher:

> Too little thought has been given to the impact of delegation on school support staff and to the need for Heads to be free from the administrative burden if they are to continue to 'manage' the learning in their schools. The possibility of group bursar posts handling the financial arrangements of small groups of adjacent schools is worth considering.

Another wrote: '(We) need very well qualified (and paid) admin. staff otherwise head teacher is overburdened with admin. and monitoring role.' The case for increasing administrative skills was emphasised by the then Minister of State, Eric Forth, commenting on the Audit Commission's report (1993) on schools' financial management:

> The report . . . says that some schools need more administrative support and that it is a false economy to skimp on administration if that means teachers end up doing clerical tasks.
>
> (Forth, 1993: 1)

We sought to examine trends in the amount of time allocated to LM by support staff. The large majority of head teachers reported an increase, for 1992 and 1993, in the amount of time support staff spend on LM. Seventy-seven per cent of head teachers reported in 1992 that the amount of time had increased in 1992 and 72 per cent reported the same in 1993. These findings were analysed by size of school and the results are similar across school size and sector.

The changing role of the administrative/clerical staff

A report on the implementation of LMS by HMI recognises that schools are increasing the amount of administrative/clerical hours but also that the nature of the work has changed:

> Schools are increasing the levels of clerical and other non-teaching support. Part of this rise is to meet the administrative cost of LMS itself . . . The amount of clerical support has been increased to deal with accounts and to operate the information technology. The nature of the clerical tasks is changing. To handle LMS administration, clerical staff often had to acquire a range of computing skills in a short time . . . Many governing bodies have reacted by increasing their working hours and linking these to a commensurate upgraded and improved salary.
>
> (1992: 25)

LM has brought a quite dramatic alteration in the nature of the work of some administrative/clerical staff. The secretary at a middle school commented: 'the coming of LM has meant considerable training and increased responsibilities for myself'. The Administrative Officer at one school had prepared a recent job description outlining the role of the school secretary. She describes the aim and purpose of her job as:

> To provide an efficient and effective financial, administrative and clerical support service for the Head teacher and staff of the school. The Secretary's duties cover all areas of the financial systems and procedures established (and developing) in line with the delegated responsibilities

associated with the local management of schools (LMS). In view of the nature of the job confidentiality is essential at all times.

and the main duties are described as:

1   Provide administrative, clerical and typing support (including word processing) to the Head teacher and school staff. This includes the organisation of the school office, maintaining both manual and computer records on the SIMS (Schools Information System) computer, origination of letters, photocopying, telephoning duties and provision of hospitality.
2   To maintain accounts for all the school budget areas, including the provision of annual balance sheets and regular balances for each budget head. Completion of summary sheets.
3   To assist in the enrolment procedures, to maintain pupil and staff databases on SIMS, together with the maintenance of class and dinner registers as necessary, ensuring that all records are up to date.

From discussion with other secretaries during our school visits, duties also include such things as raising orders, invoicing and checking for payment, reconciliation and balancing statements. Some secretaries are also expected to administer petty cash, collect dinner monies, see to minor first aid and act as the telephonist and receptionist. In some schools, on the other hand, appointments have been made solely for the financial administration of local management.

The changed role is viewed as a welcome career opportunity by some, while for others it is not the job they wanted and there are feelings of lack of consultation. Some believed that they had to either face the changes or leave. The senior clerical assistant at a primary school wrote 'I now have wider responsibilities and at a higher level' and commented that many secretaries had felt overwhelmed by the changes and had left. The change has clearly been stressful for many, although the job may now be seen as more challenging and rewarding. The secretary of one primary school reflected on the experience:

> I would like to mention the stress impact LMS has had on me, particularly during the first six months. The responsibility of maintaining the financial administration on a day-to-day basis was overpoweringly worrying! I was a school secretary one day and then after a few days' training I was a financial administrator (as well as trying to fit in all the usual clerical/secretarial duties). I now enjoy the LMS aspects of my job but still consider that certain functions may be best carried out by a specialist, centrally, at Area Education Office or County Hall level. I am concerned that too much will be delegated to schools, in areas that we are not – and should not – be expert in e.g., cleaning, grounds, salaries and wages – please no!

The senior clerical assistant at another primary school wrote:

> There is more money available to the school and more secretarial hours. Although there was a great deal to take in at first, the job is now much more interesting and I believe the school is now more efficiently run.

Re-grades and salary enhancements

The HMI report of 1992 mentioned the practice of upgrading and improving the salaries of administrative/clerical staff in line with the changed nature of their duties. In the second and third surveys we asked if the governing body had awarded any salary enhancements to 'support staff', a category which includes all non-teaching staff. In 1992, 44 per cent of head teachers reported that salary enhancements had been made to their support staff and 24 per cent reported this in 1993. Compared with our data on head teachers, deputies and teachers, support staff were more likely to receive an enhancement.

Despite this, we heard many comments about inadequate re-grades and salary improvements. A common practice was for schools to re-grade their administrative/clerical staff in line with the LEA recommendation. The secretary of a primary school expressed her feelings about this:

> I consider myself fortunate in that our governors have increased my salary above that recommended by the County Council . . . The recommended Grade 2 is insulting for the responsibilities.
>
> Since taking up my post with the school, the introduction of LM has meant a significant increase in my duties and responsibilities. I feel that this has been recognised by most bodies, but has not been reflected by a pay award in recognition of the increased duties. I have however enjoyed my increased role and enjoy the increased involvement in the way the school is run.

Another commented that 'I feel more money could be given to clerical staff owing to the amount of work and responsibility required for the job.' The senior clerk at a secondary school spoke of 'increased clerical hours, new job description, extra responsibilities' but she regarded the re-grade as being out of line with the additional responsibilities.

Two further administrative/clerical staff expressed their views on re-grades. The bursar at a primary school felt that the re-gradings did not match the quantity of work or responsibilities. The Administrative Officer at another primary school had fought hard with the LEA for re-grades before LMS and commented that the governors viewed an increase in her salary as fewer books for the children.

Recognition

From our field visits, recognition – and sometimes its absence – was mentioned by administrative/clerical staff. For some the changes have resulted in them feeling more integrated and they are now invited to meetings and training days. A clerical assistant commented on how she felt 'stressed and over-worked' but also 'more part of the school'. Another remarked that 'since LMS I have attended staff meetings'.

Elsewhere, the increase in responsibilities and duties has not been recognised by other staff who still viewed them more simply as the 'school secretary'. In one school, the administrative officer spoke of the failure of teachers to recognise the changed status of secretaries. The senior clerk at a secondary school commented that clerical staff were not recognised by the head teacher as being an important part of the school. They were never invited to meetings as members of staff. The senior school secretary at a primary school commented: 'in education, only the teachers count'.

She voiced concerns about 'money, salary and respect for increased responsibilities'. She also explained that she had to 'sign on unemployed during Christmas, Easter and the main summer holidays as not paid'. At another primary school, the secretary spoke of the closer working relationship with the head teacher who shared with her his financial hopes and concerns. This same secretary also commented, however, that the 'teachers view the school secretary as first and foremost a "secretary"'.

Caretakers/site managers

Our field visits illuminated changes in the traditional role of the caretaker. The job title has changed for some; ex-caretakers are now known as 'site managers'. Head teachers reported that caretakers/site managers now carry out repair and decoration; 'caretaker has now an active role in site management and effects minor repairs'; 'small repairs can now be undertaken by caretakers'; other schools have a full-time caretaker who carries out repairs and decoration. The deputy head at one school explained that 'the caretaker carries out more day-to-day maintenance'; at another school the caretaker and her husband decorate the building.

There is no clear evidence whether these different duties provide caretakers with additional hours of employment and it may be that duties are tending to change rather than hours increasing. Indeed, while there are instances of schools increasing the caretakers' hours, there is little evidence of change in hours from the longitudinal data on seventy-eight primary schools and twenty-two secondary schools. Table 6.4 shows the average hours per week worked by caretakers between 1990 and 1993.

Table 6.4 Average hours per week worked by caretakers

Sector	1990	1991	1992	1993	No. of schools
Primary	35	34	34	34	78
Large	37	35	35	36	63
Small	29	28	28	27	14
Secondary	86	85	70	72	22
Large	108	108	85	81	11
Small	59	57	60	57	10

The figures show that in the primary sector the number of hours has remained stable, varying by no more than one hour. The data for the secondary sector reveal some fluctuation with the number of caretaker hours in the set of larger schools declining, from 108 in 1990 to 81 in 1993.

Comments from two head teachers show that some schools are actively choosing to keep and use their caretakers:

> We have been able to keep a full-time caretaker (who has proved to be very cost effective).

> We have decided to employ a caretaker/handyman rather than opt into LEA contract.

Cleaners

The cleaning service provided to a number of schools has been contracted-out by the LEA and comparatively few head teachers were able to furnish us with information on the number of hours worked by the cleaners in their school. On our visits, there was evidence of discontentment regarding the arrangements for cleaning. At one school, for example, staff were unhappy that the cleaning contract had gone out to competitive tender as this had resulted in the governing body having to make all the cleaners redundant one day and re-employ them the next on revised contracts. The revised contracts had also meant a decline in the service provided. While we do not have detailed data on the nature of cleaning contracts, we do have data on changes in the hours worked by cleaners.

Table 6.5 presents information on the mean hours per week worked by cleaning staff in the same set of primary and secondary schools, for each year from 1990 to 1993. In both sectors there is evidence of some fluctuation in these hours.

Table 6.5 Average hours per week worked by cleaners

Sector	1990	1991	1992	1993	No. of schools
Primary	29	28	35	29	39
Large	32	30	40	33	31
Small	19	21	17	15	8

Sector	1990	1991	1992	1993	No. of schools
Secondary	155	153	92	136	9
Large	207	205	93	164	6
Small	51	50	89	78	3

Mid-day supervisors

The final group of staff we report on are mid-day supervisors. The data in Table 6.6 show small changes in the primary schools while the larger secondary schools show a clearer pattern of decline. We recognise, of course, that the overall number of schools for which we have these longitudinal data are small.

Table 6.6 Average hours per week worked by mid-day supervisors

Sector	1990	1991	1992	1993	No. of schools
Primary	34	34	30	34	82
Large	37	37	34	38	61
Small	24	23	18	22	20
Secondary	37	36	34	33	20
Large	50	49	44	38	10
Small	24	23	24	29	10

When the number of hours worked by mid-day supervisors in 1990 and 1993 is compared, thirty-seven out of eighty-nine primary schools show a reduction in hours; twenty-six increased the number of hours and another made no change. In the secondary sector, ten out of twenty-six secondary schools reduced the number of hours, two secondary schools made no change and the others increased the hours.

This section ends by detailing the impact of LM on staffing in three schools. They illustrate a number of the issues raised.

The impact on staffing: Three vignettes

These vignettes of staffing issues represent circumstances in three schools we visited and are drawn from data collected on the visits and the survey returns.

Vignette 6.3: Modest growth

The school is the product of an amalgamation in 1989 of an Infant and a Junior school on the same site. It has had full local management since April 1990, and the 1992 survey shows a roll of 288 pupils and a full-time equivalent staff of head plus twelve, all teachers being on full-time permanent contracts. The school has not made any reductions to teaching staff since LM. The head teacher's responses to attitude statements suggest that LM *will* result in more teachers on temporary contracts; she strongly agreed with the statement and added the words 'will do'. Strong disagreement was indicated with regard to the statement about redundancies but she agreed that salary considerations influenced the selection of teaching staff.

When visited, individuals at this school were asked to respond to the statement *I anticipate teacher redundancies at this school, as a result of LM.* Both the head and the chair of governors disagreed with this statement but the deputy head and the classroom teacher agreed. What became apparent during the visit was that LM had meant that the school was able to support an improved level of staffing. The head explained that under the LEA the teaching staff would have been head plus ten but now, in accordance with the governing body's staffing policy, it was head plus twelve. The governors' staffing policy is to maintain staffing levels and keep class sizes below thirty. This could involve the head teaching full-time where necessary.

Additional non-teaching classroom assistance has also been employed. The chair of governors reported that in one classroom when the numbers went over thirty, an NNEB was employed on a temporary one-term contract. This was so successful that money was found for a further term, until Easter 1993. The school was awaiting the 1993/94 budget before deciding to continue this contract.

The deputy head said that two teacher appointments had been made recently, one temporary contract to cover a maternity leave, and one for two terms in the Reception in response to the large January intake. This position will be reviewed in the light of pupil numbers. He commented on the selection: 'restricted choice – although no problem in the circumstances – but some candidates were over-priced'. He felt that salary costs were becoming a subject for consideration because of the budget implications, and he spoke of the years of experience you cannot afford.

Financing this improved staffing level had drawn upon other budget heads, including £5,000 from capitation items and £6,000 from premises. The chair of governors and deputy both commented on the impact of the large, old ex-secondary-school building on the heating and cleaning bill. The deputy felt that capitation had not been significantly affected by LM. The October 1992 Governors' Report to the Annual Parents' Meeting stated:

> Formula funding . . . provided money for Head and 10 staff, but as a result of considerable savings made in 90–91 the Governors were able to fund Head and 12 staff. These savings were made in part as a result of a negligible maintenance bill 90–91 as a result of county funded alterations for the amalgamation of the schools. In addition, the county assisted in meeting the cost of salaries during the first two years of the amalgamation.

Despite this relatively favourable staffing position, the classroom teacher interviewed expressed concern about job security. She felt that jobs were on the line each year, dependent on pupil numbers, and she described this as a constant pressure.

The chair of governors reported that the secretary's hours and salary had been increased a year ago. She felt that if the school had 'someone good you have to look after them'. The head remarked, however that the, 'secretary is overloaded. High powered job now but we cannot pay an equivalent salary'.

Vignette 6.4: Managing under pressure

A different set of staffing issues were prominent in an infant school serving a socially disadvantaged area with about half the pupils on free school meals. Full local management had been in operation since April 1991 and from the 1992 survey the school had a roll of 214 and six full-time permanent, two full-time temporary and one part-time permanent member of teaching staff. No staff had been lost through redundancy or natural wastage.

The school is a 'winner' with the change to formula funding and while this might suggest a healthy financial situation, it was not felt as such at the school. In the first year of LM the school had experienced some unsettling confusion over budgetary information. After the first year the school was informed of an £8,000 underspend which they duly spent but it was later discovered that this was an error, by which time the school was left with an £10,000 overspend. After prolonged wrangling, the LEA agreed to pay the £8,000 but left a clear sense of a tight financial situation. The head teacher said that without the parents' support 'we'd be lost', even though the economically disadvantaged parents can ill afford financial support for the school. The school actively engaged in fund raising and, according to one of the teachers, the money was being used to pay for 'essentials'.

During the course of our study, a new head teacher was appointed to the school in September 1992. The retiring head teacher's responses to the attitude statements in the 1992 questionnaire suggest that LM had resulted in more teachers on temporary contracts at the school; teacher redundancies were not expected and salary considerations influence the selection of teaching staff. The school planned to move £2,000 from capitation and £1,000 from premises to teaching staff in the 1992/93 budget plan.

It was clear that teaching salaries had been a real concern. A three-year full-time teaching contract had not been continued because of the cost. The head teacher commented: 'Lack of money for additional salaries has meant loss of special educational needs (SEN) teachers which we desperately need – will I ever be able to replace!!'. On the other hand, two newly qualified teachers had been appointed, to save money. The head described staffing as a 'continual anxiety' and wrote that the school 'had to appoint two probationer teachers and another teacher not higher than point 6 on the scale'. The head felt that given the circumstances, experienced staff were too expensive. A classroom teacher reported that 'staffing has been affected because the school is forced to take on staff that are newly qualified because they are cheap and we cannot afford experienced staff'. The loss of the three-year contract had caused a certain amount of ill feeling amongst staff. A classroom teacher with an A allowance mentioned that, although 'cheaper', newly qualified teachers meant more work in terms of support. There had also been a reduction in allowances.

The head commented that the non-teaching staff could be first in line for cuts if needed. A certain amount of anxiety was reported among the NNEBs who felt threatened by the danger, not especially at this school, but more generally that they would be replaced by cheaper, untrained people. The deputy head wrote of their concern about the place of unqualified staff – 'they cost less, so staff are threatened by this idea'. On the other hand, the chair of governors mentioned the employment of additional classroom assistants and the creation of additional posts of responsibility. The deputy reported the popular decision to employ two extra NNEBs.

The deputy head also spoke of the subtle pressure not to be absent because of the cost of supply cover: 'teachers have a lot of concern about cover budgets, long-term absence and sickness – subtle pressure not to be absent'. She had experienced an anxious time worrying about overspending and job security:

> I do know as a 'B' allowance member of staff myself, and many others, were deeply distressed and unsettled when we had a period where it was thought the budget had been over-spent by several thousand. It had not but we still felt very worried and vulnerable – we felt some of us might lose jobs or have to take pay cuts – may be this was an extreme reaction but that's how it seemed!

A classroom teacher wrote: 'Everybody feels under pressure because of extra work and fear of losing their jobs. Health has been affected by all these pressures.' Financial constraints may be a factor contributing to such feelings, although clearly there are management issues as well. The head, deputy head, two classroom teachers and the secretary neither agreed nor disagreed with the statement *I anticipate teacher redundancies at this school as a result of LM*, although the chair of governors strongly disagreed.

Vignette 6.5: Managing redundancies

This 11–16 secondary school was introduced to full local management in April 1990. The 1992 survey shows the school with 1,070 pupils and a total full-time equivalent teaching staff of 72.4. The majority (70) are on full-time permanent contracts, the remainder being part-time permanent teachers. Since LM the school has lost teaching staff through natural wastage and compulsory redundancy. The head agreed with both the statement about salary considerations influencing the choice of teaching staff, and *I anticipate teacher redundancies at this school, as a result of LM*. The head neither agreed nor disagreed that *LM has resulted in more teachers on temporary appointments at the school*.

During the visit to the school, a fuller story about the circumstances of the redundancies emerged. The chair of governors reported that in 1990 the school lost its sixth form as a result of an LEA reorganisation and this left a surplus of four staff. Three teachers left and were not replaced. This included one deputy head whose work has since been taken on by other staff. Another left through ill-health, apparently having been served with a redundancy notice while off sick. Matter-of-factly, the deputy wrote: 'unfortunately an initial trimming of staff numbers was necessary' and he saw LM as a welcome way of weeding out dead-wood and tidying up the profession'. In his view, 'poor' teachers had ended up on the supply list. The senior clerk held a similar view. She believed that schools have 'to be run on more business-like lines – staff must be seen to be earning their salary. It will become easier to get rid of dead-wood'. In the head of history's words, on the other hand, 'the first year of LMS brought major problems with four redundancies'. A member of his department 'was declared surplus to require-ments without me being consulted in any way'. However, in the second year of LM, the head reported that three new young teachers were appointed on permanent contracts and the head commented that 'relying on natural wastage we have more staff than we can afford, but not more than we need'.

Staffing levels are based on a curriculum audit that is prepared by the head of science. He feels in a precarious position because the information he prepares goes to the governors and may be used in redundancy decisions. He explained his responsibility 'for identifying staffing/curriculum needs and providing information for possible reduction in staffing. This requires delicate handling so that staff do not feel threatened by discussions'.

In response to the attitude statement *I anticipate teacher redundancies at this school, as a result of LM,* all except the chair of governors agreed with this state-ment. While the chair disagreed, the head, deputy and head of science agreed; the head of history, English teacher and senior clerk all strongly agreed. In this context, many of those interviewed understandably spoke of teachers' concern over job security. The chair of governors spoke of staff feelings of insecurity about jobs. She said that unfounded rumours abounded but there was a lack of cash. The head commented:

Teachers fear for their jobs but our staff trust the school and its open discussion of staffing matters.

The head of science spoke of the policy to appoint cheaper teachers and an English teacher wrote of 'a feeling of tension among the staff – people are con-cerned about their jobs'. She believed that 'staff numbers will be decreased in the near future if number of pupils on roll falls'. The school had experienced a falling roll in recent times. The school lost pupils to a nearby school with a sixth form. The numbers, however, have now stabilised and are increasing, in part, perhaps, because of the deputy's pro-active stance to advertising.

More positively, the head of history stated 'LMS has allowed more flexibility in employment of, for example, technicians'. The head wrote of increases in non-teaching staff: 'the senior clerk had had her hours increased, a new job description with extra responsibilities. She had been re-graded with the introduction of LMS but not in line with the increased responsibilities.'

These three vignettes illustrate the autonomy of locally managed schools and the need for them to address and overcome problems. They illustrate also the different perceptions of role holders, those in less senior positions feeling more vulnerable and, in that sense, less autonomous than before. While they are largely left to respond using their own initiative and resources, schools are not entirely alone. Despite the delegation that has occurred, LEAs continue to hold resources at the centre which are to be used to support schools. How schools assess this role is the focus of the next section.

THE ROLE OF THE LOCAL EDUCATION AUTHORITY

In this section we consider the head teachers' perception of the role of the LEA. Local management of schools has dramatically affected their role and responsibilities and their relationships with schools. It has re-shaped the degree of autonomy a school has and altered accountability relationships in significant new ways. We examine the range and quality of the services provided by LEAs and leave our discussion of the new accountability relationships to the next chapter.

The policy context

A major objective of recent education policy has been to re-define the role the LEA has in relation to the schools under its control (Audit Commission, 1989; Raab, 1992; Ranson, 1990; Tomlinson, 1989). Government legislation has fundamentally altered the role of the LEA, essentially shifting power to schools and governors, diminishing the influence and power of the LEA. The Conservative Government elected in 1992 made clear that it wished to continue this process of restructuring:

> to continue to press for even greater delegation . . . Some LEAs are already considering maximum delegation of budget to their schools . . . LEAs offer a range of educational advice, support and training services to their own schools and to others. They also provide museums, the school library service and peripatetic music teaching and other music activities . . . The government expects that increasingly the private sector will step in to provide such services.
>
> (DfE/Welsh Office, 1992: 31–2)

Whether those in schools accept this view may be doubted. The stalling of the grant maintained initiative is one important piece of evidence, attitudes to LEAs and their services are another.

Central services

Assessing the quality of services

On the first questionnaire we provided a list of services typically provided centrally by the LEA and asked head teachers to rate them on a five point scale, from very good to very poor. These ratings are presented in Table 6.7 and suggest that head teachers, on the whole, were not unhappy with the quality of the services provided by the LEA. For each service, over 70 per cent of replies assess their quality as average, good or very good; the two least well-regarded services – site management and educational psychology – being regarded as poor or very poor by 29 per cent and 30 per cent respectively. When the sectors are considered separately, there is little difference between the ratings given by primary and secondary heads.

Table 6.7 Quality of LEA services/support

LEA service (% average or better)	Very Good	Good	Average	Poor	Very Poor	Number of cases
Personnel (91)	24	43	24	8	1	512
Legal (90)	24	36	30	7	2	406
IT (90)	21	42	27	7	2	503
LMS Advisers (89)	32	38	19	7	4	524
Financial Information (86)	25	39	22	12	3	556
Curriculum Advisers (84)	15	38	31	12	5	547
Health & Safety (84)	11	30	43	12	4	464
Advisory Teachers (81)	11	36	34	11	8	506
Resource Centres (80)	10	36	34	11	8	470
Pupil Welfare (80)	12	34	34	14	6	594
Site management (71)	9	26	36	17	12	441
Educational Psychology (71)	14	32	25	18	12	564

Written comments from head teachers reinforce the view that they believe further delegation will affect the quality of services offered by the LEA:

My fears are that schools will move to grant-maintained status in a bid for 'easy-cash' or that more and more will be devolved to schools through government pressure. I fear this because it would mean that I would lose the professional support of the LEA. Their role is essential both in supporting us in local management and the INSET role of staff development – advisory teachers etc. If this happens the non professionals (governors) could have an undue influence in the running of schools and this could be detrimental.

I hope LEA services (e.g., educational psychologists, peripatetic music, library services etc.) are not delegated as I fear these valuable services will be lost if they are.

Excellent support formerly provided by LEA is being eroded by ever increasing delegation.

Clearly, there appeared to be high regard for many LEA services in 1991, a view reflected in head teachers' attitudes to further delegation.

Attitudes to further delegation

From a list of services provided in a questionnaire, head teachers were asked to identify areas of LEA activity where delegation would be welcomed. The majority of head teachers appeared not to want more LEA services delegated, although there are differences between primary and secondary schools in attitudes towards more delegation.

The data in Table 6.8 suggest that heads of both primary and secondary schools were not seeking a very significant extension of delegation in 1991, although secondary heads showed a notably greater desire for further delegation in certain services. The majority of secondary heads would like to have greater responsibility for the budget on the in-service training of teachers, the peripatetic curriculum service delegated and responsibility for link courses and peripatetic music.

Table 6.8 Delegation of services

SERVICE Retained by LEA	Delegation Welcome (total number)	
	Primary	Secondary
INSET	50% (302)	77% (69)
Peripatetic Curriculum	39% (370)	56% (77)
Peripatetic Music	38% (360)	47% (90)
Special Needs	31% (406)	36% (90)
Education Psychologists	30% (440)	41% (97)
LEA Initiatives	20% (350)	34% (80)
School Meals	19% (367)	33% (81)
Education Welfare	19% (431)	39% (96)
Library Services	18% (396)	41% (87)
Museum Services	16% (341)	28% (81)
Residential & Field Centre	15% (326)	34% (82)
Link Courses	12% (238)	47% (53)
Teachers' Centres	11% (375)	28% (85)
Home Tuition	9% (350)	18% (91)
Crossing Patrols	9% (344)	12% (72)
Home/School Transport	6% (360)	11% (87)

Head teacher views on the delegation of specific LEA services contrast to some extent with their responses to a statement on the first questionnaire, which read: *I would welcome greater levels of delegation.* The percentage of head teachers agreeing with this statement is higher than might be expected, although the sector differences are apparent: 70 per cent of secondary head teachers either agreed or agreed strongly with this statement. In contrast only 42 per cent of primary head teachers would welcome further delegation.

Of those secondary heads who would welcome greater levels of delegation 45 per cent were heads of smaller secondary schools and slightly more than half, 55 per cent, were heads of larger secondaries. In the primary sector, 67 per cent who responded positively to the statement were heads of larger primary schools and only 33 per cent were heads of smaller primary schools.

One head of a large primary school, while supporting in principle the transfer of responsibilities from the LEA to schools, did not wish to see the 'demise of the LEA':

In principle I support local management . . . I welcome the idea of a considerably 'slimmed-down' LEA but *not* the demise of the LEA.

However, another wished to eventually see 'a fully delegated system':

I feel that LMS has revolutionised the way in which schools are managed. It is something that was long overdue and it is a process which I as a head welcome. I hope that ultimately it will take place within a fully delegated system outside local authority control.

A head of a small secondary expressed the 'hope for extended delegation', while another hoped for 'maximum delegation and a cheque book soon'.

Since these data were collected in 1991 there has been further delegation of LEA services. Responding to concerns that many schools may seek GM status, several LEAs devised schemes with more extensive delegation. Even if such policies achieved their purpose of limiting opting-out, however, it may have been at the expense of the preferences of many heads who, in 1991, were apparently satisfied with the retention of many LEA services. This extension of delegation caused us, in the 1993 survey, to seek views on the delegation of services previously retained centrally by the LEA. The statement read: *The LEA is now delegating funds for some services which I think would best be provided centrally.* In the primary sector 59 per cent of head teachers agreed that their LEA is now delegating services best provided centrally, as compared with 43 per cent in the secondary sector.

Changing relationships and the role of the LEA (1): Concerns

Through the questionnaires and visits to schools, head teachers commented quite extensively on the changing role of the LEA and their school's relationship with the local authority. The changed role of the LEA is sometimes a cause of concern, notably the loss of dedicated, skilled staff; the loss of a strategic planning role; undermining of some services; and the need for retaining some services at the centre. There was some anxiety about losing the support of the LEA: 'I would be worried to lose the backing of the LEA which has proved most supportive'. A secretary told us that she liked the school 'being in control' with the 'back up' of the LEA. A deputy head liked the 'umbrella image/concept of a supporting LEA'.

The loss of dedicated, skilled staff

Local management shifts power from the LEA to the school and its governing body. A result of this shift in power, some would argue, is the demise of the LEA and consequent loss of expertise. A chair of governors commented: 'Power is being given to lay people at the expense of LEA office/adviser experience, particularly on senior staff appointments'. One head teacher wrote of her 'concern about . . . loss of, or excessive cost of, little used but crucial specialist services e.g., legal advice, advice on redundancies etc., as more money is delegated'. A deputy head felt strongly about this loss and commented 'it is a loathsome spectacle to see dedicated and able people scrapped'. Some heads argued that some duties are more efficiently or effective organised by the LEA:

LEA has people who can do the job better than me. I am now learning their job – how can that make me (or them) more effective?

and another agreed with this sentiment, observing:

Delegation does not automatically improve efficiency. Some tasks are best performed by dedicated staff at LEA level. Transport for instance.

The 'danger that excessive delegation could lead to loss of economies of scale and duplication', is also mentioned by one head teacher, and another notes the 'transfer of clerical work from city education office to school'.

Loss of strategic planning

A recurrent theme in the comments of heads was a concern about the implications that LMS could have for the strategic role of the LEA. One head stressed the inability to plan in long term, seeing LM as 'hastening the demise of local authorities – to the detriment of planning education provision, strategic planning etc.'. Similar sentiments were expressed by another:

Loss of LEA role in planning for educational provision locally and handling placement of children in local schools when over subsidised in a fair manner.

Other head teachers argued that:

There is an increasing chance that the demise of LEAs as planning bodies will occur, despite efforts to prevent this.

and that:

It (LM) is causing fragmentation of the whole system – LEAs will not be able to have any co-ordinating system, e.g., special needs provision.

LEAs are seen as playing a central and valuable role in the planning and co-ordination of school places and services. In particular, some feel that LM and extended delegation will undermine the provision of certain services and result in their loss.

Undermining services

A fear of the loss of services was voiced by one head teacher with the words 'local authorities . . . no longer have the scope to develop centrally funded provision, like special needs support'. The demise of other services is mentioned by head teachers, one writing of the 'disruption of LEA services – psychological help for pupils, peripatetic music instruction, advisory service'. Another spoke of the LEA having 'no discretionary resources to support schools with particular problems/needs'. The decline of the LEA was not welcomed by some, who saw 'vital services' being 'cut . . . children with special needs are not being given their entitlement in resources'. Extended delegation exacerbates this problem:

> Excellent support formerly provided by the LEA is being eroded by ever-increasing delegation.

With increasing delegation of funding for central services, if insufficient numbers of schools buy back into the services, there is a danger that they will disappear, or become prohibitively expensive:

> Some services which could not realistically be provided by individual schools are being undermined and there is a danger that they will be replaced by commercial ventures and eventual increased costs.

Clearly, then, some head teachers are alert to the 'danger that services will disappear'. One head told us that 'we have always enjoyed the support from advisers and feel very sorry that this is diminishing'. Those who are unhappy with the delegation of some services argue for their central retention.

A call for the retention of services

The following statement argues for the central retention of some services and the end to further delegation:

> More generally, I think devolved funding has gone far enough. LEAs must be able to keep enough money back for flexibility to direct funds to where they are needed. This applies equally to educational psychologists, leading innovation, property repair, etc. Needs are not equal, so there has to be discrimination in provision.

In practice, the government has now mandated that the services of educational psychologists and the educational welfare service are 'protected' as exceptions to the Potential Schools' Budget. There are other services which some wish to see retained at the centre:

> Educational Support Services must be kept alive and well for the support of the primary sector – ever the poor relation of the system.

LEAs are needed – only they can offer certain centralised resources e.g., SEN provision.

We (teachers) are . . . very concerned about the changes in central support services, e.g., literacy support etc.

A specific concern of some head teachers is the threat to professional development programmes posed by the reduced role of the LEA.

Central role in professional development

'The delegation of GEST funding could militate against professional development of a personal nature'. This concern was expressed by a head teacher who viewed the reduction of LEA advisory staff as 'resulting in greatly diminished programmes of staff development'. The threat to the career development of staff is identified by this head teacher who writes:

If LEAs are forced to delegate funds that are currently used for inspection/advice/INSET it could lead to considerable problems in career development of my staff and also in their response to curriculum development. We have good provision and support from the LEA at the moment in this area and I am concerned it might cease. LEAs still have an important but different role.

It would be misleading, however, to suggest that all of the changes to the role of the LEA are seen by head teachers as unwelcome developments. Many have mixed views, voicing concern about, for instance, the loss of some services, and delight at the development of a more responsive and less paternalistic LEA. It is this change that we consider first in our exploration of the perceived benefits, or welcome changes to the role of the LEA and its relationship with schools.

Changing relationships and the role of the LEA (2): Benefits

Less bureaucracy

Some head teachers quite simply speak of local management as the 'removal of bureaucracy' or the 'release . . . from the bureaucracy of the LEA'. Others comment on less time 'involved in unnecessary bureaucracy'. More specifically, LM has given schools the 'ability to move money in order to make extra purchases where most needed without involvement in LEA bureaucracy'. One head teacher writes:

It has . . . freed us from some bureaucracy although in general our LEA officers are excellent and very helpful.

Cutting out this 'red tape' is perceived as improving decision-making processes at some schools.

Improved decision-making

Locally managed schools no longer have to wait for LEA approval on their spending decisions and, finance permitting, the needs and priorities of the school may more easily be identified and met. Head teachers speak of 'decision making at the local point rather than LEA decision making and priority rating' and 'more flexibility to use funds without referring to the LEA'. The secretary at one school we visited commented that 'staff do not have to wait for decisions from the LEA'. As other comments reveal, being able to respond to local needs without having to wait for LEA approval is welcomed:

> Money is now spent meeting the needs of the school as we see them and not the perceived needs of the LEA.

> It has been beneficial to have control of budget for items such as maintenance, furnishings etc., and to be able to control expenditure on these items according to a plan (rather than waiting for the 'office' to see to it – or not).

> Being allowed to spend money without first having to seek approval/permission from LEA.

The resulting additional workload on head teachers is seen as worth the effort, as two head teachers explain:

> This has increased my workload, but for once it has been well worthwhile, for decisions taken locally have received immediate support so that priority decisions have been implemented without undue delay. Many of the frustrations have been reduced, if not totally removed and this has made for a much happier staff.

and:

> Although I do spend more time on LM as Direct Services contracts come up for re-negotiation and more is delegated, and I find some of the admin. very boring, on the whole I enjoy it because I have skills I am now using and because I can get nearer to achieving our vision for the school. I have much more power re the LEA which benefits our school.

Some head teachers also express desires for further delegation.

Desire for further delegation

Many requests for further delegation are specific to certain items or are in the context of a wish to remain with the LEA. For example, one head teacher writes:

> I've enjoyed the development and would like to see some further delegation of areas that are still administered by the LEA, particularly regarding external maintenance.

and another:

> I would like the elements retained by the LEA to come to schools so that we could 'buy in' support services as we deem the need.

while a third observes:

> The LEA still has a tendency to be paternalistic but will hopefully delegate more in due course of time. The tendency for schools to move out of a corporate system can eventually only damage the service as a whole.

The deputy head at one of the schools we visited believed that if a school had successfully proved itself capable of managing the LM budget, further funds should be delegated:

> If schools are good enough and capable of improving the educational provision through the prudent management of their budgets then they should be given responsibility for the whole budget. At present LEAs still influence too much and provide poor value for money in some areas. The school should be able to purchase that which it needs in addition to redirecting resources otherwise held by the LEA to more urgent priorities within the school.

For others, requests for extended delegation are associated with the longer term desire to seek grant maintained status:

> After 100 plus years of State (county council) run education, the emphasis is at long last at the point of delivery – and I regret nothing for the past – every change in LMS funding and in inception is a huge plus – long may change continue – 100% plus will satisfy me.

and:

> I like the full delegation and can't wait for a cheque book. I would like to opt out because I feel we have more resources for children's benefit.

The desire for a 'cheque book' is voiced by several:

> What we really need is the money so that the best deals can be achieved – some obviously would benefit from 'cash in hand' sooner than waiting for all the process of payment to be made by LEA.

The administrative officer at one school with a cheque book extols its virtues:

> Since April 1992 we have had our own bank account which has benefited the schools even more. Dealing with suppliers on a personal basis, instead of through the Authority, has improved these relationships.

A rare view is a preference for maximum delegation which forces schools to rely on their own capacities:

Give us as much delegated power and decision-making as possible. Cut the centre (LEA) to the absolute minimum . . . (LM) the best thing that ever happened to Education – ineffective schools should be allowed to fail and be taken over by effective managers (or close).

It is evident, however, that the overall assessment of local management is more balanced than this observation and is reflected in our concluding summary and comments.

CONCLUSION: DELEGATION IN PRACTICE

Schools in England and Wales not only manage the larger part of the expenditure on schools but welcome that role. Over 90 per cent of head teachers welcomed the responsibility and the flexibility it is seen as providing. It appears to have contributed to changes in spending priorities and the creation of contingency funds to allow for future uncertainty. Schools have been cautious in their total spending and this has led to underspending and a continued effort at raising additional funds, although these are very small in volume. There is evidence of head teachers taking on the role of management while administrative staff handle more routine procedures but this is by no means universal. This delegation has led to a greater awareness of the cost of things among head teachers and other staff, an awareness which includes the cost of the staff themselves.

Reinforcing this heightened greater awareness of costs is the evidence that salary has become a consideration when appointing teachers. The use of temporary contracts for full and part-time staff has also increased and there has been a deterioration in the pupil–teacher ratio. Among non-teaching staff, the average number of hours worked by non-teaching assistants has increased in the primary sector while the secondary sector shows little change. In addition, however, the role of administrative/clerical staff has changed significantly, not always with matching change in grades and salaries. Some administrative/clerical staff report feeling a greater identity with the school while others speak of a lack of recognition. The role of the traditional school caretaker has also changed; more often referred to as site managers they commonly have responsibility for minor maintenance work.

Finally, the majority of head teachers see a continuing role for the LEA and do not wish to see it reduced further by the delegation of more services to school level. None the less, the delegation that has taken place is welcomed and the majority of head teachers believe that the LEA is now more responsive than in the past and provides a better service.

The evidence on the practice of delegation cited here points to a welcome for the opportunities it creates to set spending priorities. Alongside that advantage is the more challenging task of judging relative priorities when the choices include the trade-off between salary and experience when making staff appointments or the priority of spending on staff as against other resources. Few schools wish to be wholly self-managed, however, our surveys indicating support for a continuing role for the LEA.

Taken as a whole it is an account which shows head teachers employing their greater autonomy over the management of resources. What cannot be discerned from this evidence is its significance for learners. What is clear, however, is the impact of local management on teaching and support staff. This takes a variety of forms but, for many, the greater concern about tenure and the use of temporary contracts is likely to create a sense of loss of control or autonomy over their lives. As with so much change, benefits for one group can create problems for others. How it all manifests itself for pupils is a theme we consider in Chapter 8, following an examination of the new accountabilities in Chapter 7.

Chapter 7

Accountability and decentralisation

DIALOGUES OF ACCOUNTABILITY

The delegation of resource management to schools is a specific and limited form of autonomy and must be distinguished from an autonomy which means that, in certain areas of action, individuals or groups have an unfettered right to self-determination. The freedom schools have to make their own spending decisions, for example, is contingent upon it being used responsibly. This means that decisions on resources must be taken in the context of a statutory duty to implement the national curriculum: spending decisions must give primacy to meeting the requirements of the national curriculum. Second, the continued right to delegation is contingent upon how it is exercised; if schools plan to overspend their budget, for example, an LEA has a duty to suspend the powers of delegation. Third, the exercise of their powers is subject to a regular financial audit and a four-yearly inspection. The latter leads to a published report which includes a judgement on how well resources are being used and whether the school is providing value for money. In extreme cases of poor management, the head and governing body can be replaced.

By citing these examples of the distinctive nature of autonomy in delegation, we begin to identify the forms of accountability through which autonomy is constrained and delegation monitored. While the study upon which this book draws does not include data on all these forms of accountability – the regular cycle of school inspection, for example, began as our surveys concluded – we are able to examine some aspects. Most substantially, we examine evidence on the nature and scope of the accountability relationship between head teachers and their governing bodies and, to a lesser degree between schools and their LEAs. We regard the first of these relationships as a central component of the accountabilities created by the 1988 Education Reform Act. The Act and its consequent regulations and circulars are clear in the emphasis they place upon governing bodies as the key agency for discharging the new responsibilities placed upon schools:

> the governing body will control the running of a qualifying school within its delegated budget ... the governing body and the head teacher will have

freedom to deploy resources within the school's budget according to their own educational needs and priorities. They will determine the number of both teaching and non-teaching staff at the school, will select for appointment and will be able to require dismissal, taking account of the professional advice of the Chief Education Officer and the head teacher.

(DES, 1988).

The identification of the Chief Education Officer in this quotation represents a continuing role for the LEA as a source of professional advice which, together with its duty to suspend powers of local management where these are abused, indicate its position as a body to which the school – head teacher and governing body – remain accountable. As argued in Chapter 2 and Chapter 6, however, there is little doubt that the 1988 Act and later legislation has limited the capacity of the LEA as an active agent of accountability and, while we draw upon further evidence of their role, our principal emphasis is on the role of the governing body.

In examining emerging relationships we give particular attention to what we identify as a *dialogue of accountability* between and among the stakeholders who have a legitimate interest in the work and achievement of schools. As it is around this concept that we have organised the remainder of the chapter we examine briefly the conditions for supporting these dialogues. Subsequently, we provide vignettes on the involvement of governors in five schools and we end with a brief conclusion.

Schools need structures and processes whereby decisions about the allocation of resources are made in ways that are well-informed about the standard and quality of the core activities that support learning; decisions which are based upon poor information can lead to a mis-match of resources to needs. The information required is predominantly qualitative and teachers and head teachers have a key role in judging needs. Outside observers, however, can also participate in making that judgement. One of the challenges of delegated management is identifying the means by which other stakeholders, such as the governing body and the LEA, can obtain information about the school which enable them to contribute to judgements about the school and its needs. Meeting this challenge has three main components, all of which are related to the nature and quality of information: the structures of decision-making; the dialogue between interested groups; and the sources of information.

A principal aim of delegating resource management is to improve the match between resources and educational needs and, therefore, the *structures for decision-making* must provide for a link between resource decisions and the assessment of needs. Since the governing body is accountable for resources and learning, any committee structure that is created should ensure that decisions about resources are properly informed by an assessment of educational need. The nature of any *dialogue of decision-making* over resources and educational needs is another crucial test of accountability.

What is discussed at meetings of governors and head teachers is one test of this dialogue and we examine those areas in which governors are involved. We also provide perspectives on how the involvement of governors and their participation in decision-making is changing. Finally, the nature and source of *information* contributes to the quality of the dialogue. Effectively matching resources to needs requires good information on the teaching and learning which we take to be the prime purpose of schools. The accountability of professionals requires governing bodies to have access to information and to be able to use that to make independent judgements. We draw upon data on the role of head teachers which raise questions about the impact of delegated management on the availability and quality of that information.

We would include a note of caution before we proceed. The theme of accountability was a limited part of the surveys we undertook as part of the LMS 'Impact' Project. We see our data as no more than illuminating a much larger area of inquiry, some of which is explored in a partner study to this and includes a fuller discussion of the theme of accountability in an examination of the characteristics of a cost-effective school (Thomas and Martin, 1996).

STRUCTURES OF DECISION-MAKING

In 1993, the then Secretary of State for Education outlined the challenge of being a school governor as:

> a fulfilling and challenging form of active citizenship. Governorship has become a real job with real responsibilities. A governing body of a large secondary school can have control of well over £2 million a year. Decisions over staff appointments and increasing discretion over rates of pay now come under the control of the governing body. Contrary to some views many people find these duties a challenge rather than a burden.
>
> (Patten, 1993)

On the assumption that membership, attendance and meetings are basic prerequisites for discharging their responsibilities, it is with descriptive information on these issues that we begin.

The Education (No. 2) Act 1986 specified the constitution of governing bodies. For schools with fewer than one hundred pupils, the governing body is made up of two parents, two LEA nominees, one teacher, three co-opted governors and the head teacher if s/he wishes. Controlled schools have just one co-opted governor, and two foundation governors. Schools with one hundred to two hundred and ninety-nine pupils have an additional parent, LEA and co-opted or foundation governor. Larger schools (300 to 599 pupils) have an extra parent, LEA, teacher and foundation/co-opted governor. The constitution of governing bodies of schools with over six hundred pupils is five parents, five LEA nominees, two teachers, six co-opted members and the head if s/he wishes. Controlled schools have four foundation and two co-opted instead of six co-opted. Thus, the largest schools may have a governing body with nineteen members although, as Sallis (1987) explains, 'LEAs have the option to drop the largest category and treat schools of over six hundred pupils in the same way as those of 300–600, thus establishing sixteen as the top size of governing board'. The arrangements for aided and special agreement schools are different. Sallis explains:

> Regardless of size:- at least one LEA governor. In primary schools, at least one representative of the minor authority, if any; at least one parent governor; at least one teacher governor in schools of under 300; at least two teacher governors in schools over 300; the head if s/he wishes; foundation governors sufficient to secure majority. . . . There shall be a majority of foundation governors of two over all other interests in boards up to 18 members and three in larger boards. One foundation governor must always be a parent of a pupil.
>
> (1987: 27)

From the one hundred and eight primary schools providing us with data on the number of governors necessary for a full complement in 1992 and 1993, the most common number was twelve (38 per cent of schools in 1992 and 32 per cent in 1993) or sixteen (24 per cent in 1992; 22 per cent in 1993). The most common number of governors in the secondary sector was sixteen (32 per cent in 1992; 35 per cent in 1993).

In the first survey, head teachers were asked if they and their deputies attended and were members of the governing body. Responses showed that head teachers attend almost all meetings of their governing bodies and three-quarters of these heads are also members of the governing body. In over one-third of the cases, deputy heads are also members of the governing body and, in about half of those cases where the deputy is not a member, s/he attends the meetings.

The first survey also collected information on the frequency of meetings of the full governing body in the year to April 1991. Many governing bodies (39 per cent) meet for the statutory minimum of three times annually with 19 per cent meeting four times. Ten per cent met more than six times annually and one governing body met on thirteen occasions. Head teachers were also asked to report the 'average' length of these meetings and 84 per cent lasted between two and four hours. Typically, governing bodies had established committees to conduct some of their business, the most common being for finance, staffing, curriculum and premises.

Despite expressions of concern about schools attracting enough people to act as governors, national data and our own survey data suggest that this has not been a great problem. In a survey following the first cycle of replacements after the 1986 Act and 'the challenge of replacing up to 150,000 school governors whose terms of office had ended' (all governors serve for four years), Patten observed:

> There were those that said that people would not come forward. In fact the figures we now have show a vacancy rate of just 6.9 per cent across the country. . . . Governing bodies invariably carry vacancies mainly because people move house or change jobs and find that as consequence they have to resign.
>
> (1993: 1)

Set against this positive national evidence are expressions of local concern about recruitment. One deputy head teacher commented: 'due to school area we find it difficult to get parent governors', and a chair of governors observed: 'They are very hard to come by as people are reluctant to take on the responsibility'. Among those who do become governors, the nature of the dialogue of decision-making between governors, head teachers and teachers is examined below.

THE DIALOGUE OF DECISION-MAKING

The role of the governing body and the relationship with the head teacher and other members of staff takes many forms. Given the extensive powers of governors, how are they being exercised in practice? Is there a difference between their theoretical powers and the use of those powers in practice? To what extent are 'amateur' governors led by the educational 'professionals'? Does the involvement of governors enhance the decision-making process or slow it down and cause frustrating delay? These questions are raised by comments made by those we interviewed on the school visits and are represented in statements made by head teachers on the postal surveys. Governors are 'new centres of power' and their roles and relationships are still emerging. Golby asks:

> Can they take these powers without diminishing the powers of professional staff and local authorities (which remain, except in the case of schools which opt out, the legal employers of the teachers and owners of the schools)? Is it desirable that they should do?
>
> (1992: 165)

Sallis reports on confusion about their role: 'Most governors who write to me say, in different ways, that they are confused about their role, whether they are in effect supporters, inspectors, ambassadors or go-betweens' (1991: 217). A study for Sheffield City Council reports the involvement of governors in reaching decisions on resource allocation:

> The common practice across all the sites was one whereby governors had delegated all decisions concerning resource allocation including financial

decisions to the head. In this sense, governors were often placed in a position whereby they ratified decisions which had been taken by head teachers and full time members of schools. However, it should be emphasised that governors were not bystanders but were interested and supportive members of schools within which they worked.

(Burgess *et al.*, 1992: 32)

Our surveys provide examples of governing bodies both fitting this description and departing from it. One head teacher commented on his own governors as 'reluctant to interfere or control – they enjoy the involvement but prefer to monitor rather than innovate'. Participation by some governing bodies in the decision-making process amounts to the discussion of the head teacher's recommendations and another head teacher described this role of governors in decision-making as hearing the head teacher's explanation of the management of the school 'rather than entering into the management at the decision-making stage'. The HMI report on the implementation of LMS reiterates some of these comments on the involvement of governors:

> During the early phase of LMS the degree of involvement of governing bodies varied widely. . . . Gradually, in part a result of training, more governors are gaining confidence and becoming directly involved, although most continue to leave the initiative to senior management of the school.
>
> (1992: 15)

We discuss data on the roles and relationships of governors under a number of headings, providing examples of positive, 'successful' relationships as well as difficult ones. We give voice to those desiring greater governor involvement and to those who do not welcome the increased involvement.

Areas of involvement

Head teachers were asked to identify those they felt to be 'principally involved in decision-making' in a given list of areas. Greatest governor involvement in decision-making was in the allocation of responsibility allowances, where the survey showed 65 per cent of governing bodies/chairs as 'principally' involved. The second highest level of governor involvement was in decisions on the use of premises out-of-hours (60 per cent), much the same as their involvement in decisions on the total number of teachers (59 per cent). This was followed by involvement in decisions on the maintenance of premises (56 per cent) and the number of support staff (33 per cent). Twenty-three per cent of head teachers reported governors as being principally involved in the preparation of the school's Development Plan. In summary, governors appear principally to be involved in resource decisions related to staffing and premises. When asked to identify decisions where governors *insisted* upon involvement, staffing issues dominated (64 per cent).

Head teachers in the first survey were also asked to respond to statements on the involvement of governors in decision-making. Replies from 172 smaller primary schools, 249 larger primaries, 51 smaller secondaries and 51 larger secondaries showed general agreement with the statement *Since LM decision-making is more widely shared with governors.* Sixty-seven per cent of head teachers in smaller primary schools and 73 per cent of heads of smaller secondary schools agreed with this statement. Agreement was greater still among the heads of larger primary and secondary schools: 78 per cent of heads of larger primary schools agreed and 82 per cent of heads of larger secondary schools.

Head teachers and others recognised the increased involvement of governors. One head commented that 'governors are more involved and interested in what happens and the way the school is run' and another: 'there is now far greater governor involvement in the running of the school'. A third head teacher noted the 'excellent working relationships with governors, and their greater involvement with the day to day running of the school'. The deputy head at one school commented: 'governors are more involved and encouraged to liaise with school' and one of the teachers felt 'more involved with the governors. They are all known to us and each class has a governor attached to it . . . We can all work together'. This was reiterated by another teacher who said: 'governors are more closely linked and identified with school; my class has its own governor who visits the children'.

From their comments, some saw this greater involvement positively, the chair of one governing body saying:

The increased involvement of the governing body had led to more co-operation with the head teachers and to some extent the staff. I feel that in the long term this will increase to the betterment of the school.

Others felt that the changes had brought real purpose to the governing body, several commenting that governors no longer 'rubber-stamped'. A chair of governors told us: 'governors do have powers and responsibilities – previously we were a rubber stamp'. Another chair of governors commented that 'more governors are getting directly involved rather than rubber stamping' and that the meetings had changed from 'tea parties' to 'business meetings'. He saw the role of the governors as wicket-keepers catching the odd stray ball.

While recognising that the governors relied on the head teacher to inform, the chair of governors at a third school felt much more involved now, no longer rubber-stamping. On the other hand, one of the teachers commented: 'governors now have powers to make decisions but do not have necessary knowledge. In practice they . . . go along with whatever is presented'. Whether the level of governor knowledge is commensurate with their responsibilities is discussed later.

In the first survey we sought responses to the statement *The involvement of the governing body is about right.* Fifty-four per cent of the larger primary heads agreed with the statement and 41 per cent of heads of smaller primary schools; in the secondary sector, 74 per cent of the heads of larger schools, and 58 per cent of the head teachers of smaller schools agreed.

The need for greater involvement

Responses to the statement *The governors still need to become more involved in decision-making on LM* generally complement the previous statement. Levels of agreement were greatest among heads of smaller primary schools, who also showed least agreement with the statement about the involvement of the governing body being about right. Forty-seven per cent of heads of smaller primary schools agreed that governors still need to become more involved and 41 per cent of heads of larger primaries agreed. In the secondary sector, just 5 per cent of heads of larger secondaries and 32 per cent of heads of smaller secondaries agreed.

Some governors have clearly become more involved with the school and its decision-making processes. However, there are indications that some governors are more reluctant. The head teacher at one school, for example, has governors that 'need to be more involved in school affairs to comment on, advise on and govern the school. LMS has frightened and mystified them'. The chair of governors at this same school thought that the increased role of the governors was 'very interesting and enjoyable but time consuming' and that it was 'difficult getting all governors involved'. The chair of governors at another school also points to patchy involvement, commenting that '*all* governors need to have close links with school and head'.

The welcome for greater involvement

In the second and third surveys, we asked head teachers to respond to the statement *I welcome the increased involvement of governors in the running of the school.* Responses from one hundred and twenty-one primary head teachers show that 48 per cent agreed with this statement in 1992, dropping slightly to 46 per cent the following year. The thirty-nine secondary-school head teachers showed 38 per cent agreeing with the statement, increasing to 46 per cent the following year. In both sectors fewer than half of head teachers *welcome* the increased involvement of governors in the running of the school. A head teacher in the third survey noted 'more interference in day to day running by some governors'; another also mentioned governor interference:

> Regrettably some governors find it an excuse to interfere with the internal running and decision-making in schools and this has led to some friction.

and one head teacher warned that

Governors can be tricky to handle – even for an old lag like me. . . . To be a new head can be very difficult when governors think they should run the show.

In the second and third survey, head teachers were asked to respond to a statement about the suitability of governors in deciding upon discretionary payments. Replies from one hundred and twenty-one primary and forty secondary head teachers show that less than a quarter (24 per cent) of primary heads agreed in 1992 that *The governors are a suitable body for deciding upon discretionary payments* and this declined to just 16 per cent in 1993. Responses in the secondary sector are similar: 25 per cent agreeing in 1992, reducing to 20 per cent in 1993. When this issue was explored during school visits, considerable differences emerged between groups. Sixty-eight per cent and 69 per cent of teachers and deputy heads *disagreed* with the statement, and more than half (51 per cent) of heads disagreed. On the other hand, 65 per cent of chairs of governors *agreed* and more administrative/clerical staff agreed than disagreed. One head teacher, on the third questionnaire, commented:

Governors are not professionals and they cannot possibly be expected to make decisions over pay etc. How do they assess? . . . The differentials between head/deputy and top paid teachers should be uniform throughout the country and not left to governors to decide. It is not fair to expect them to do this.

Our data suggest that governor involvement in decision-making has increased, although there is some evidence that not all heads welcome this, sometimes because of a more prolonged decision-making process.

Prolonged decision-making processes

From comments in the second and third surveys we found some head teachers voicing the opinion that involvement of governors in decision-making, although welcomed in some respects, prolonged the process to an extent which some found frustrating. One wrote that 'governor structures to ensure accountability are slowing down management decisions and making change harder'. Others point to the length of time and the extra work:

Governor support/advice often *slows down* decision-making process. Governing body meetings are very laborious – first one ended 11.35 p.m. . . . Prefer 'rubber stamp' governing body who would trust professionals to do their job and refer only exceptions to them. Case in point, new pay structure requires new Pay and Staff Policy to be agreed by whole governing body and implemented by 1.9.93. Means extra whole governing body meeting and much extra work for the head teacher.

and

> Greater flexibility for decision-making in the distribution of finance . . . has involved more meetings with governing body sub-committees in order to discuss policies/decisions. Consultation can slow down some decisions that need to be made. . . . I am concerned about the gradual realisation in some governing bodies of the power potential available. Already . . . some governing body senior management decisions (head teacher appointments) have drastically changed the climate of appointment and job tenure.

One head teacher described the governing body as 'a pain in the neck' and their greater involvement as a 'millstone rather than helpful'. He made the decisions, and the job of 'persuading' the governors simply prolonged the process. He commented: 'the process is long-winded but the result is the same'. This view raises an important issue about the nature of accountability. It might be argued that, in order to provide a reasoned case to his governors, this head may have had to review his position more carefully. In this sense, even if governors only listen and approve, they have fulfilled a role in ensuring that options are more carefully considered. It may be the case, however, that governors have too little information in order to assess the arguments and judgements put to them by their head teachers. We consider this theme in the next section.

INFORMATION FOR ACCOUNTABILITY

The quality of head teacher–governor accountability must in some degree depend on the knowledge governors have of the issues on which they must decide. We begin our consideration of this by reviewing evidence provided by head teachers of their own familiarity with events in the classroom. We do this on the grounds that information about classroom activity – teaching and learning – is the critical base for making decisions on resources: matching resources to needs requires good information on needs. As governors depend heavily on the information provided by head teachers, the quality of information from that source is a key issue. Evidence from our surveys suggests that heads may now be less informed about events in the classroom.

The information base of head teachers

In all three surveys head teachers were asked to respond to the statement *The demands of LM mean I am less familiar with events in the classroom.* Over half the heads from both sectors agreed with this statement in 1993 and their responses suggest that experience of LM has *not* improved this situation. In the primary sector (one hundred and twenty-one schools) 77 per cent of heads agreed with the statement in 1991, 71 per cent in 1992 and the same in 1993. There is no consistent relationship with size of school. Given that LM may have had a greater impact on the knowledge primary heads have of events in the classroom, how did secondary heads respond to the statement? Their responses have remained fairly stable from 1991 to 1993, about 58 per cent agreeing that the demands of LM had resulted in them being less familiar with events in the classroom. In summary, a high proportion of heads feel that the demands of LM mean that they are less familiar with classroom activities. Their comments suggest that they are alert to this:

> I am not as aware of classroom practice and feel I am not supporting staff as I used to. I rarely teach and when I do it is in an emergency and I am totally unprepared. The stress level on head teachers is high – many of us have experienced sleepless nights and feel de-skilled and de-valued. It has obviously improved with time and experience but I personally feel that the cost has been too high.

In the third survey, many head teachers spoke of the changed role and the increased workload taking them away from educational matters. They wrote about the 'more time consuming non-educational work and responsibility', which takes them 'away from educational matters' and said that LM 'has meant considerably less time teaching children'. One head teacher said that workload does not allow time to 'give priority to the children's learning'. Some find themselves spending 'more time on maintenance and buildings' than 'on education'. Others comment:

> The principle of LM is good, but authority support is insufficient and extra work is unacceptable. Less time for heads to consider 'education' and support teachers in classrooms.

> I thought I was trained as an educationalist – far too much time being taken up for administration and in particular with reference to LM. . . . Checking out that contractors are completing their contractual duties is an absolute pain!

> While it is difficult to disentangle the effects of LMS from other recent developments, I spend most of my time doing things that I did not have to concern myself with a few years ago. I have tried not to decrease the support I give staff, but involvement with children and the curriculum is much less.

In order to maintain a role in matters directly educational, some head teachers have sacrificed life after school to catch up on administrative tasks. One head teacher felt that the duties he now undertakes will do nothing for educational standards:

> I waste time trying to find out who can cut the weeds or unblock drains cheaper than the LEA. Meantime we have lost our Special Needs teacher, but I cannot help those children because I have to spend time ringing the Finance Department about expenditure wrongly coded to our school. This will do nothing to 'raise educational standards' and compete with other countries to create the wealth needed to pay for education.

While the majority of head teachers have welcomed local management the consequence of less awareness of classroom practice may be affecting the quality of the information on which decisions on resources are made. This may have an effect on decisions by governing bodies who, in any event, face a challenge in becoming well informed.

Lack of knowledge and understanding

A number of comments point to a concern about the lack of understanding and knowledge of governors about educational issues. One head teacher told us: 'I feel that sometimes the governors are not well enough informed . . . I welcome the closer involvement . . . (but) question their suitability to make some of the decisions being asked of them.' On the second survey, a head teacher expressed his 'main concern' as 'governors' involvement in decision-making that they barely comprehend'. Others indicate that the effort needed to keep governors informed adds to the head teacher's burden. A teacher told us: 'I don't feel that governors are always qualified and much effort is needed to inform on the head's part'. Other head teachers comment:

> The workload has been rather high particularly as a number of governors have little real understanding of issues.

> I am finding it difficult to motivate governors to take real decisions. Are they in fact sufficiently qualified or informed to do so or can their role ever be more than monitoring?

A head teacher described her need to 'lead governors through the minefield'. Another said 'governors find great difficulty dealing with the meanings of new regulations etc.'. The additional task of explaining information to governors is noted by another who writes:

> There has . . . been a growing awareness that many governors have neither the time nor the ability to assimilate the deluge of information from the DFE. Consequently, an extra burden is placed upon the head teacher who is frequently seen as an easy source of reference, little consideration being given to the fact that heads also have to assimilate new regulations as well as perform their statutory duties.

The ability of governors to make financial decisions related to staffing seemed to be an area of particular concern, one deputy head commenting that 'budgetary constraints caused a lot of problems particularly on staffing. Governors in the school felt completely inexperienced to deal with the problems it presented.' A teacher interviewed during a school visit voiced concerns about the 'increased involvement of governors on financing and staffing'. He thought that governors were not in a position to make financial decisions because they did not know the 'practice', only the 'theory'. He said it was like him going over to JCB (a large, local vehicle manufacturer) and telling them how to spend their money. One head teacher believed that 'the voluntary status of governors does not always guarantee the right people to deal with issues that were skilled jobs in the LEA e.g. personnel issues.'

Other comments raise specific concerns about the involvement of non-educational amateurs in school management. One teacher stated: 'I don't think this influence and power in the hands of people who know little about education is a good thing', and a head teacher wrote: 'devolving power and authority to groups of amateurs is not the way to guarantee improvement'. A teacher at another school commented on 'more power in the hands of non-specialists – not for the better'. The deputy head, however, felt that these governors 'seem wary of their new responsibilities and are largely happy to leave work to the professionals'. More governor training might alleviate this concern, as one head teacher suggests:

> Governors now have a more defined 'real' role to play – however, more training needs to be provided for them to enable them to make informed decisions.

On the other hand this may not be an entirely helpful recommendation, as one governor warned:

> Too great a volume of material/training has over burdened some to the extent that they have had to give up being governors.

A quite different perspective on the role of governing bodies as part of the processes of accountability is whether the powers vested in them are too great.

Too much power

Put simply by a teacher, 'the head teacher needs to be in control – approved by governors, not vice versa'. One head teacher expressed his views on the powers of governors in some detail:

> It is right that heads should manage the money but . . . the notion that governors have legal responsibility is flawed. At present we have a well-paid 'manager' implementing decisions taken by only partially informed amateur governors. The powers presently vested in governing bodies should be allocated to head teachers – the governors should retain one power only – to dismiss the head teacher if he does not inform them of the decisions he is taking and why, does not consult them for their opinions, and then is seen to have taken the wrong decisions. At present governors determine the policy and if it is wrong they resign but the head is left carrying the can.

One chair of governors also wished to see a reduction in the powers of governing bodies:

> I would like the budget area, encompassing salaries, to be divorced from

the total budget. Thus governors would be responsible for overseeing the school budget but not the finances of the staff.

Another chair of governors voiced his view that governors have too much power although, having the job he uses it and 'flexes his muscles'. He felt that governors are not a suitable body on their own; they require clear advice from the professionals. He does not like the governors' ability to appoint staff, only having to take the *advice* of the LEA officials, who are the real experts, and he worries greatly about the process whereby professional advisers may be marginalised – 'they've gone too far in giving powers to lay people'.

By contrast, there are others who view the powers of governors as illusory. One head wrote: 'governor control has proved a complete illusion – it is head's control. Information gives power', and, in a similar vein: 'the notion of governors' responsibility and involvement is a nonsense, as our governors have neither the time nor the inclination to be involved'.

Some of these statements explain why some head teachers have not welcomed the increased involvement of governors in the decision-making process. There are others, of course, who have welcomed greater governor involvement, and experience positive and supportive relationships with their governing body. We consider such examples next in an examination of the quality of accountability.

THE QUALITY OF ACCOUNTABILITY

Positive and supportive relationships

Some schools are in the fortunate position of having, in their view, a positive and successful relationship with their governing body. A chair of governors described the relationship as 'informal, happy . . . very supportive'. The head teacher at another school welcomed 'their support, friendship and advice'. Elsewhere, governors seemed supportive of staff and respectful of the teachers' professionalism. They were persuaded by educational arguments, asked questions and sought educational justifications. A teacher described the relationship with the governors as 'excellent. . . . Very supportive both ways – when anything big is going down, we are all involved'. A co-opted chair of governors commented:

> I feel that the governors and staff have formed a team which is very personal to the school, its children and parents and is providing the very best form of management they can for that school.

At another school, the head teacher felt that the governors were not a 'walkover', although they had supported all her decisions so far. This support was the result of a lot of hard work, in terms of the head keeping them informed and public relations; she worked at the relationship. Another head needed to put less effort into the relationship but recognised their support as a vote of confidence: the governors 'have always been supportive. . . . There has always been a feeling that the "head knows best" and I am grateful for the continued confidence'.

At some schools this 'supportive' role may be interpreted as *more* passive, the governors handing over, rather than being led by the 'professionals'. For example, the relationship with the governing body at one school was described by the head teacher as 'very supportive'. Apparently the chair of governors had told the head that they employed him to run the school. The chair of governors at another school saw governors in a supportive role which left the decision-making to the professionals. A deputy head commented that the governors were 'very supportive of all that is done. Very little influence – just rubber-stamping. Works well'.

A 'supportive' governing body clearly means different things to different people. There is a distinction between the support of a governing body which has properly participated in decision-making and been persuaded by the educational arguments of the 'professionals', as against the passive support of governors who have handed over decisions to the head teacher. Some heads are less than happy with these uncritically supportive governors:

> My governors are very supportive and tend to leave it to me – I'm educating them gradually!

Our data suggest that the nature of governor involvement in the running of schools varies. Might it be that governor involvement and the extent of their understanding of educational issues are linked to the skills and abilities of individual governors, and might this in turn reflect the community the school serves? Our study did not directly explore this, although it was an issue raised by head teachers.

Availability of 'able' governors

Several heads raised concerns about the uneven distribution of 'able' governors across the whole community. One commented:

> Areas such as where this school is situated do not have a supply of 'professional' people willing and able to carry out fully the duties of governors – therefore an additional burden falls on the head teacher.

One teacher commented that the governors at the school tended not to be so 'well-educated' and that it was not 'fair that more affluent areas had "better" governors'. On the other hand, the chair of governors at another school felt 'lucky' because the governing body was quite 'able'; he pitied 'more disadvantaged areas'.

One head teacher was making moves to recruit governors with 'expertise', such as local business people. Another informed us that the school did not have 'high calibre' governors and indicated that schools were unequal in this. One of the teachers said the school was lucky if parent governor vacancies were filled. While this was unusual, a more general problem related to governors nominated by the LEA, an issue we consider together with evidence on the changed nature of the relationship with the LEA.

Accountability and the LEA

The paradox of accountability

In formal terms, locally managed schools remain the responsibility of the LEA to whom they are accountable for the standard and quality of provision. There appears to be little evidence of this accountability in practice. Indeed, there is far more evidence of schools believing that LEAs are now accountable to them. This is perhaps particularly evident with respect to the services still provided by the LEA.

Writing about Hillingdon LEA, Higgins states:

> The culture had changed recognisably from one of control to one based on service with a sharp client/customer focus.
>
> (1993: 19)

Such a cultural change has been recognised in our study, and on our visits to schools we heard heads and others describing the 'much more client/supplier relationship' with their LEA; LEAs 'advising rather than telling'; being 'much more client-oriented'; 'providing' rather than 'controlling'; shifting the emphasis from 'control to service'; 'willing to listen and react – we are no longer supplicants'. A deputy described the change: 'having been "big brother" watching over the school, the LEA is now operating on a client-provider model'; and a head spoke of the:

> total change from the paternalistic dictatorship of yesterday to an emerging position of genuine partnership and provider of services.

Two comments reflect the emphasis in our comments that it is the LEAs who are accountable to schools:

> I am pleased by . . . the increased school relevance and accountability of LEA staff – inspectors, officers, educational psychologists etc. . . . The (slow growing) decline in LEA paternalism.

> The single most important issue is still emerging and relates to the changed relationship between school and LEA. The whole culture has changed from one of paternalistic central control to providers of services in partnership. Where this leads in the end is still unclear – if the LEA continues to devolve yet more funds, at what point does it become irrelevant so far as the school is concerned?

One head recognised that the LEA is more 'our servant than our employer'. Comments such as these emphasise the comparatively weak role of the LEA in terms of accountability. This appears to extend to the way in which LEA governors, ostensibly a link between schools and the LEA, undertake their responsibilities.

LEA governors

From our visits to schools it became apparent that some had very specific concerns about the motivation and commitment of LEA governors. One head felt that LEA governors were the worst: there had been no response from the new LEA governor on being invited to the school. On the other hand, parents and co-opted governors were very committed and more visible in the school. The head teacher at another school thought that governors, like parents, who had the interests of the school at heart, were great. He was suspicious of the motives of others, naming LEA nominees as examples. The deputy head referred to such governors only doing it for their own self promotion.

Another head teacher and the chair of governors talked of the problems of politically motivated governors. One chair, an LEA governor himself, talked of the political bias of some LEA nominees. He felt that there was a danger that they would disagree with a view because of who made it rather than disagreeing with the issue. This was reiterated by the chair at another school, again an LEA nominee, who felt that some county council nominees were politically motivated and 'collected governing bodies like scalps'. A co-opted chair of governors described LEA governors as being 'as useful as a chocolate tea-pot' explaining that they never turn up, are political appointments and are not interested in the school. It would be unfair, however, to generalise from these comments and, indeed, a number of the governing bodies of the schools we visited were chaired by an LEA nominee. It is with this more general observation that we lead into five vignettes, which provide a more qualitative perspective on the role of governors in decision-making and implications for how accountability is exercised in practice.

ROLES, RELATIONSHIPS AND GOVERNOR INVOLVEMENT: FIVE VIGNETTES

Vignette 7.1: A working partnership

The first vignette is a large junior school with over 300 pupils on the roll. The chair of the governing body is co-opted. This school provides an example of a 'successful' relationship between the governing body and the school. The chair of governors gave his view of the relationship between the governors and the teachers saying, 'partnership and respect is . . . the key note. Governors' increased involvement is a potential opportunity for both sides'. On the relationship with the head teacher, he spoke of 'mutual support and respect'. The head teacher felt that 'closer working relationships and greater consultation leads to more involvement of governors in school decisions'. Although he thought that it would be 'far simpler not to have to consult the governing body', in the sense of being more 'efficient and quicker', 'you do have to take the governing body with you'. He described the decision-making process: 'recommendations from me are made to one of the governing body sub-committees, then to the full governing body. This takes longer because of the need for consultation. . . . Governors are happy to agree if the money is available'. The deputy head teacher at the school commented: 'being able to discuss finance with people who work in different industries has helped my understanding'. The chair of governors recognised the importance of 'able and committed' governors, agreeing that 'the decision-making process seems sound but depends upon the availability of (such) governors', then adding that 'we all have to work hard, but loyalty and commitment pay dividends. I pity more disadvantaged areas here'. One of the teachers raised a couple of tempered notes of anxiety about the governing body: 'I'm very conscious of having governors' children in the class, though all have been very pleasant. Recently I applied for compassionate leave to the governors and didn't feel it desirable they knew my personal details'.

Vignette 7.2: A tense relationship

In contrast, the relationships with the governors in the second school were much more unfortunate. On our visit to this primary school (with about 250 pupils on the roll) we did not meet the chair of governors, perhaps because relationships were soured, as reported by the head teacher. He described the governors coming into the school 'all guns blazing' to 'sort it out', the 'hard-nosed businessmen' saying 'if we can't afford them, sack them'. This had created tensions. The head teacher explained that 'relationships were very strained at the beginning, as people were exercising newly found authority with less than equanimity. This situation reached crisis point before changing course. It is difficult to verbalise real advantages to the school for the new role of the governors . . . . Governors may make life very painful for the head and staff if they attempt to "throw their weight about", even going beyond their authority'. Things had since improved, the head commenting that 'they now treat me like a human being'. One of the teachers felt that the governors saw them as well-paid child minders. She commented on the governors' 'too little involvement in observation and communication with staff' adding that 'more closeness would improve relationships: we would feel that their decisions would be better informed'. Another teacher at the school described the relationship with governors as 'sometimes problematic, e.g., they stopped dancing sessions in school', for what she saw as 'petty power reasons'. The deputy head teacher was 'not sure they are aware of how accountable they should be'. It is unfortunate that we were unable to meet a governor.

Vignette 7.3: An active partnership

A third vignette is a secondary with over 1,000 pupils on roll. The chair of governors is co-opted. From interviews with a number of people at the school, it became apparent that the governing body took an active role in the decision-making process. The chair of governors was a member of the senior management team (SMT), having 'overall control on how the budget is spent'. The deputy head commented that the governing body as a whole was happy to take the lead from the SMT. The chair of governors had mixed views on the responsibilities, describing them as 'sort of welcoming but also terrifying', making particular reference to staffing appointments – especially the impending head teacher appointment – and redundancies. The deputy head thought that, depending on the governing body, governor involvement in staffing decisions was an improvement on the Chief Inspector old-boy network. The chair's relationship with the deputy head was closer than with the head teacher. She thought that the head was 'out of touch' and felt that he was happy to have the governing body 'carrying the can'. Although the relationship was a good working one, she would welcome a head teacher who participated actively and was 'more on the ball – at the last meeting he said nothing'.

Some of the teachers had a more cautious view on this governing body. One teacher felt that there had been 'some occasions when lack of expertise on the governing body and the failure to listen had caused problems'. Another commented: 'they are seen as remote and have little contact with staff'. The chair of governors seemed aware of these feelings and told us 'I feel staff are slightly wary of the governing body . . . due to insufficient funds'.

The chair of governors made two points in relation to the increased powers and responsibilities of the governing body. She felt that powers and responsibility had transferred to the governing body but there were no expenses and commented: 'I feel we are often the scapegoats for the LEA and central government'.

Vignette 7.4: The challenge of local management

A second secondary school with over 700 pupils on roll. The chair of governors is a representative of the LEA. The first year of LM had been traumatic, ending with a deficit, which resulted in three staff redundancies. This had affected relationships. The chair of governors explained: 'LMS led to compulsory redundancy procedures for three staff. This naturally caused a deep rift between staff and governors. This has improved but I still feel there is a deep and understandable mistrust'. The staff had lost confidence in the governing body because of the redundancies and a staff/governors liaison committee had been set up. It initially met monthly but now just in response to issues. It had no 'powers' but provided a forum for talking. The school had appointed a new head teacher and the chair thought that 'the appointment process under LMS has laid strong foundations for a good relationship'. This new head teacher believed it was generally highly desirable to have more governor involvement, so long as governors are good, and 'ours are'. One of the teachers thought that the governing body contained many very committed and professional people. In contrast, another teacher felt that the more visible governors were all part of the 'big stick' mentality.

The chair of governors made comments about the pressures of being a governor: 'I suspect the pressures on governors to attend frequent meetings and to take on decision-making may explain two early resignations'. There was some feeling that governors were being over-loaded. The deputy head spoke of the 'much closer involvement' and the 'huge impact on governors in terms of time and responsibility'. He felt the situation was 'much improved . . . but do they know the school well enough to take these decisions?'.

Vignette 7.5: Governor over involvement?

Our final case is a secondary high school with a roll of about 500 pupils. The relationship between the governors and the school was interesting. The deputy head described the governing body as very supportive, taking note of the professionalism of the school. He felt that governing bodies are as good as the people on them, 'but the potential for damage by thoughtlessness or bee-infested bonnets' had been 'greatly increased'. The head teacher found the governing body 'very parochial' and felt that they were unable to make simple decisions on their own. They were reluctant to set up committees, preferring all to be involved and hear 'chapter and verse'. He gave an example of it taking one meeting of the full governing body to decide on horizontal or vertical blinds. The head believed that the governors viewed the school as a medium-sized business with the head teacher as managing director, the governors as the board of directors and the school as shareholders. He was not completely happy with this analogy, as he saw it as undermining the educational role of the school. The chair of governors, an LEA representative, had strong views on LM, saying 'you ask me what I think of it and I'll tell you, it stinks'. He saw the underlying intention as the weakening of the LEAs and saving money by getting governors to do it for nothing. He commented on the 'surfeit of unwarranted correspondence, advertisements, folders, extolling the virtues of "opting out"'. He also expressed concerns about the sorts of people who were governors – the demands on time meant that they were likely to be retired and he had concerns about aged governing bodies.

CONCLUSION

In this chapter we have examined the role of governing bodies and, to a lesser extent, LEAs as stakeholders to whom schools are accountable. On governing bodies, we have examined the means by which they exercise their accountability and reviewed evidence of their involvement in the affairs of schools. While most governors tend to be supportive, there is a question over whether this support is always sufficiently critical, and we have evidence of involvement being nothing more than 'rubber-stamping' decisions. Many governors recognise the professionalism of the head teacher and their own amateur status, and some head teachers have expressed concern about governors' lack of knowledge and their involvement prolonging the decision-making process. Attention was also drawn to the uneven distribution of 'skilled' governors and the possible consequences this may have for schools serving socially disadvantaged areas. With respect to the role of LEAs, we observed a paradox of LEAs being more accountable to schools rather than schools being accountable for how well they use the resources allocated to them by the LEA.

These findings suggest that, in many cases, governing bodies and LEAs currently provide a rather weak form of accountability. It is an important illustration of how policy intentions and legal frameworks and responsibilities may lead to a practice which is different. As governing bodies and LEAs are the principal administrative agents of accountability, this evidence must be of some concern. Set against this are the quasi-market arrangements for securing accountability through competition and the related introduction of formal inspections and the annual publication of 'league tables' showing how pupils have performed in national examinations and assessments. We should also recognise, however, that the professionalism of head teachers, teachers and other staff in schools includes a concept and practice of accountability which may be as powerful as these other means. How some of these accountabilities link with delegation to affect the overall efficiency of schools are themes we examine in the next chapter.

Chapter 8

Decentralisation and efficiency
The impact on learning

EFFICIENCY, COST-EFFECTIVENESS AND UNCERTAINTY

As has been argued in Chapter 4, our use of the word efficiency is not to be equated with cheapness and the definition we apply gives equal status to 'what is got out' as well as 'what is put in': what is obtained from resources as well as the resources themselves. We note a tendency by governments to focus on measurable educational outcomes, but our position is that an assessment of efficiency in education entails a qualitative judgement based on a range of information.

> There are no guidelines from research and practice, for example, on the effects of spending different proportions of the school budget on teachers as against support staff. Will it ever be possible to advise a school that they are spending the right amount on books, as against other learning resources?
>
> (Thomas and Martin, 1996: 20)

To these uncertainties about resources, we would add the limited information available to head teachers as to what is actually taking place in the classrooms of their schools: most of what occurs in classrooms is unobserved by anyone other than the teacher and the class. In terms of the management of a school, this clearly creates difficulties in ensuring that there is a sufficiently informed dialogue so that resources are allocated in ways which reliably match needs and priorities: the less that is known or understood about events in classrooms, the more likely the mis-match of resources to needs. Difficulties in clearly articulating the link between resource decisions and learning is a general problem, as identified in the annual HMCI report.

> Inspectors judged the *evaluation of cost-effectiveness* by governors and head teachers unfavourably in nearly two-thirds of the primary and nearly half of secondary schools. Few of the primary schools had, for example, procedures to monitor the effectiveness of their deployment of support staff; and while awareness about cost-effectiveness is increasing in secondary schools, few schools evaluate the cost of their procedures and

plans . . . Many schools require more rigorous methods for assessing the costs and opportunity costs of alternative plans.

(Ofsted, 1995a: 24)

The problems and uncertainties that Inspectors have in making such efficiency judgements should not be ignored and, on the basis of analysis of inspection reports, Levacic and Glover (1994) have reported on these difficulties. It is essential we also recognise that some important processes and outcomes of schools are amenable only to a qualitative judgement. While these judgements should be based upon evidence – such as an account of what occurs in the classroom – we have to recognise and accept the role and the responsibility of the professional educator in making these judgements. The nature of school inspection illustrates this role: inspectors must use their professional judgement when assessing what they observe and not be dominated by the 'objective' measures of exam and test results. The latter provide important information about aspects of academic achievement but are so heavily influenced by the nature of the pupil/student intake they tell us little about the quality of the education being provided in the school.

Uncertainty about the relationship between resources and outcomes, limited information about classroom activity and the role of professional judgement in assessing the quality of learning illustrate the uncertainty which is endemic to schools as organisations. Where then does this leave us in assessing efficiency or cost-effectiveness, as well as our appraisal of the impact of decentralisation on learning? In responding to that question, we propose to draw upon some of the findings from the literature on effective schools and some recent work on the nature of the cost-effective school. We do so on the basis that those schools which are identified as effective or cost-effective will, *prima facie*, be those who have found ways of managing in the uncertain conditions we have outlined.

Two studies provide the sources we draw upon in shaping those factors which we shall focus on in the remaining parts of the chapter. The first of these is the study of fifty London Junior schools (Mortimore *et al.*, 1988), which identified a set of twelve *key factors* that were associated with the range of effectiveness measures used. These are:

Purposeful leadership of the staff by the head teacher; the involvement of the deputy head; the involvement of teachers; consistency among teachers; structured sessions; intellectually challenging teaching; the work-centred environment; limited focus within sessions; maximum communication between teachers and pupils; record keeping; parental involvement; positive climate.

(Mortimore *et al.*, 1988: 250)

This study pre-dates decentralisation and so we add some of the attributes of the cost-effective school proposed in a more recent theoretical and empirical study of resource management in twelve secondary schools. These are to:

> periodically undertake a radical audit of resources . . . improve information on costs . . . use the expertise of relevant staff on resource priorities through some internal delegation . . . limit the dangers of complacency . . . by ensuring that the structure of decision-making provides for a dialogue of accountability . . . reduce the detachment of management by using team meetings, appraisal and surveys to collect information on the quality of teaching and learning from teachers, parents and pupils; . . . develop sources of information which are independent of head teachers and teachers.
>
> (Thomas and Martin, 1996: 42–3)

Our study makes no claim to embrace all the factors listed here. Moreover, we do not take account of theorising on pedagogic practice which is omitted from existing empirical studies of school effectiveness and limits the insight they provide. We did not systematically visit classrooms, for example, and cannot, therefore, comment upon the several factors referring directly to classroom practice. We undertook one-day field visits to forty schools but the remainder of the data were collected by postal questionnaires completed by head teachers. While these circumstances limit the scope of our commentary, the factors associated with effective and cost-effective schools do, none the less, provide a framework against which we can report on the impact of local management on learning. It has three main components.

The first recognises the role of **purposeful management and leadership**. The data from both the studies we have cited recognise the role of the head teacher in giving and conveying a clear sense of purpose to others in the school. In view of the contemporary requirement placed on schools in England and Wales to prepare school development plans, we would also expect to see the planning process as a prominent means for communicating this sense of purpose. In this section we will also review evidence on the management of financial resources which relates to the radical audit of resources and the quality of information on costs. The second component of our analysis is focused upon **participation in decision-making**. Mortimore *et al.* (1988) note the involvement of the deputy head, teachers and parents in aspects of decision-making and, in view of their new role in managing schools, we would expect to see governors more prominent than in the past. The third component is a **focus upon practice**. Data from Mortimore *et al.* (1988) and Thomas and Martin (1996) emphasise the attention that effective and cost-effective schools give to the practice of teaching. Our account of this is clearly more limited than could be obtained from a more extensive study located at the school site but we are able to report evidence on how resources are being used in ways which are close to classroom practice.

PURPOSEFUL MANAGEMENT

Matching resources to needs

The view of the government is that LM has given the governing body and the head teacher powers to determine their own needs and priorities (DES, 1988). In this relationship, the government recognises the central role of the head teacher, expecting governing bodies to 'delegate the management of the school's budget to the head teacher' (DES, 1988: 29), but it also lays emphasis on the planning process. A past Permanent Secretary at the DES has written of the impact of LM on school management, claiming that it has been 'an enormous stimulus to the development of more systematic management'. He continues:

> Without good management, schools cannot control their income and expenditure in the way they now have to. Governing bodies have had to . . . determine priorities for the school within the funds they have at their disposal. They have to oversee the preparation of school development plans, budget plans and be directly responsible for staff selection. . . . LMS and grant-maintained status have allowed schools to give real meaning to their own priorities. These are key initiatives in getting management decisions taken at the right level, closer to the point of delivery of the service . . . They can decide for themselves whether to refit the library, to establish an additional reception class, or to carry out swiftly those irritating repairs.
>
> (Caines, 1992: 19–20)

This view of the potential of delegated management and the place of development planing in ensuring its success is echoed by the Audit Commission:

> The key to success in locally delegated management is a process of planning, action and review which encompasses schools' financial and educational responsibilities and integrates them into a coherent system of school development planning.
>
> (1991: 41)

The extent to which more systematic management through development planning has actually taken root is less obvious. In a study of sixty-three schools published in 1992, HMI observed that 'the management focus is being sharpened and staff are participating more fully in forward planning' (HMI, 1992). A more recent research report observes that development planning can mean that the requirement to write a plan is observed, but that its use as a means of securing educational change does not always occur (MacGilchrist et al., 1995). It is an analysis that reflects weaknesses in monitoring and evaluation by schools, the evidence suggesting that schools can identify needs and devise strategies of implementation but are less successful in evaluating the impact of change (HMCI, 1994). Some of these findings corroborate our own evidence.

The role of school development planning

Commenting on the most important consequences of LM for her primary school, one head teacher writes of 'more effective planning':

> Decisions made specifically for our school. Increasing confidence to use money between compartments and have more effective planning. Increasing staff awareness of funding and delegating into compartments has made for more considered purchases. We are able to forward plan better. We are fortunate to have a steadily increasing roll. We have especially gained by being able to improve our building more quickly than we had anticipated. We are getting more precise with our SDP and successfully targeting money. We have yet to crack how really to optimise the INSET budget and how to keep effective track of supply expenditure.

Our survey of head teachers in 1991 requested information on the preparation of Development Plans (DP). Although at the time of the questionnaire, school development plans were a recent innovation, they were already prepared in almost all schools. The adoption of a DP had led more than half of the schools to review their statement of aims: an indicator of schools seeking to clarify their purposes. Most of these heads reported that DPs help in planning, prioritising and evaluating. Only 9 per cent reported that its preparation had not been helpful. LEA guidelines were normally available and two-thirds found them helpful. Only 4 per cent found them unhelpful.

No specific questions on the preparation of the SDP were asked on the follow-up questionnaires, although head teachers were asked to respond to a statement on the value of preparing DPs. In 1993, 81 per cent of primary heads and 83 per cent of secondary heads *agreed* that the preparation of the DP was worthwhile.

One component of the planning process is monitoring and evaluation, and schools reported (in the 1991 survey) the use of more information for monitoring their performance. Typically, they were more likely to use exam results than in the past, but the replies provided were diverse (Arnott *et al.*, 1992). Enhanced accountability, a theme addressed in Chapter 7, is recognised by some head teachers:

> There is a greater feeling of controlling our own destiny. Individuals are more directly accountable for their actions.

> Head and staff feel more accountable where finances are concerned and value being able to get things done straight away.

The advantages LM brings to management and planning, in terms of the freedom to make decisions locally, control resources, prioritise and respond to needs, were revealed in comments made by head teachers in response to a question on the third survey asking 'what are the most important consequences of LM?'. Heads spoke of:

- greater flexibility in allocating monies
- greater financial/management freedom
- greater flexibility in resourcing the school's work, especially in the areas of capitation
- personnel (support staff) and maintenance
- more flexibility – action can be taken more quickly
- increased flexibility of management – decision-making nearer the user
- more flexibility in prioritising issues
- ability to allocate funding where it is needed
- the ability to spend money where we choose – particularly for pupils rather than heating
- opportunities to determine own priorities
- being able to prioritise needs and fund them in accordance with the SDP
- the ability to target individual school needs through the SDP
- use extra money as required
- feeling of ownership and decision-making – knowing where the money goes
- greater freedom to control our own destiny and work to our own priorities
- the much greater sense of independence and of having more control over our own destiny
- we have been able to make our own priorities and to meet most of them
- the ability to follow through plans with a greater deal of control over financial implications

One head believed that decisions being made 'by the people who have to implement them, and whom they affect' is 'good news surely'. Another wrote that 'LMS has given me direct control over staffing and the flexibility to make financial decisions that have been of positive benefit for the school'; and a third: 'most importantly we are able to respond more quickly to needs, whether a broken window, or teaching resources. We are able to prioritise expenditure for ourselves, which allows us to target more accurately'. In the view of one head 'the school has improved significantly in the last two years and LM has given me the freedom to do what I have wanted to, to achieve that'. The most important consequences for another school were listed by the head teacher as:

(i) managerial expertise used much more effectively; (ii) much tighter control over costs involved in running the school; (iii) greater feeling of 'control' over the school's destiny; (iv) greater significance of the School Development Plan – determining long-term planning.

In some of the schools we visited, head teachers informed us of their planning process. At one school for instance, the budget setting is policy driven, beginning with the question, 'what do we want to do?'. Needs are then prioritised through the development-planning process. The deputy at another school believed that the idea was not to be budget-led, but rather to 'create the perfect plan and then prioritise as budget allows'. It is apparent, however, that the state of the budget affects perceptions of local management and whether it is seen as an opportunity or a constraint.

Planning and the budget

Managing budgetary opportunities

Greater budgetary control, and sufficient funding, has enabled some schools to achieve improvements 'undreamed of':

> The ability to decide 'on the spot' what is right and needful for this partic- ular school has been the most important consequence as far as we are concerned. I have been able to provide facilities and resources undreamed of ten years ago.

> The advantages have been that we can control and direct resources to where we perceive needs to be. We have achieved more here in 18 months than in 18 years!

Management of the budget has given many heads the opportunity to improve the school environment:

> The school environment is more pleasing. We have been decorated for the first time in 24 years! Alterations have been possible (minor); there is more equipment and staff are aware of budget constraints or allowances.

> Greater control over all areas of resourcing has led to improved planning and efficiency. The school is now better decorated, more efficiently maintained and better resourced (in terms of curriculum materials).

One head teacher, however, drew attention to the furniture replacement and redecoration programmes that were part of the pre-LM system.

Given sufficient funds, control of the budget can facilitate the implemen- tation of SDPs, which may, commonly, include a programme of redecoration. At one school for example, such improvements have been instigated, although the head recognises their 'fortunate' position:

> We are able to prioritise spending in a way that suits us. Our school is bet- ter decorated, we have made improvements and we are able to decide on our PTR and not have an official from County Hall allocating staff. However, we are fortunate, we have very good, supportive parents and an active PTA raising funds for the school.

Another recognises the necessity of adequate funds:

> We welcome the increased decision-making that occurs within school and the flexibility achieved through virement but this can only take place when there are adequate funds.

A more limited budget, however, can cause understandable frustrations. Committed costs, notably for staffing, can leave little flexibility or room to manoeuvre and a view that local management is less about opportunity but means limited scope for action and even retrenchment.

Managing budgetary inflexibility

It is easy to be positive if your school has gained under formula funding. More money has meant more resources and time between decision and implementation has been considerably reduced. To date we have benefited – the future is less promising.

There has been an increase in budget flexibility but there is very little one can do in a budget of this size once salary costs have been taken into account.

HMI found that 'LMS is achieving its objective of giving schools control over their money, and with it greater flexibility'. They also recognised, however, that the extent of this flexibility is determined by the state of the school's finances:

The ability to realise some benefits, however, depends on schools' under-lying funding, which has sometimes proved uncertain. Many schools have been understandably cautious and those faced with reductions in funding have had to use their new responsibilities to make good any shortfalls or, in a few cases, to make staff redundant. Financial planning needs to be better integrated into long-term development plans for schools as a whole.

(HMI, 1992: 34)

In recommending schools to improve the integration of financial and long-term development planning, HMI highlight the greater need for planning when resources are limited. Perhaps it is all too understandable that schools do not respond in this way but instead adopt an approach closer to crisis management. One head teacher commented: 'I find myself penny-pinching all the time in order to make ends meet or to allow a carry-forward in order to meet known future expenses'.

Complaints about decisions being led by the budget were heard in several schools. One teacher spoke sceptically of the 'façade of democratic decision-making but the outcome is always determined by financial considerations. . . . Financial constraints are now a major factor in decision-making'. At another school the head felt that it was easy to make decisions on how to spend money but quite different if the school was trying to make ends meet. One of the teachers commented: 'any need is discussed with the head teacher – then we laugh because we haven't any money'.

At one secondary school it was apparent that decisions were limited by the need to make ends meet. The chair of governors recognised that 'decisions are restricted because of finances'. The school had gone through the process of identifying a member of staff for redundancy. A consequence of this, perhaps, was the feeling among staff of not being involved in the decision-making processes. The head of one department felt that 'decisions are . . . forced upon us'. One of the teachers believed that staff 'should be involved more and kept informed about staffing etc.'.

Another head teacher is unhappy with the cultural shift in schools which has led some to being overly cost-conscious:

> I deplore the fact that so many colleagues are overtly unprofessional in their pursuit of what they consider to be right for their school at the expense of others. This was always so but LM raises the stakes. Too many good young staff question whether they want to be part of a profession which is now so money oriented, the old adage holds good: too many people know the cost/price of everything and the value of nothing.

Another questions the fairness of the system:

> Many colleagues are suffering from reducing numbers on roll leading to staff losses (physically) and general stress. If a school is in a good area with supportive parents it has the opportunity to do very well under LMS. The opposite also applies. Is this a fair system?

Changing rolls is only one aspect of the uncertainties affecting budgets and which have an impact upon how budgetary control is seen as a means of improving management and planning.

Managing uncertainty

> It is precarious planning where funding is totally dependent on formula funding in a catchment area where numbers are difficult to predict.

Late knowledge of the school's budget and information on any carry-over to the following year, as well as the impact of changing pupil numbers on future budgets, makes long term planning difficult. This problem was voiced by some on our visits to schools. The head teacher at one school complained that the school did not know the budget until the beginning of the financial year, thereby 'making long term planning difficult':

> Very frustrating when finances don't adequately meet our needs. Not able to plan very far ahead as funding and requirements are forever changing.

Planning with purpose?

It is apparent that the planning and budgetary opportunities created by local management differ substantially as between schools. Superficially, development planning has been seen as an opportunity to create a better framework for managing schools but it is not apparent that these are closely linked to the budgetary contexts of schools. In a rational planning model, the link between the development plan and finance would be the same regardless of whether funding was increasing or decreasing: priorities would be set in the context of available resources. It is not apparent that this model of planning is always present in these schools. The account that emerges seems highly contingent upon the financial context of a school: buoyant funding creates the impression of opportunity while retrenchment leads to penny pinching, the role of the development plan in either of these circumstances not being readily apparent. The integration of development plans and budgets is not clear.

This is not to say that development planning has not assisted schools in defining their purpose and giving a focus to their energies. In this important respect, local management is contributing to purposeful management. Several of the accounts we have cited also show evidence of funds being committed to meet needs defined by the schools. Set against this is evidence about the unwelcome changing role of the head teacher, notably their concern that increased workload arising from local management has made them less familiar with events in the classroom, evidence which we cited in Chapter 7.

PARTICIPATION IN DECISION-MAKING

The case for participation

While the formal responsibilities of local management are delegated to governing bodies and head teachers, the government's guidelines for the new system recognised the importance of involving staff in decision-making. This is consistent with the discussion in the previous chapter on how accountability can be sustained by a dialogue between stakeholders. The influential early report prepared by Coopers and Lybrand also recognised that heads would need to consult with others but warned:

> It will be important to ensure that any such consultation does not unduly slow down decision-making, nor reduce management flexibility.
>
> (1988: 34)

Some of the early national training packages, such as that prepared by a major consortium of local education authorities, placed considerable emphasis on the range of stakeholders who should participate in decision-making (LEAP, 1990). This emphasis on participation and involvement is consistent with evidence from studies of effective schools. The comment made by one head teacher recognises the potential for such participation in securing commitment to shared purposes:

The involvement of staff/governors in the decision-making and planning process has increased a sense of ownership and commitment.

There are, however, clear tensions between the direct management responsibilities of governors and head teachers on the one side, and the demands for wide participation in decision-making on the other. In an analysis which is sceptical of the consequences of local management, Halsey argues that local management forces schools away from collegial management:

> The delegation of schools budgets, coinciding as it has with the introduction of personnel policy changes (appraisal and performance related pay), is driving a wedge between management and staff . . . The process of 'consultation' with staff has overtones of a formal procedure which is legally mandatory, rather than discussion between fellow-professionals. To take another illustration, policy-making in many schools now follows more or less formal guidelines developed by subcommittees of governors and staff, and based on an 'Institutional Development Plan'. These may use responses to questionnaires in which individual members of staff say, anonymously, what aspects of the school should, in their opinion, have priority in the allocation of staff time and other resources. The management team is not bound by the results of this procedure. The appearance of broader involvement in school decision-making may divert attention from deeper changes which reduce staff participation.
>
> (1993: 55)

Set against this view about the actual nature of staff participation, an early assessment by HMI points to 'greater openness' but an awareness of its limited progress:

> In most schools there has been a greater openness in financial planning and some re-structuring of management and administration arrangements for the school as a whole. But alterations in management structures and decision-making have yet fully to engage departments in secondary schools and many staff in primary schools. The concepts of delegation and shared decision-making need to move into other layers of school life.
>
> (HMI, 1992: 35)

In our 1991 survey, head teachers were asked to respond to statements on decision-making and their replies suggested that, in some schools, LM had led to greater staff involvement in decision-making: 53 per cent agreed that *since LM decision-making is more widely shared with staff*, and few (16 per cent) agreed that *decision-making has not changed with LM*. How participation occurs in practice and develops over time will partly be a consequence of the management style of individual head teachers although, as we shall see, the nature of the decisions required also determines who is involved.

Areas of participation

The role of governors in decision-making was discussed in Chapter 7. Our focus here is on the involvement of teaching staff. With respect to development planning, if we exclude the head and senior staff from the total, other teaching staff were reported as being *principally* involved in 51 per cent of the schools.

When we visited schools, the diversity of involvement in the preparation of the SDP was apparent. In some schools staff seemed to feel very much part of the decision-making processes. Teachers, for example, spoke of the 'great emphasis put on consultation', one teacher commenting that 'decisions are made as a whole staff and staff have opportunities to decide what will be included in the SDP'. Elsewhere, staff views on the school's needs and priorities were gathered via a questionnaire. In one instance, all staff are asked to identify their priorities by anonymous questionnaire, the final SDP being drawn up by the SMT (head, deputy, the finance and INSET co-ordinators). One teacher voiced some scepticism about the implementation of the SDP, suggesting that in practice it did not influence decisions.

The 1991 survey asked head teachers to reply to a question asking them to 'list those people **principally** involved in decision-making' in areas which we specified. When we examined these replies across categories of resources, different groups emerge according to the type of resource.

Decisions on the allocation and deployment of teachers, the allocation of training opportunities, the deployment of support staff and the involvement of LEA support services were typically made by the head teacher and senior staff. Across these five areas, between 14 per cent and 21 per cent of heads identified staff – other than the head and senior staff – as being principally involved. Decisions on the allocation of responsibility allowances were taken, typically, by the head, senior staff and governors. This was also the principal combination for decisions on the out-of-hours use of premises. Decisions about the total number of teachers and support staff also involved them, although the LEA was involved in many schools.

In contrast, there were much higher levels of staff involvement in decisions on the identification of training needs (39 per cent), the purchase of books (49 per cent), educational equipment (50 per cent) and the involvement of parents in support of learning (66 per cent).

Among the schools we visited, the involvement of staff in deciding spending priorities varied widely. It was not uncommon for curriculum leaders to have considerable autonomy over spending the 'capitation' budget for their area, although it was more unusual for teaching staff to be involved in deciding how the funds were allocated between the curriculum areas, or the overall size of the 'capitation' budget. For example, all teachers at one school have a budget for book buying, based on numbers of pupils and, although staff meetings are used to discuss spending priorities, teachers felt decisions had been made in advance of the meeting. One teacher said she would like to have more of a say but did not have the time.

Lack of time affecting involvement in decision-making was often identified. One teacher observed: 'I'm not involved so I am happy'; another 'would like more involvement in finance decisions but unable to attend any more meetings'. At another school, curriculum area budgets are 'agreed by staff' although it is recognised that they are too busy to be more involved: the deputy head commented that 'perhaps teachers are not consulted as much as they should be'. However, teachers at this school felt that 'all decisions are shared' and that there is 'good consultation with all involved'. The deputy head at a different school remarked that the school did need 'to involve staff more fully – but time is a limiting factor and many staff see this as part of the management role of the head and deputy and don't want to be involved'. Interestingly, one of the teachers commented: 'most of the decisions . . . are made by the time I am informed. I would like to be involved more in the planning stages'.

A new head teacher had resulted in a changed management style and greater in-school delegation at one of the schools visited. The head explained that 'all funds for consumables/resources are delegated to co-ordinators', and one of the teachers told us that the head informs staff of the global sum at a meeting and then the sizes of the slices are argued out, influenced by the SDP. At another school one teacher commented: 'consultation procedures are well established with clear lines of communications laid out, with all staff having the opportunity to input into the decision-making process'. In a different school the head led 'all decision-making about apportioning money, staffing etc.' but also 'shared the good and bad news' with the staff. The deputy head, a classroom teacher, welcomed some involvement but did not seek it. One of the teachers described feeling 'very satisfied with decisions and methods of the head – feel consulted and valued'.

Staff at one school seemed to have considerable involvement in decision-making. Commenting on staffing decisions, the deputy explained: 'as there is more decision-making at school level, the whole staff has been involved in discussions about number and type . . . There is more discussion between teachers, for example at staff meetings, about use of resources . . . Staff are involved as much as possible in decisions which affect them'. However, on staffing, one teacher felt that decisions were 'fed to us in a way which makes us feel we've made the decision, but we haven't really'.

In some areas, responsibility for resources is delegated within the school, a factor we cited earlier as being an attribute of a cost-effective school. The next section focuses specifically on the delegation of funds to curriculum-leaders and departmental heads, as well as systems of bidding for funds for curriculum development projects.

Internal delegation

An HMI study commented on the practice of in-school delegation and the bidding system:

> The management focus in schools is being sharpened and staff are participating more fully in forward planning. Delegation to departments in secondary schools and subject co-ordinators in primary, appears to improve managerial and resourcing awareness . . . . The practice of subject co-ordinators bidding for and controlling their own purchasing is gathering momentum in primary schools. The schools which are ahead in the field have carefully planned curricular audits which accurately match their school development plans and prioritise spending in both the short and the long terms. However, there are many schools which have still to link their planning to resource allocation.
>
> (1992: 11, 21)

Different management structures were in evidence in the schools we visited. Some schools had introduced the delegation of budgets to curriculum co-ordinators; others had simply extended a system of delegating the capitation budget already in operation prior to LMS. For example, in one school, the capitation budget had previously been delegated to curriculum leaders and with the introduction of LM greater sums of money were delegated within-school. Speaking of involvement in LM one teacher stated: 'my only specific involvement is how my own budget is spent which has obviously increased as a result of LMS'. Another teacher told us of 'more involvement in how the money is spent'. The deputy head spoke of the teachers' greater 'responsibility for resourcing curriculum areas'. One teacher welcomed these changes:

> I am now given an amount of money over which I have complete control, after consultation with other members of staff. . . . As we are now in control of our own budgets, there is far more consulting one another and decision-making being made.

Elsewhere, internal delegation was being used to support staff development:

> Internal budget holders are now better informed, and better managers. Our staff development can be much more focused with GEST delegation

In another school, where 'capitation' budgets were delegated to key stage co-ordinators, the deputy head felt that although more money was not available, 'the involvement I now have makes me feel that what is available is used to its best advantage'.

There are clear instances of autocratic decisions by head teachers who made most budget decisions in comparative isolation. The head teacher at one primary school believed in a 'democracy of one': he decided the spending priorities, set the budget and reported at the Annual Parents' Meeting the total budget the school received and informed the meeting that the 'budget balanced'. Teachers were not involved in deciding the amount of money to be allocated to the various curriculum areas, although there seemed no great desire for involvement on their part. The head teacher of another school described the school as 'very democratic although as far as management goes it's very autocratic. . . . As far as financial aspects are concerned, I am left to my own devices'. He held the view that teachers 'don't know a lot about LM – even my deputy. I don't think it's affected them'.

The way in which funds were allocated to departments or curriculum-leaders varied. In some instances allocations were based on carefully devised formulae taking account of numbers of pupils and periods taught, on the phased introduction of the national curriculum. In addition to a formula allocation, departments/co-ordinators in some schools could bid into a curriculum development fund for special initiatives. These were sometimes carefully assessed by the SMT or discussed in staff meetings and related to the SDP. One school uses a formula based on pupils, lessons and weightings to delegate funds to departments and also has a bidding system for curriculum development. At another school one teacher explained: 'co-ordinators consult with staff over needs for curriculum areas and put in bids for equipment. These are then submitted to the head teacher who refers it to the sub committee for finance'. The head teacher told us that the priorities for capitation spending were linked to the SDP. One school distinguished between 'tick-over' and 'growth' budgets for curriculum areas. At another school 'middle management' were able to 'decide on own expenditure and make long-term budget planning an essential part of their curriculum area' (teacher). The SDP at another school is used to identify an area of the curriculum each term and this informs budget-setting for the next year.

In other schools the system of delegating funds had met with problems, most often in schools where budget problems led to funds already delegated to departments being clawed back for more urgent expenditures. This had a clear and negative impact on the holders of these budgets, encouraging them to spend the money as soon as it was allocated so avoiding claw-back. This was the case in one school where funds delegated to departments were withdrawn mid-year if money in other budget areas had been exhausted. The head teacher commented: 'the problem is not with *how* decisions are made but with the financial background which forces these decisions'.

Effective participation?

The survey data and our school visits point to some growth in participation in resource decisions but to quite a diversity of circumstances. Our data show some schools securing high levels of staff participation and internal delegation while others preserve an autocratic approach to decisions on resources. In this respect, our evidence supports the conclusions of the 1992 HMI report about some 'greater openness': there does appear to be greater participation in some areas of financial decision-making.

However, the data also suggest a demarcation in decision-making with staffing issues reserved to senior staff and governors. In this respect the data offer some support for Halsey's view that change in personnel policy is 'driving a wedge between management and staff'. We do wonder, however, whether such demarcation has always existed in those schools where head teachers and governors made decisions on staff appointments. We conjecture that the demarcation becomes a more substantial issue at times of retrenchment. An interview with a head teacher who had experienced both LMS and pre-LMS forms of financial delegation illustrates the effect of redundancy decisions on the relationship between management and staff:

> I remember way back in the training days, when the course leader stood up and said 'the greatest effects will be the fact of separating your senior staff from all the other staff'. I remember taking him up and saying I didn't believe it, but that has certainly occurred, there's no doubt about that, there's very much a feeling of 'us and them'.

> (Thomas, 1996: 187)

Taken together, it would seem that local management has increased staff participation in certain areas of school resources, principally in areas closer to the day-to-day concerns of staff. In a number of schools this includes forms of internal delegation of responsibility. How all this is contributing to learning by pupils and students is, of course, the critical question.

IMPACT ON LEARNING

Securing improvement

The government sees LMS as 'a key component of (its) strategy for raising standards of teaching and learning in schools' (DES, 1988: 45), and HMI have observed that LMS has two main objectives: 'to increase schools' control over resources' and 'to improve standards' (HMI, 1992: 8). In the Coopers and Lybrand Report, the 'major benefits from delegation' are set out:

> It will increase the accountability of schools for providing value for money; it will give schools the flexibility to respond directly and promptly to the needs of the school and its pupils in a way which will increase the effectiveness and quality of the services provided.

> (1988: 7)

The belief that LMS can contribute to improving standards has led to a more extended delegation and a greater emphasis on pupil-led funding:

> (the Secretary of State's) aim is to build on the progress that has already been made towards pupil-led funding and delegated management, so as to

increase schools' control over resources and thereby improve the standards of education which they provide.

(DES, 1991: 3)

The emphasis on pupil-led funding aims to reward schools which are successful in attracting pupils as well as adding to pressure for schools to compete for them, another factor viewed as a key to improving standards. Speaking about the extension of delegation and more emphasis on pupil-led funding, Michael Fallon claimed to be:

> delighted to announce these radical steps which fulfil our undertaking to give more powers of decision-making to the governors and head teachers of schools. They also give genuine choice to parents which will drive up standards as schools and parents take advantage of the freedom to make their own decisions . . . Taken together, these two measures will ensure that our schools control more of their budgets, and the size of these budgets is determined by the number of pupils they attract. This will ensure that our primary and secondary system is more responsive to customer choice which will drive up standards.

(1990: 1–2)

The role and impact of competition is a theme we examine in Chapter 9. In this section our purpose is to report our data assessing the reported impact of LMS on learning, and to examine those factors related to it, which are perceived as affecting learning.

Assessing the impact on learning

It is easy to obtain enthusiastic affirmations for local management from a wide range of sources. The fundamental test of delegation, however, must be in terms of its effect on pupils in schools which, as Levacic observes: 'is the $64,000 question to which diametrically opposing answers are hotly but speculatively debated' (1992: 27). She is right to identify 'proponents' of LMS who claim that it contributes to improved effectiveness, but she is equally right to resist an easy judgement on this; in practice comparatively little work has directly addressed this question. An early HMI assessment of locally managed schools reported:

> There is little evidence yet of LMS having any substantial impact on educational standards, although specific initiatives have led to improvement in the targeting of resources and staff, and so to improvements in the quality of educational experiences.

(HMI, 1992: 11)

An OECD (1994) synthesis of studies in nine countries on the effectiveness of schooling and education resource management recognises the problem of assessing the effects of delegated resource management. It observes that researchers have 'had difficulty demonstrating direct empirical links between school organisation and student outcomes, in part because the research to date has lacked the necessary depth and time scale to draw out such effects' (para 21). Taken as a whole, the synthesis warns against drawing unproblematic conclusions. It is against a background of comparatively little work in this area that we ponder the $64,000 question!

In all three of our annual surveys, we invited head teachers to respond to the attitude statement *Children's learning is benefiting from LM*. In reporting these data, we begin by considering the responses of one hundred and seventeen primary heads.

In the 1991 survey, fewer than one-third of these primary heads felt that LM had brought benefits to children's learning. The percentage agreeing with the statement, however, grows with experience of LM: 30 per cent agreed in 1991, 44 per cent in 1992 and the percentage rises to 47 per cent in 1993. In the primary sector therefore, almost half of these heads are able to recognise benefits to children's learning from the introduction of LM. When we consider the figures for smaller and larger primary schools we find that in both groups the percentage agreeing has increased and greater proportions of heads of larger primary schools are able to identify benefits to children's learning, although these differ according to the size of the school. In the set of smaller primary schools (twenty-seven schools), the percentage agreeing that learning was benefiting rose from 15 per cent in 1991 to 33 per cent in 1992 and 41 per cent in 1993; for the larger primary schools (eighty-eight schools) the figures are: 34 per cent in 1991, 46 per cent in 1992 and 50 per cent in 1993.

In the secondary schools included in the three-year survey, the number of heads perceiving benefits also increased with time and are not dissimilar to those in the primary sector: 34 per cent agreed in 1991, 46 per cent in 1992 and 50 per cent in 1993. The proportions agreeing in the set of larger secondary schools (twenty schools) however, are quite different than those in the set of smaller schools (twenty schools). Heads of larger secondary schools show considerably greater agreement: the percentage increases from 65 per cent in 1991 to 70 per cent in 1992 and 80 per cent in 1993. In the set of smaller secondary schools, the figures are: 45 per cent agreeing in 1991; 25 per cent in 1992 and 30 per cent in 1993, an interesting decline over time. Moreover, a comparison of the responses between heads of smaller secondary schools and heads of smaller primary schools shows fewer of the former group believing that learning is benefiting from LM.

We should exercise caution in drawing conclusions from the small set of secondary schools. These data clearly suggest, however, that the heads of smaller secondary schools in this sample are more sceptical about the effect local management is having at classroom level and are uncertain about the extent to which LM has improved children's learning. Most of their colleagues in larger secondary schools, however, believe that learning has benefited.

During our field visits we presented this attitude statement to those we interviewed. For each group – heads, deputies, teachers, chairs of governors, clerical/administrative staff – at least one-third of the respondents felt unable to agree or disagree with the statement. Among these groups, the highest level of agreement was from head teachers, 41 per cent (of thirty-nine heads) of whom believed that children's learning had benefited from LM. This was a similar proportion of deputy heads, 39 per cent of thirty-three deputies and chair of governors, 39 per cent of thirty-one. Teaching staff were slightly more sceptical, however, fewer than one in three being able to identify benefits to learning, 31 per cent of seventy teachers and just 20 per cent of clerical/administrative staff, thirty-five in number, agreed with the statement; in this last group many felt unable to judge, 63 per cent neither agreeing or disagreeing.

These responses point to a complex set of responses from head teachers and others about the perceived benefits from LM for children's learning. There are cases where head teachers are clearly able to identify benefits to learning and many heads of larger secondary schools seem able to do so. There are also signs, particularly in the primary sector, of increasing recognition of benefits to learning. However, in comparison with head teacher responses to many other statements about the benefits of LM, there is more caution in assessing its impact on learning.

This caution is also apparent on responses to the attitude statement *As a direct result of LM, standards of education have improved in my school.* In each sector, smaller percentages of heads agree with this statement than that on perceived benefits to learning. In the 1993 survey of the primary sector, fewer than one-third, 30 per cent, of one hundred and twenty-three heads, agreed that standards of education had improved, although this is an increase of 9 per cent on the 1992 figure. As with the statement on learning, heads of larger primary schools are more positive than those of smaller schools. In the set of twenty-nine small schools, the proportion agreeing with the statement increased from 17 per cent in 1992 to 28 per cent in 1993; in larger schools the level of agreement increased from 22 per cent in 1992 to 32 per cent in 1993. As compared with this, in the secondary sector a higher proportion of heads agreed with the statement, although those in smaller schools were significantly less convinced than their counterparts in larger schools. In the smaller secondaries (nineteen): 32 per cent agreed with the statement in 1992 and 32 per cent in 1993; in the larger secondaries (twenty) agreement rose from 50 per cent in 1992 to 65 per cent in 1993.

During our visits to schools, interviewees were cautious in their response to the statement *As a direct result of LM, standards of education have improved in my school.* For all groups, except head teachers, at least half neither agreed nor disagreed with the statement. Most agreement, 32 per cent of thirty-nine, was found among head teachers, although 27 per cent disagreed. Few deputy heads (12 per cent of thirty-three), teachers (16 per cent of seventy) and administrative staff (15 per cent of thirty-five) believed that 'standards' had improved. Teachers reported the highest level of disagreement (31 per cent) with the statement. From their responses to attitude statements about the impact of LM on children's learning and standards of education, many heads are cautious in viewing the changes as generally beneficial. Some of this may be explained by the scope of change:

> I am worried about whether our children are receiving a better education. So many changes have led to so much of the teachers' time being used for administration. They are very stressed.

We do well to also recognise that the experience of LM will differ between schools, something that becomes apparent when we examine the factors perceived as affecting its impact on learning.

Factors affecting the impact on learning

Having examined the perceptions of how LM has affected learning, we examine in this section the range of factors that shape those perceptions.

Increases in provision

On all three questionnaires, head teachers were asked to respond to the statement *I can show a number of increases in provision as a result of LM*. Responses to this statement are reported here because improved provision is judged by many to have an impact on pupils' learning. Some head teachers hold the view that the level of funding has a direct impact on the quality of provision and make such comments as 'drops in numbers or government cuts . . . all affect the quality of educational provision'. Others mention how improved resources and facilities lead to improved educational experiences, as in the following examples:

> School is very well resourced due to fact that money can be spent as we wish, for the overall benefit of the children . . . quality resources make for improved education. (teacher)

> Great benefit to the children in the quality of education they receive. Better planning – curriculum resourced very well. Environment can be enhanced. Taking control over the things you want in your school. (teacher)

> Students have benefited from increased resources and an improved environment. (assistant bursar)

> It is time consuming. However, the environment and PTR have both improved considerably, both have improved standards of education.

When the responses of primary head teachers are examined, we find that the majority are able to point to a number of increases in provision as a result of

LM. The proportion was 55 per cent in 1991, increasing to 69 per cent in 1992 and effectively constant at 68 per cent the following year. These relatively high proportions would include instances of heads being able to identify increases in some areas while also having made reductions elsewhere. The percentages agreeing are higher in larger primary schools: in these schools (eighty-nine), 60 per cent agreed in 1991, 74 per cent in 1992 and 72 per cent in 1993; in the smaller primary schools the figures are 39 per cent in 1991, 54 per cent in 1992 and 57 per cent in 1993. On the first questionnaire only, heads were also asked to respond to the statement *I can point to actual reductions in provision as a result of LM*: 35 per cent of the primary heads agreed.

In the secondary sector (forty schools), the percentages who agree with the statement *I can show a number of increases in provision as a result of LM* have remained stable over the three years: 68 per cent agreed in 1991 and 1992 followed by a slight fall to 65 per cent in 1993. The responses of heads from smaller secondary schools are, however, markedly different from heads of larger schools: we find a *decline* in the proportion of heads of smaller schools agreeing and an *increase* in the number of heads of larger schools agreeing. Among smaller secondary schools, 65 per cent agreed in 1991, falling to 60 per cent in 1992 and a further fall to 50 per cent in 1993. In the larger schools, the 70 per cent agreeing in 1991 increased to 75 per cent in 1992 and to 80 per cent in 1993. On the first questionnaire only, heads were also asked to respond to the statement *I can point to actual reductions in provision as a result of LM*: 37 per cent of the secondary heads agreed.

The pattern of school responses shows some similarities to those on perceived benefits for children's learning: both show size differences in the secondary sector. This led us to examine the relationship between those heads agreeing that children's learning is benefiting from LM with those reporting increases in provision. Looking at the responses of the two groups of schools in each sector, for the three years, there are nine groups where there is a statistically significant correlation between the responses agreeing that LM has benefited children's learning and those able to show increases in provision and vice versa (Bullock and Thomas, 1994a). That is, it is those heads who are able to identify increases in provision who are likely also to report benefits in children's learning. The implications of this finding merit consideration. Does it mean that LM may have brought benefits to learning in schools where the financial situation is healthy while a reduced budget could result in unwelcome consequences for children's learning? Such a view would be consistent with the statistical correlation and with a strong taken-for-granted view in the teaching profession of a positive relation between resources and what can be achieved in schools. It is against the background of this analysis that we consider other factors, all essentially about resources, which may be affecting the impact of LM on learning.

Staffing and the management of time

While a number of the staffing issues arising from local management are examined in Chapter 6, in this chapter we consider three staffing issues relating directly to its impact on learning: whether staff time for the support of learning has been reduced, whether more meetings are focused on administrative issues, and what impact funding has had on staffing levels.

In all three surveys, head teachers were asked to respond to this statement about staff time and the support of learning: *LM has led to reduced staff time for the direct support of children's learning*. Here we examine the responses of the one hundred and eighteen primary and thirty-nine secondary school head teachers who participated in each survey. Among primary head teachers, agreement with this statement falls sharply from 40 per cent in 1991 to 24 per cent in 1992, with a slight increase to 27 per cent in 1993. The perceptions of these head teachers depend upon the size of the school. The figures for the smaller primary schools (twenty-six schools) are: 58 per cent in 1991, 39 per cent in 1992 and 35 per cent in 1993; for the larger primary schools (ninety schools): 36 per cent in 1991, 20 per cent in 1992 and 24 per cent in 1993.

Viewing their responses as a group, the secondary-school head teachers were less likely to agree with the statement than their primary colleagues. Over the three years, the proportion reporting agreement that LM had reduced staff time in support of learning changed from 21 per cent in 1991 to 26 per cent in 1992 with a fall to 10 per cent in 1993. As with the primary schools, there are clear differences according to the size of school: for smaller secondaries (twenty schools): 20 per cent agreed in 1991, 35 per cent in 1992 and 15 per cent in 1993; for the larger secondary schools (nineteen schools): 21 per cent agreed in 1991, 16 per cent in 1992 and 5 per cent in 1993.

In most schools, then, the data suggest that LM has not led to reduced staff time for the direct support of children's learning. There are schools, however, notably in the primary sector where staff time has been reduced; there is also a difference between small and large secondary schools' assessments of the overall impact of local management on learning.

How schools spend their time in meetings is an aspect of their effectiveness, an important issue being the focus of such meetings and the extent to which they may be devoted to issues which are not directly linked to teaching and learning. We view this issue as consistent with the importance of involving teachers in decision-making but in ways which focus their attention, and that of their colleagues, upon matters of curriculum and learning. In each year head teachers were asked to respond to the statement: *As a result of LM, more meetings are taken up with administrative issues which lessen our attention on pupils' learning*.

In the primary sector the percentage agreeing with this statement declined over three years from 69 per cent in 1991 to 57 per cent in 1993. Thus, three years after the implementation of local management half of primary head teachers agreed that more meetings are taken up with administrative issues and affect the attention given to children's learning. When these schools are analysed by size, substantial differences are evident: of the twenty-eight smaller primary schools (two hundred or fewer pupils), the level of agreement with the statement was 82 per cent in 1991, 64 per cent in 1992 and 71 per cent in 1993. For the ninety larger primary schools (more than two hundred pupils), 66 per cent agreed in 1991, falling to 56 per cent in 1992 and 46 per cent in 1993.

As a group, fewer secondary head teachers agreed with the statement that there were more meetings on administrative issues which diverted attention from learning. The overall figures showed a decline from 54 per cent in 1991 to 49 per cent in 1992 and to 31 per cent in 1993. Differences in school size are also evident here, although less marked than in the primary sector: for the smaller secondary schools, the percentages agreeing declined from 68 per cent in 1991 to 53 per cent in 1992 and 37 per cent in 1993; for the larger schools the change was from 40 per cent in 1991 to 45 per cent in 1992 with a sharp fall to 25 per cent in 1993.

Despite some sector differences, the results support the view that more meetings are taken up with administrative issues and these lessen attention on pupils' learning, although we recognise a downward trend in the perceptions of head teachers on this issue. What may be more significant is the difference of view within the sectors between head teachers of smaller and larger schools, a finding that is consistent with responses to other statements.

In Chapter 6 we reported the incidence of reductions in the number of teaching and non-teaching support staff, an issue which clearly matters in terms of the learning opportunities available to children. The size of the budget was an issue which arose in many of the questionnaires and school visits:

> Lack of money in the primary budget means that LMS is a burden with very little benefit for the education of the children – we cannot plan to spend money which does not exist.

The head teacher at another observed that the school has 'insufficient money . . . to fund adequately the teaching and support staff requirements'; its impact on pupils being stated succinctly: 'without teachers children do not learn'. Another reported that 'staffing levels will be reduced by two FTE in September (from 15 to 13)' and anticipated 'yet further reductions in April 1994'. These cuts are seen as placing 'severe constraints on the service we offer our pupils'.

Although not requiring cuts to staffing, the budget at some schools is considered insufficient to an extent which, nevertheless, has a detrimental impact upon work with children. The head teacher at one school believes a stage has been reached 'where curriculum developments (which need an input of money) are threatened because there isn't any money'. Another head teacher made a similar remark:

> local management and formula funding are affecting the funds I have available for the development of the curriculum. We are having to rely more heavily on PTA fund raising to meet the expenses.

The teacher at another school viewed LMS as 'penny pinching at the children's cost'. One clerical assistant commented:

> Theory is good but in practice problems in large old school with experienced staff as monies eaten up on wages and repairs. I feel the children may suffer educationally because of lack of money.

One head teacher makes the link between the level of funding and the benefits or the lack of benefits arising from local management, drawing attention, usefully, to the distinction between the size of the budget and devolved management:

> The children in the school have not benefited from LMS – although it is the *size* of the budget that is at fault, not the delegation to schools of the responsibilities for the budget.

The links being made here between the availability and use of time and staff with the learning opportunities provided by schools reinforce the earlier analysis of the relationship between evidence of increases in provision and assessment of the effect of local management on children's learning. It is a view reflected in other ways in which local management has had an impact on learning.

Flexibility to target resources

LMS enables schools to target resources, including staff, in ways which could lead to improvements in the quality of work in the classroom. One head teacher writes that 'LM has provided me with an opportunity to manage the school's resources more flexibly to the advantage of pupils and staff'. Another told us that spending on 'school-defined needs' had enhanced the 'learning and the environment'. The deputy head at this school reiterated this, seeing the school's ability 'to target expenditure upon the priorities it identifies' as 'a most important consequence of LMS' – the school had done this successfully, 'to benefit children's education'. Such sentiments are echoed by others:

> To manage the budget is an essential part of managing the curriculum which is the only way to ensure we give the service to the children.

> Whatever my misgivings about the political motives behind LMS, in practical terms I think that I can deliver a better service to my pupils through the increased flexibility and independence that the system provides.

This flexibility to target resources, however, is clearly easier in schools where the financial situation is healthy, as is suggested in the following three remarks where reference is made to 'sufficient', 'greater amounts of', and, 'more' money:

> We have sufficient money to meet the needs of our pupils to a more effective extent than ever. More staff, more decisions made quickly, happier staff – and the ability to react to needs and requests quickly. More generally, LMS has raised the status of the school as the whole, place is better looked after and cared for and pupils have excellent equipment bought competitively.

> Greater freedom to influence events. Greater amounts of money spent on pupils. A betterment of overall provision.

> We seem to have had more money and choice in how we spend it for the benefit of the children.

By contrast, another head teacher welcomes 'the opportunity to have greater control over the school's budget' but regrets that, in his view, 'primary schools remain the poor relations of the secondary sector'. Perhaps this may explain why he feels that his school is 'only gradually . . . getting better at exercising our control for the benefit of our pupils'. The link between the ability to target resources to the benefit of children relates more specifically to a school's opportunity to enhance the school environment and improve educational resources (including staffing as well as books, materials and equipment).

Improved environment and resources

Head teachers point to improvements in the school environment and facilities as a means of enhancing the educational experience for pupils. Improvements 'in human resources and facilities for the children' are believed to have 'improved education' at one school. Another head comments on the improvements and the 'happy pupils':

> I have been a head for 17 years in three different schools, the last three (years) locally managed and handling our own budget. The best time of my whole career. I have a much better school, better resources, more staff, better premises, happy pupils, satisfied parents, high morale among staff. . . . Never had it so good.

Many head teachers write about how LM has enabled them to work through programmes of redecoration and purchase new equipment. These, clearly, could have indirect benefits for children. The following are examples of such comments:

> I enjoy the freedom which LM gives us, and my pre-1990 school which was badly decorated and not too generously equipped has now been completely

redecorated internally, and we have large amount of equipment, books and beautiful new furniture everywhere. LM is house-keeping on a large scale, and has been a great and enjoyable challenge.

This school is better staffed, equipped and is in better decorative order than it has been for a long time.

The most important consequence of LM has been the opportunity to provide much better facilities for the pupils – i.e., new laboratory, curtains, carpets etc. In terms of the curriculum it has led to being able to buy expensive items beyond our means before – especially computers.

The school is better furnished. Extra staff allow better delivery of the national curriculum. Generally good for school, both staff and children.

In these schools, financial delegation has enabled the head teacher and governors to enhance the working environment and improve educational resources. The budget has been sufficient to accommodate these decisions. In contrast, there are schools where the budget is insufficient for their perceived needs resulting, in some cases, in cuts to resources, including staffing, with consequential affects on the quality of educational provision. These aspects of local management caused some head teachers to reflect on the inequalities associated with the change.

Inequalities

It is argued by some head teachers that LMS has increased inequalities between schools. There is a concern that disadvantaged children will be adversely affected. One head teacher made this point on both the second and third questionnaires:

In general, LMS increases inequalities between schools and those with the most disadvantaged children suffer most.

LMS aggravates differences between schools. The rich get richer, the poor poorer. The main sufferers are disadvantaged children.

Such concerns are related to more open enrolment and the pressure on schools to compete for pupils with the additional fear that schools popular with parents will move to select pupils and less popular schools will be forced to close:

I fear that schools will be pressurised into CHOOSING pupils and that those with special needs (or socially less acceptable) because they pull down the scores, will not be able to go to the school of their choice, i.e., sink schools will develop.

The weak going to the wall is OK in business but not when you are dealing with pupils' once and only opportunity to learn.

The option that some schools will seek grant maintained status is seen as exacerbating this situation, threatening to widen the gap between schools in terms of some principles of equity:

> Fragmentation will not improve education. . . . Education will be more diverse, providing unequal opportunities for children.

The impact of the grant maintained sector on the schooling system is not explored here: our focus is on the impact of local management, although we recognise that the two initiatives are part of a whole which cannot be entirely understood in isolation. In this chapter, we conclude our discussion of the factors affecting the impact of local management on learning by considering comments made to us on a shifting emphasis to financial matters.

Shifting the focus from 'education' to 'finance'

Head teachers report a shift in emphasis away from matters directly educational toward a greater concern with financial issues. In everyday terms this may be manifested by some head teachers being apparently more interested in 'cheque books and fax machines':

> Focus of attention moving from the child to management – when a group of head teachers meet they don't talk about children any more – just cheque books and fax machines etc.

Another head teacher comments on meetings for head teachers saying that they 'tend to be on financial aspects instead of addressing educational issues'. Comments by teachers reveal their concern about the effect of linking funding directly to pupil numbers:

> The focus has also been on encouraging pupils to come here. Marketing of the school is now an important part of things – are we losing sight of actually teaching children?

> Children are now seen as financial assets with a price on their head – and there is despair when families leave the area because they affect the budget. The head seems to have less time for maintaining the ethos of the school and is becoming a financial manager – with little time for teaching and curriculum leadership.

Both of the above comments were made by teachers in the schools we visited. Related concerns were made by other classroom teachers, reflecting anxieties that budgetary or financial issues were taking precedence over 'educational matters':

> I like to think that we are in more control of the future of our school but worry that teacher/pupil time and problems relating to educational issues may become overshadowed by 'budget issues'.

The senior management are very heavily involved in financial discussions and have no time to 'waste' discussing educational matters.

One head teacher believes that 'LMS has brought advantages but, if taken further, schools will be run as businesses to the detriment of education'. Another sees 'finance' as setting 'the whole tone of "opting out". It appears money-led rather than educationally led'. How this view relates to wider evidence on the impact on learning we consider in the next section.

Improving practice?

The survey data over the three years show head teachers becoming more positive in their assessment of whether local management is benefiting children's learning. While this trend is apparent among primary and secondary school heads, we have discussed clear differences according to school size in each sector.

In understanding these differences of perception, the financial situation of schools appears to be a major factor. When we examined responses to statements on increase in provision there is, in both sectors, a difference according to the size of the school. This also applies to assessments on the impact of local management on staff time and its use in administrative roles. These findings contain echoes of an earlier analysis we undertook comparing the historical and formula budgets of over 2,000 schools, which showed that small secondary schools were among those schools losing most in the change to local management (Thomas and Bullock, 1992a).

The data reported here suggest that assessing the impact of local management on children's learning is linked with the resource context of the school: local management is viewed by many as providing flexibility to target resources to the needs of children, allowing the purchase of materials, employment of extra staff and spending to improve the working environment. Where budgets are constrained, however, head teachers are less positive about the impact of local management and more concerned about deterioration in the educational services offered to children. It would seem that if funding is declining, having the means to choose between alternative ways of making cuts may not be a welcome addition.

CONCLUSION: LOCAL MANAGEMENT AND COST-EFFECTIVENESS?

In organising our discussion of the impact of local management on learning, we have tried to represent three key areas identified in the literature of effectiveness and cost-effectiveness: purposeful management and leadership; participation in decision-making; and a focus upon practice.

On purposeful management and leadership, we have received accounts from some schools which affirm the positive contribution made by local management to this aspect of schools as organisations:

> Decision-making at local/school level has made the notion of 'management' more realistic to all staff. School development planning is seen as a positive, real exercise with visible results.

> Consequences for this school have been: (i) the opportunity to manage more effectively, by having money to meet the needs of the school; (ii) the ability to monitor and make savings in such areas as maintenance of building, heating, lighting and water consumption; (iii) a feeling of ownership of the school, which leads to more effective management of the school by all staff.

Our data confirm that LM has affected planning, management and decision-making in schools, although the extent to which it has brought benefits seems to be affected by the financial situation of the school and the management style of the head teacher. The responses of head teachers to statements about LM resulting in 'more effective' and 'better' management, suggest that, in their view, LM has improved school management. Indeed, on the first questionnaire 56 per cent of heads agreed that *LM has meant that the school is more effectively managed.* An increasing number of heads believe that *schools are better-managed as a result of LM.* Sixty-eight per cent of primary heads agreed with this statement in 1992, increasing to 75 per cent in 1993; in the secondary sector, 90 per cent agreed in 1992 and 1993 with little difference in opinion from heads in larger and smaller schools.

This self-reporting on how local management has contributed to management effectiveness should not be disregarded but it should also be treated with some caution. Head teachers are, after all, commenting on their own performance. For example, while development planning has been seen as an opportunity for creating a better framework for managing, our data suggest that these are not closely linked to the budgets of schools; although, it does appear to have contributed to developing a sense of purpose. However, we have noted that additional workload has made heads less familiar with events in the classroom, a matter of real concern as an awareness of practice is a keystone for matching resources to needs.

Set against this, our survey shows some schools securing high levels of staff participation and greater internal delegation of some decisions on resources. Such participation is subject to demarcation, some areas being restricted to senior staff and governors. Some of the best outcomes of local management for participation are reflected in one comment:

> LM has provided the opportunity to have a complete overview of the whole school, both in educational and financial aspects. It has created an awareness of how each is dependent on the other and the necessity for a strong management team to bind it into a cohesive whole. The involvement

of staff in the LM development plan and the devolvement of knowledge of procedures has created an appreciation of the complexity of management which, to many, was previously an unknown quantity.

What this all means for children's learning and their standard of education remains the fundamental question. Our data show head teachers becoming more positive in their assessment over the three years of the survey, although there are clear and persistent differences according to sector and school size. This is related to the financial position of a school, which appears to be a critical factor in shaping judgement of the impact of local management.

In their earlier report, HMI were unable to conclude that LMS had directly affected 'the quality of teaching and learning or the standards which pupils achieve' (DfE, 1992: 21). In their summary they stated that 'It is too early . . . to conclude how far LMS is contributing to any general improvement of standards, and difficult to disentangle its influence from the web of other initiatives' (p. 34). It is evident that the impact of local management is complex, recalling some of the earliest evaluations of the financial delegation scheme in Solihull in the early 1980s (Humphrey and Thomas, 1985, 1986). These showed that the opportunity to make decisions on the school site was appreciated, making head teachers positive in their attitude to delegation, but it did not mean that it was possible to attribute to delegation clear learning benefits for pupils. In making this observation however, we should not discount the opportunities it creates for influencing the school environment and the resources supporting learning. In this respect, we must also recognise some of the concerns expressed about the impact of local management in equal access to resources.

We have also noted the comments of some head teachers who are concerned about an apparent shift in emphasis away from matters explicitly 'educational', towards a situation where decisions are based more on financial considerations. We should also recognise the diversity of effect on schools, some benefiting while others seem disadvantaged by a decline in resources. Where the balance lies in its impact on the learning opportunities of different groups of pupils is a theme we consider in the next chapter.

Chapter 9

Diversity and equity in decentralisation

EQUITY, ENTITLEMENT AND NEEDS

In Chapter 4, we explained that a central question in evaluating decentralisation is related to issues of equity: 'who benefits?'. We recognise that equity entails asking questions not only about the distribution of educational opportunity *between* social groups, but also *within* social groups, and further, that concern with disparities within and between social groups must not overlook the needs of individuals. Because of different needs, a commitment to greater equity can mean the acceptance as well as the rejection of *some* diversity: judging what to accept or reject will involve the moral reasoning to which we referred in Chapter 4.

In the case of this chapter, our moral reasoning is embedded in the equity-centred examination of decentralisation which follows. The studies upon which we draw deal solely with aspects of the financing and resourcing of schools in England and Wales; they do not, for example, examine issues of equity raised by the national curriculum. The chapter has four main sections. In the first of these we examine how pupils of different ages are funded and how this varies across the country. The second section describes and analyses evidence on funding pupils with additional needs, some reflecting the needs of individuals and others arising from membership of social groups. This is followed by a review of some evidence on the impact of the re-structured mixed economy of schools and the pressures created for schools to compete in attracting pupils. The concluding section reflects on this range of evidence for some of the issues of equity with which we have begun.

FUNDING BY AGE OF PUPIL

Public funds provide by far the largest share of the finances of maintained schools in England and Wales and they are an essential component of school development. They provide much of the means upon which schools draw in order to meet their aims and objectives and, to an extent, they set limits to what can be achieved. Describing how these public funds are distributed make explicit the preferences-in-practice of the planners who decide how much to allocate to different children and schools. One of the virtues of LMS, therefore, is that since April 1990 funds are allocated to schools by LEAs on the basis of public and explicit formulae. These make more explicit the judgements by LEAs about the funding implications of different educational needs and include judgements on: the needs of children aged from two years to nineteen years; schools of different size; schools serving communities assessed as socially disadvantaged; and schools with children identified as having special educational needs but who are not statemented. In this section we examine data on the funding of pupils according to age.

Schools in England and Wales are required to provide a national curriculum which specifies the programmes of study for all children from five to sixteen years. How much money a school receives for providing for these children can differ widely. In Table 9.1 we provide data on the allocations of funds to pupils at seventeen age intervals; in the contemporary jargon, these are age-weighted pupil units (AWPUs) and are the funding levels used in the financial year ending in April 1991. We have data on AWPUs for seventy-one LEAs and show maximum, minimum and mean expenditures for the sample as a whole. Since the data on all seventy-one would be indigestible, however, we have selected ten cases to illustrate some general points. Their choice was based upon AWPU8 (pupils aged eight years), normally the unit of lowest value in the seventy-six LEAs, and we have included in our sample all those LEAs where the AWPU8 was within 2 per cent of the group mean. The group mean was £800, so we include LEAs with a range of £784 to £816. Whilst we begin our discussion with the set, we draw as necessary upon other examples.

The funds distributed on the basis of the age-weighted pupil units (AWPUs) are not the whole budget of a school and we should be cautious about simplistic comparisons. In an early summary of schemes, George Thomas (1990) warns that inter-LEA comparisons of AWPUs ignore the proportion of the General Schools' Budget which is delegated through the formula. One LEA may have AWPUs of a lower value than another but provide more support to schools through the non-delegated part of their budget. Differences may also arise because of the construction of a formula, the rules which determine the distribution of the Aggregated Schools' Budget (ASB). One LEA may allocate more of its ASB through the AWPU component of the formula compared with another which may give more emphasis to non-AWPU special factors, such as additional funding for small schools. There are, however, some limits to these differences and government policy is directed to reduce them further. At present, for example, a minimum of 80 per cent of the ASB must be allocated through the AWPU element of the formula. There are also differences in funding levels between LEAs which arise because of the current arrangements for funding local government. For all these reasons we shall largely avoid discussion here of

Table 9.1 The value of age-weighted pupil units

Age	Local Education Authority										71 LEAs Summary stats			Age
	Cleveland	Coventry	Derbyshire	IoW	N. Yorkshire	Redbridge	Somerset	Sunderland	Tameside	Warwickshire	min	mean	max	
3	976	1252			941	1258	921	1108	1186	789	12	984	1651	3
4	856	1064	887	801	861	1031	921	1124	1145	789	704	935	1285	4
5	856	803	783	801	816	804	921	827	837	789	634	840	1092	5
6	856	803	783	801	816	804	921	799	837	789	634	831	1017	6
7	814	795	802	801	792	804	806	799	812	789	614	804	1025	7
8	814	795	806	801	792	804	806	799	812	789	614	800	935	8
9	814	795	806	869	792	804	806	799	812	789	617	810	987	9
10	814	799	806	869	792	804	806	799	812	789	617	820	1002	10
11	1139	1239	1135	869	1146	1272	1133	1309	1170	1073	869	1128	1468	11
12	1139	1239	1135	869	1146	1272	1133	1309	1170	1073	869	1148	1468	12
13	1139	1239	1135	1302	1221	1272	1133	1309	1170	1073	913	1179	1468	13
14	1453	1594	1381	1302	1435	1525	1484	1368	1495	1436	1105	1383	1633	14
15	1563	1724	1497	1392	1607	1525	1591	1368	1609	1436	1217	1475	1901	15
16	1917	1732	1792	2325*	1921#	2148	1901	1664	1869	1862	1428	1843	2325	16
17	1917	1798	1803	2325*	2062	2148	1901	1664	1934	1862	1501	1878	2325	17
18	1917	1798	1803	2325*	2062	2148	1901		1934	1862	0	1865	2630	18
19		1798		2325*	2062	2148	1901		1934	1862	0	1828	2325	19

* indicates different funding for 'A' Level and non-'A' Level students in the Isle of Wight
£2317 for 'A' Level
£2331 for GCSE in the 6th Form

# indicates different funding for 16 year olds in North Yorkshire, reflecting the additional costs in respect of exam fees: £1,890 (non-exam) and £1,952 (exam)

inter-LEA comparisons. By including the maximum, minimum and mean data, however, we do indicate that there are very considerable differences between LEAs which need to be better understood. There is certainly a need for a methodology which allows comparability so that the equity implications of these funding levels for children of the same age in different parts of the country are better understood.

Making comparisons within LEAs are somewhat less problematic, although we should be alert to specific circumstances which may explain notable differences. With these caveats, what can be said about these ten LEAs and the set from which they are drawn? In eight of the ten LEAs, the lowest cash values are for seven- to ten-year-olds and, in this respect, they typify the larger set. The exceptions are Derbyshire and the Isle of Wight (IoW) where some infant years are less well-funded. Why these LEAs differ in their view of the resource requirements of these year groups is a legitimate question, although of a lesser order, perhaps, than why the junior years should be the cheapest. The overall chronological pattern is of a decline in funding levels for the junior years from the infant years and then substantial increases into the secondary years. This again is the pattern for the seventy-one LEAs, although the IoW and Warwickshire differ by not giving a premium to any of the early years by comparison with the junior years. Why?

The move from the primary to the secondary sector is demarcated by additional resources amounting to a mean of 46 per cent for eleven-year-olds compared with ten-year-olds. Within the set of ten LEAs this ranges from zero in the IoW, explained no doubt by its pattern of middle schools, to 64 per cent in Sunderland. Whatever historical explanations might explain the additional funding at eleven years, do they remain tenable in terms of differences in the requirements of the National Curriculum and the wider educational needs of the child? Should national and local planners review these and other relative weights in view of the national curriculum created by the 1988 Education Reform Act? In a recent national review of these disparities by the Education Committee of the House of Commons, the final report observed:

> The witnesses with secondary school backgrounds regarded the disparity between the phases as being relatively small, but not so small that it could not be adjusted without serious disadvantage to secondary schools. Those with primary school backgrounds and most of the neutral witnesses thought that the disparity was too large and should be reduced. We are persuaded that the latter are right.
>
> (HC, 1994: xliii)

and

> In the light of our present knowledge, though our view may be modified by information coming from the research on activity-led staffing that we

propose above, we believe that the funding of schools should begin to show less differentiation based simply on pupils' age.

(ibid.)

The inter-sector difference is most marked in the comparative funding of eight-year-olds as against sixteen- to nineteen-year-olds, and here also there are sharp differences in intra-LEA ratios. In the IoW, for example, the value of AWPU16 (£2,325) is 2.9 times greater than the weighting of AWPU8 (£801). This compares with Sunderland where the value of AWPU16 (£1,664) is 2.08 times that of AWPU8 (£799). The summary data from the seventy-six LEAs in Table 9.1 show that the *minimum* value of AWPU16 (£1,428) is greater than the *maximum* value of any LEA's AWPU4 to AWPU10 (National Curriculum Years R to 6). Whilst these inter-year differentials reflect the tradition of higher levels of resourcing for older children, and itself raises questions about educational needs, the different *relative* judgements within LEAs suggest an area worthy of closer examination. It would also be pertinent to compare the funding levels of sixteen- to nineteen-year-olds in schools compared with further education. A final example notes the different assumptions about the perceived needs of Reception year children (AWPU4) in different LEAs, our sample of ten having a range from £789 in Warwickshire to £1,145 in Tameside.

Clearly, the comparative weights of all year groups is an area that would benefit from further examination with respect to the implied judgement of need. What are the rationales which underlie these differences, and are some more compelling than others in meeting contemporary needs? The differences and the similarities shown here raise questions about differences in local circumstances and in local interpretations of educational needs. One of the great merits of funding by formulae is that they make more public the preferences of policy-makers and resource planners. They offer no answers but they suggest that, to the extent that resources contribute to the quality of educational experiences in schools for children of different ages, there are differences within and between LEAs which merit further investigation. They suggest a need for internal reviews within LEAs but also point to national reviews to better understand the differences which exist.

If resources matter, these allocations are of crucial significance in shaping the opportunities that schools can provide for their children. The more public process for allocating those funds promises circumstances where the rationale for the funding of schools will be subject to more discussion – as in the House of Commons inquiry – and where the relationship between resources and educational needs will be more clearly articulated. It is a system that does allow for easier comparison, more easily allowing questions to be asked about differences in funding comparable children in different LEAs and different children in the same LEA. The evidence so far is that funding differences according to age exist in ways which mean substantial disparities *between* age groups in different LEAs and *within* age groups in the same LEAs, raising pertinent issues for the equity of current patterns of funding.

FUNDING ADDITIONAL EDUCATIONAL NEEDS

A framework for re-distribution?

LMS has led some commentators (Ball, 1990a; Ball, 1990b; Wragg, 1988) to express concern that the reforms are socially divisive and threaten the future of schools serving disadvantaged pupils. Ball writes:

> Clearly *some* schools and *some* pupils will benefit from the redistribution of resources which the LMS provisions of the Act will bring about. But it is important to emphasise the some. Others will lose out, most likely those situated in the inner cities. Those pupils who receive their schooling in the most economically disadvantaged areas of the inner cities will be faced with declining resources, a scarcity of experienced teachers, poor plant and facilities and in some cases their schools will eventually close.
>
> (1990a: 21)

We would regard these observations as a reasonable prediction about the possible effects of local management. They are based on the assumption that local management creates a more competitive environment between schools. The prediction is, that as a result of the quasi-market components of local management, schools will compete for pupils *and* that, as a consequence, schools serving the 'most economically disadvantaged communities' will be the most likely losers. There are good arguments for regarding that view as an important hypothesis about the effect of LMS. In terms of the typology in Chapter 3, however, it is an hypothesis which arises by defining LMS as an exclusively market-oriented change where behaviour is characterised by non-altruistic modes of behaviour and by schools 'cream-skimming' local neighbourhoods for pupils expected to do well in examinations. However, we would wish to add some necessary qualifying statements to this view of local management.

The funding formula used by each LEA has the capacity to direct resources to schools with pupils – and pupil intakes – with a variety of additional educational needs (AEN). Indeed, in terms of our definition of equity, it is apparent that the guidelines on AEN have implications for all three of the elements of our definition of equity: influencing disparities between and within social groups as well as for individual needs. Moreover, the guidelines could have been interpreted by some LEAs as a means for *increasing* their support to schools with a high proportion of pupils with additional educational needs. In terms of the typology in Chapter 2, this could be the case for those LEAs which adopt a 'collective' view on the allocation of resources; there we would expect schools with high proportions of pupils with AEN pupils initially to be net beneficiaries of the new funding system. Obvious exceptions to this would be any LEAs which before LMS were allocating levels of resources for AEN which could not be matched under the government's guidelines.

How these 'market' and 'collective' elements of local management interact over time will shape the distributive effects of local management, although loss of pupils alone will be insufficient evidence of its effects upon schools. The overall effect of pupil loss on a school will depend upon the interaction of competition with the level of support provided – through the formula – for pupils with additional educational needs. Even if schools in the inner cities lose pupils as a result of competition, therefore, its impact upon their overall funding will depend upon the share of their budget coming through additional educational needs. The scale of change in pupil numbers will be significant here; an issue which leads to a rather different problem.

There is an overall demographic shift in population away from the inner cities in England and Wales. Data showing declining pupil numbers from schools in these areas, therefore, cannot alone be taken as evidence of the competitive effects of local management. Assessing its impact in terms of changes in pupil numbers will require some account to be taken of the scale and pace of earlier population movements, as well as information on housing policies in local areas. Isolating the effect of competition is a complex process. The devil is in the detail. Only by examining the application of local management in detail are we able to draw conclusions about its distributive effects. This section contributes to that process by examining the use made by LEAs of their discretion in this area.

We have done so by drawing upon school level budget data for all schools in a set of thirteen LEAs – almost 2,800 schools. The set provides a source of examples of the use LEAs have made of AEN elements within the funding formula and the level of such funding; the national guidance illuminates the problem of exploring some of the equity issues in this area.

Advice and guidance

Within the framework of LMS schemes detailed by the DES (1988) and Welsh Office (1988) the additional costs of meeting special educational need is recognised:

> the Secretary of State will expect LEAs to include in their formulae provision for taking into account the incidence of pupils with special needs in schools covered by their schemes. This includes both statemented and non-statemented pupils with learning difficulties as defined in the Education Act 1981. . . . In addition, the LEAs will be free to take into account any other factors, such as the incidence of social deprivation among pupils in different schools and the distribution of gifted pupils.

(DES, 1988: 24)

This guidance (DES, 1988) distinguishes, therefore, between different forms of special needs. There are those special needs defined in the Education Act, 1981, a factor *expected* to be included in each LEA's formula, although an LEA can treat expenditure on statemented pupils as a discretionary exception. In our definition of equity, this is an approach to differentiating needs which is based upon a recognition of individual needs, such as specific learning difficulties. There are other forms of special needs, however, such as social deprivation, a factor which is essentially concerned with differences between social groups. This is a factor whose inclusion in an LEA's funding formula is *optional*, a difference which we judge to reflect the political preferences of the government which set up local management. It is also the government which set the limit to allocations for special educational needs or social disadvantage. Funding all special factors, including AEN, small schools, salary variations and premises factors, must not exceed 20 per cent of the Aggregated Schools Budget, the remainder being distributed on the basis of age-weighted pupils. In addition, some AEN factors may be funded from the pupil-led component but must not exceed 5 per cent of this factor.

While noting this restriction, we must also recognise that this funding of AEN does not necessarily account for all the support provided for special needs. Some services remain centrally provided by LEAs and their funding is not included within the formula allocation. This often applies to educational psychologists and welfare services, advisory and peripatetic teachers, home tuition, as well as funding for special units in mainstream schools and provision for statemented pupils; Lee (1991b) reports that most of these services were kept under central control.

In exploring how LEAs have used the additional educational needs factor within the formula, two related issues are raised. The first is the problem of definition: what are 'special educational needs', 'social disadvantage', 'social deprivation'? The second is the question of eligibility criteria: how are such needy pupils identified?

Problems of definition and eligibility criteria

In considering the advice and guidance issued by the DES and Welsh Office it is apparent that no single term was used. Reference is made to 'pupils with special needs' (a blanket term), 'special educational needs', 'statemented pupils', 'non-statemented pupils with learning difficulties defined by the Education Act 1981', 'non-statutory special needs' and 'social deprivation'. Lee (1991a) suggests *additional educational needs* (AEN) as a helpful umbrella term to represent 'a wider range of factors thought to impact unfavourably on children's education'. Doing so only emphasises the problem of distinguishing between those equity policies that focus on the needs of social groups as against those which recognise the needs of individuals with quite specific needs. AEN can *include* factors related to the social disadvantage of pupils' backgrounds, an individual's special educational needs and the language needs of certain ethnic minority children. This is not comprehensive: George Thomas examined LMS submissions and identified the following in a definition of 'special needs':

- statemented pupils,
- 20% of the pupil age group as defined by the Warnock Report,
- pupils with severe socio-economic disadvantages, e.g., deprived social catchment area, one parent families, unemployed parents, families where the main language is not English, etc.,
- pupils with severe learning difficulties,
- pupils with severe behavioural problems,
- pupils with physical handicaps, e.g., hearing impaired,
- gifted children.

(1990: 26)

What is not clear, however, is how these various items relate to the apparent distinction between non-statemented special *educational* needs (a factor *expected* to be included in funding formulae) and *social* disadvantage (an *optional* factor). When LEAs' formulae for funding are examined this distinction is often confused. Lee (1992b) reports that in many cases the distinction between the allocation of resources for non-statemented special educational needs, and social disadvantage is blurred. George Thomas makes a similar observation:

> Some divide the identification of learning difficulties from socio-economic disadvantage, while others make no such division.

(1991: 88)

This confusion is apparent in the thirteen LEAs whose school level budgetary data we are reporting. Table 9.2 lists the AEN factors and eligibility criteria for these LEAs:

Table 9.2 Additional educational needs factors and eligibility criteria for thirteen LEAs

LEA	Factor(s)	Distribution Criteria
County A	socio-economic needs	FSMs take up
County B	special needs additions social deprivation	reading scores, statemented pupils FSMs entitlement
County C	compensatory provision	FSMs take up, clothing grants, unemployment, census data
County D	social needs service schools	FSMs entitlement children of service families
County E	special needs element pupil turnover element	FSMs entitlement pupil turnover figures

LEA	Factor(s)	Distribution Criteria
Borough A	social disadvantage	FSMs entitlement, clothing grants
Borough B	special needs related	proportions of pupils from socially disadvantaged backgrounds
Borough C	social element special needs	FSMs entitlement statemented pupils
Borough D	social deprivation secondary special educational needs	FSMs entitlement FSMs entitlement
Borough E	positive action (social deprivation) special needs (learning difficulties)	FSMs entitlement FSMs entitlement
Borough F	social needs related special needs related	FSMs entitlement reading and verbal reasoning tests
Borough G	learning difficulties special unit integration	reading tests special units
Borough H	socio-economic need minority ethnic community	FSMs entitlement DES statistics

These thirteen alone demonstrate (individual) special *educational* needs factors (e.g., Borough G), (group) *social* disadvantage factors (e.g., Borough A) and combinations of both elements (e.g., Borough E) within funding formulae. At least two forms of confusion are apparent. The first is the absence of a clear relationship between the factors in the government's guidelines and those of the LEAs, a problem which may partly be rooted in the lack of clarity or consistency in all parts of the guidelines. A second confusion lies in the criteria used to allocate the funds linked to those factors.

On the first confusion, the column showing the factors included by our thirteen LEAs has a range of terminology for representing special educational needs and aspects of social deprivation. These include factors such as 'compensatory provision', which begs the question of whether the provision is to compensate for problems arising from special educational needs as included within the 1981 Act or some form of social deprivation. Of 'service schools' and the 'pupil turnover element', are the factors to be regarded as proxies for the needs defined by the 1981 Act or for those arising from social deprivation, or both?

As to the second confusion, difficulties are evident when we examine the eligibility criteria shown in column three. Free school meals (FSMs) are used extensively, sometimes for factors titled special needs (County E) and sometimes for social deprivation (County B). It is sometimes used by the same LEA for both factors, as in the cases of Borough D and Borough E.

Within this confusion, there are, none the less, clear attempts made to select criteria which distinguish the factors. This is evident in County B, Borough C and Borough F. In these cases, data on achievement scores of different kinds are linked to a special educational needs factor and entitlement to FSM is linked to a social deprivation factor. There is also a clarity of usage in County A, Borough A and Borough H, where a socio-economic criterion is used to assess eligibility for resources allocated on a social deprivation factor. The same clarity is evident in Borough G, where learning achievement data are used as criteria for eligibility for special educational needs resources, and County D. However, this leaves five LEAs where the description of factors and the choice of eligibility criteria are less than clear.

That there should be confusion here is due, in part, to the inter-relationship between factors associated with special educational needs and social deprivation. Our review of a larger group of LEA schemes shows some LEAs making the relationship explicit. For example, in the Wolverhampton document it is stated that 'it is evident that there is a high degree of correlation between free school meals entitlement, social deprivation and educational disadvantage'. The Leeds (1990) scheme, similarly, states that 'the 1981 Act refers to some 20 per cent of pupils having special needs' and claims that 'there is a correlation between such needs and the eligibility of pupils for free school meals'. In the Warwickshire (1990) scheme it is argued that aspects of social deprivation provide a broad and consistent identification of pupils with learning difficulties and Warwickshire too plumps for the provision of free school meals as a key determinant of need. The criteria adopted by these LEAs is reflective of the findings of much research into the relationship between family backgrounds and pupil achievement. Sammons reports the:

> strong tradition of sociological and educational research into the impact of socio-economic and family background factors upon pupils' achievements in school . . . . Such research has shown that various factors, including low family income, low social class, parental unemployment, large families, one parent families, incomplete fluency in English and membership of specific ethnic groups, are associated with poorer educational attainment at all stages of pupils' school careers.
>
> (1991: 1)

She reports that it has been argued since the Plowden report (1967) that schools in socio-economically disadvantaged areas should be given extra resources because of the greater educational needs of their pupils. None the less, Lee (1992a) is correct to observe that 'what the exact correlation between needs and free meals numbers is, and whether it holds constant between LEAs, are matters which both require research'. We agree. It is one thing to show correlation between a set of measures of social deprivation and levels of pupil attainment but another to argue that one measure – FSM – is a sufficient criterion to represent a range of deprivations and educational needs.

The problem in using a single indicator is the greater when, as Lee also notes, 'the incidence of free meals in schools is particularly susceptible to changes in the rules governing entitlement to social security' and that governors, parents and campaign groups have 'challenged the use of free meal numbers to allocate resources under LMS. They see no reason to believe that social security entitlement is correlated with educational need'. Huckman (1991) has drawn attention to the problem of using the take-up of free school meals, arguing that some parents may not use the provision for cultural reasons.

If LEAs have shown some diversity in defining additional educational needs and in developing means for measuring allocating resources to meet those needs, they have shown greater diversity in how much money to allocate. The national guidelines for funding schools have allowed LEAs sufficient latitude in regulating the funding of pupils with additional educational needs that substantial differences exist in the funding of comparable pupils in different LEAs, an equity issue in terms of different treatment of pupils *within* the same social group.

The level of funding

When we examine formula allocations to individual schools, we find that funds for additional educational needs can account for nothing or, at the other extreme, more than 20 per cent of a school's formula budget before any transitional adjustments. Table 9.3 presents information from 1990/91 on the additional educational needs funding, adding together allocations from both social and special educational factors, as a percentage of each school's formula budget.

Table 9.3 Additional educational needs allocations as percentages of formula budgets

AEN as % Formula	no. of schools	valid %
0	468	17
more than 0 to 1	637	23
>1 to 2	396	14
>2 to 3	212	8
>3 to 4	185	7
>4 to 5	197	7
>5 to 6	153	5.5
>6 to 7	77	3
>7 to 8	82	3
>8 to 9	73	3
>9 to 10	50	2
>10 to 15	163	6
>15 to 20	57	2
more than 20	42	1.5
Total	2792	

From the 1990/91 data for almost 2,800 primary and secondary schools in thirteen LEAs, it can be seen that 17 per cent of schools are not eligible for AEN funding. For a further 37 per cent of schools, sums allocated for AEN are greater than zero and up to 2 per cent of their formula budgets. AEN funding is between 2 per cent and 5 per cent for 21 per cent of schools; 5 per cent to 10 per cent for more than 16 per cent of these schools, and more than 10 per cent of their formula budget for over 9 per cent of the schools. When the information is considered for each LEA in our data set, and reported in the main research report, considerable variation is found (Bullock and Thomas, 1994b).

In our research report, we provide a more detailed analysis of the AEN provision in each of our thirteen LEAs. Following such descriptions, we explore whether and how the change to formula funding has affected the level of funding of schools serving pupils with additional educational needs. We compare each school's historic budget[3] with its formula budget, dividing schools into two groups: 'winning', in the sense that a school's formula budget is more than its historic budget, and 'losing', in the sense that the formula budget is less than the historic budget. The size of the loss or gain has also been calculated, as a percentage of formula budget. We then ask whether there is any relationship between the size of the loss or gain and the size and the AEN allocation. Is it the case, for instance, that schools with comparatively large AEN allocations are more highly represented in the 'losing' group? Or is it the case that, as the percentage of formula allocated on the basis of AEN increases, so the size of the loss decreases? In turning to consider the impact of the change to formula-funding on schools with additional educational needs, we enter an initial caveat. Schools with additional needs are defined in terms of each LEA's own formula. That may mean that, on different criteria, other schools could be identified as having additional needs. We regard this internal comparison as valid, on the basis that we are assessing the effect of an LEA's local interpretation of the national guidance.

For ten of our thirteen LEAs we were able to explore such hypotheses. In this chapter we illustrate that data with three cases.

County A

At the time of the study, this county had one AEN factor which distributed 5.1 per cent of the total budget share, funds being allocated on the basis of FSMs take-up. Within the Scheme, the allocation of funds is described:

> Depending on the proportion of pupils in receipt of a free school meal, the pupil numbers in the school are weighted by a factor (see below). The weighted pupil numbers for each school are expressed as a proportion of the total for all schools and this proportion is applied to the amount of the ASB allocated by this factor.

The percentage of FSMs take-up is banded and weighted as follows:

Primary:

% take-up of FSM:	0 to 4	>4 to 8.5	>8.5 to 13	>13 to 20	>20
total pupils weighted by:	0	0.5	1.0	1.5	2.0

Secondary:

% take-up of FSM:	0 to 2	>2 to 5.5	>5.5 to 9	>9 to 12	>12
total pupils weighted by:	0	0.75	1.0	2.0	2.5

Thus, in the primary sector, schools with 4 per cent or fewer pupils in receipt of FSMs will not be eligible for additional AEN funding. This eligibility percentage is 2 per cent in the secondary sector. A school's socio-economic needs allocation is calculated as the number on roll multiplied by the appropriate weighting, multiplied by the cash amount. In the year 1990/91 this amount was £89.

In exploring whether the change to formula funding has affected the level of funding of schools serving pupils with additional educational needs, we correlated the size of loss/gain with the percentage of formula on social needs. This gave a correlation value of 0.49**.[4] The positive association suggests that the more (proportionally) a school receives for AEN, the greater the size of the gain. In other words, schools which are high on the AEN factor are more likely to be 'winners' in the transition to formula funding. When primary and secondary sectors are considered separately, a stronger positive association is found in the primary sector.[5]

In short, whether intentionally or not, the change to formula funding has tended to favour schools in County A serving AEN pupils.

Borough B

This borough's formula includes a special-needs related factor that is based on the proportion of pupils from socially disadvantaged backgrounds and accounts for 3.2 per cent of the LEA's total budget share. For the year 1990/91, primary schools were banded, 'placement being related to criteria reflecting the socio-economic composition of the school's catchment area'. The additional allocations for each band were equivalent to increases in the element for teachers' salaries. Primary schools in Bands 1 and 2 received no additions; Band 3 schools gained 3.3 per cent; Band 4, 10 per cent and Band 5 schools 16.6 per cent. In the secondary sector also, schools received additional funding related to the socio-economic composition of the catchment area, although these schools were not actually banded. Examples of allocations in the primary sector include £5,599 for a Band 3 primary school with 314 pupils on roll; £23,349 for a Band 5 school with 226 pupils. All schools in the secondary sector received in excess of £50,000 for special needs and two received over £100,000.

The results of the statistical correlation between size of loss/gain and the level of special needs-related funding are given below:

All schools	Primary	Secondary
-0.44**	-0.31**	-0.72**

The association between the two variables is negative. It is strongest in the secondary sector, suggesting that secondary schools in catchment areas with high levels of pupils from socially disadvantaged areas tend to be the more sizeable losers: in other words, the size of the gain diminishes as the proportion of AEN funding increases. However, if the three biggest losers are excluded, a non-significant correlation value of -0.15 is given. The negative association is weak in the primary sector and reduced to -0.26** with the exclusion of the biggest loser. These associations suggest that in both sectors, schools serving disadvantaged communities are more likely to be 'losers'; a finding which may in part be explained by a system prior to LM which generously resourced such schools. A pupil-driven funding formula may have made it difficult to replicate these funding levels.

Borough C

Borough C's AEN factor comprises a social needs element (based on entitlement to FSMs and amounting to 7 per cent of the LEA's budget share) and funding for special needs (using numbers of statemented pupils and amounting to 0.5 per cent of the total budget share). Social needs funding is calculated as £557.44 x FSMs numbers. For special needs, each statemented pupil receives an additional £1,162.

Shown below are the correlation values for the AEN variables and the size of loss/gain variable. Funding for statemented pupils, the special needs factor, was not found to be associated with size of loss/gain: none of the correlation values, for all schools or schools by sector were statistically significant (any association may have been due to chance).

	All schools	Primary	Secondary
special needs	-0.17	-0.17	-0.51
social needs	0.67**	0.65**	0.46
both AEN factors	0.64**	0.63**	0.30

In the primary sector alone, however, a strong association was found to exist between level of social needs funding and size of loss/gain. In the secondary sector, on the other hand, there was no significant association. The positive direction of the primary correlation value suggests that as the proportion of the allocation based on social needs increases so the size of gain increases. Put another way, generally the less money (proportionally) a school receives for FSMs pupils, the greater the size of loss. Similar correlation values are produced when the two AEN factors are combined.

In brief then, although correlations tell us nothing about causal relationships between variables, there are some indications that Borough C may have devised a formula that favours primary schools serving pupils with additional educational needs.

Since Borough C has two AEN factors, we explored the association between them: would there be indications that schools serving pupils with social needs were a similar set of schools with statemented pupils? The correlation figures[6] show no association between the AEN factors in the first instance, although, after excluding outliers a weak correlation ($r=0.28**$) is given for all schools. Such correlations suggest an association between the two AEN factors, such that schools eligible for social needs funding tend to be similar to the set of schools serving statemented pupils. The correlations are, however, weak.

Additional needs and equity

Although in many ways the DfEE and Welsh Office framework for local management is prescriptive and restrictive, evidence from our set of LEAs shows the scope for diversity in local policies. For schools serving pupils with additional educational needs, the analysis shows substantial differences in the nature of local management schemes. It appears from our analysis that the national framework for local management has been sufficiently flexible to allow some LEAs to direct resources in such a way that the greatest beneficiaries have been schools with the highest proportion of pupils with additional educational needs. Far from being a regressive change, in these LEAs LMS has led to an apparent initial re-distribution of resources benefiting the least advantaged. Equally, in other LEAs the effect of LMS has been in the opposite direction, those schools with a high proportion of pupils with additional educational needs being the losers in the change of funding.

Without further study, including interviews with key participants in the design of a formula, we cannot provide an account of how these outcomes occurred. What is evident, however, is that the initial *change* to LMS has not had a simple one-way effect leading to greater disadvantage for pupils with additional educational needs. What is not easily extracted from the data is how these funding mechanisms contribute to meeting the needs of individuals with specific learning difficulties as against children from certain social groups. One reason for this is that the criteria used for allocating funds obscures the distinction. Another is that how the money is spent is a matter for individual schools who are free to set their own spending priorities.

The account we have provided is a snap-shot at the time when the new arrangements were introduced and does not allow us to predict *future* patterns of resourcing additional educational needs. Some evidence on how the dynamic of local management has affected 'who benefits' can be obtained from the longitudinal drawn from our three-year survey of schools.

EQUITY AND THE MIXED ECONOMY

The pupil-led formula

Excepting the special circumstances of denominational schools and selective schools, schools are now required to admit pupils to their physical capacity, a requirement which gives greater weight to parental preferences. We have already described how school budgets also reflect the significance of parental choice, the larger part of the money allocated to schools being based on the number of pupils. Given the explicit nature of formula funding, and, setting aside the impact of competition, it is a system which is potentially of great significance for achieving a more equitable school system. The diversity of its effects on schools, however, is caught by a set of views from head teachers on the pupil-driven formula:

> Formula funding is working for this school as our numbers are increasing.

> The pupil-driven formula funding leads to too competitive an 'atmosphere' between schools.

> As a Middle School with a contracting roll, I anticipate severe problems in the near future as more and more areas of the budget use pupil numbers in their calculation.

> LMS looks very well within the school, the school is popular in the area and is at present over-subscribed, so there is no shortage of money.

Our own surveys endeavoured to assess some of the effects of the change on the stability or otherwise of pupil admissions to the schools in our study.

The impact of changing pupil numbers

The scale of roll change

Despite the direct link between number on roll and school budgets, we are not aware of national data for the extent of annual changes in school rolls. The illustrations above begin to indicate the effect a falling or rising school roll might have on a school's budget. For example, an additional ten Year 7 pupils attending a school could mean an extra £11,280. But to what extent are schools experiencing such roll changes? For a set of primary and secondary schools, we are able to track the changes in number on roll (NoR) over a period of three years. We begin by considering the average size of schools in these sets.

In each of our three questionnaires (returned in the summer terms 1991, 1992 and 1993), head teachers were asked to indicate the number of full-time equivalent pupils currently on roll (including summer leavers). We have comparative data on a set of one hundred and sixteen primary and thirty-six secondary schools. In both sectors, a consideration of the mean NoR (to the nearest whole number) shows an overall rising roll. In the primary sector, the mean number of pupils in this set of schools was 258 in 1991, increasing to 260 for 1992 and further, to 265 in 1993. In the secondary sector the mean roll for 1991 was 668 pupils. This increased to 693 in 1992, and to 712 in 1993.

Although the overall rolls are increasing for these sets of schools, some individual schools are experiencing a loss of pupils. When the 1991 roll is compared with the 1992 roll, fifty-four out of one hundred and seventeen primary schools experienced a falling roll; for six schools the NoR remained unchanged; the remainder (fifty-seven) had increased the number of pupils. When the size of the loss or gain of pupils is calculated as a percentage of the 1991 roll, we find that one school's roll has reduced by 14 per cent. This compares with one school increasing its roll by 28 per cent. The set also includes one school that increased its roll by 45 per cent through amalgamation.

One hundred and twenty of our primary schools provided NoR data for 1992/93. Of these schools, forty experienced a fall in roll; in twelve schools the roll remained the same and in sixty-eight the NoR increased. As a percentage of the 1992 roll, a drop of 16 per cent was experienced by one school. On the other hand, another increased its number of pupils by 21 per cent. Two schools in the set had amalgamated with other schools in this period. For one the amalgamation represents a roll increase of 65 per cent and for the other 77 per cent.

We have also compared the roll of the set of one hundred and twenty primary schools in 1991 and 1993. When we look at these years we find forty-five falling rolls, six remaining the same and sixty-nine increasing. One school's roll has fallen by 19 per cent. This contrasts with eight schools increasing their NoR by more than 20 per cent.

Finally, we have considered the roll changes across these three years. From the set of one hundred and sixteen primary schools, 41 per cent are experiencing *fluctuating* rolls – the number is rising/falling year on year. For thirty of these schools the NoR fell between 1991 and 1992 and then rose the following year. Eighteen schools experienced a rise in roll in 1992 and a drop in 1993. For some schools the roll pattern is more consistent: in thirty-three schools the roll increased each year; in nineteen schools the roll decreased each year. The other sixteen encountered some stability with rolls remaining stable across at least two of these years.

We can make similar comparisons of the data on schools in the secondary sector, although here caution needs to be exercised since the number of schools in the set is small. We have thirty-eight secondary schools where we can compare the roll in 1991 with that in the following year. In eight of these the roll fell; three rolls remained the same and the others increased. The largest drop, as a percentage of the 1991 roll, is 8 per cent; the largest increase is 23 per cent.

We can compare the 1992 and 1993 rolls at forty-two secondary schools. Eighteen of these experienced a falling roll; for four there is no change and for twenty the rolls increase. Far more secondary schools had a decreasing roll in 1993 than did in 1992. The maximum fall and rise is greater too: one school's roll decreased by 11 per cent; another rose by 33 per cent.

Thirty-six secondary schools provided NoR data in 1991 and 1993. For nine of these the roll decreased; three remained the same and twenty-four increased. The maximum decrease is one of 10 per cent, and the maximum increase 40 per cent.

We also considered the roll change across these three years. Of the thirty-six secondary schools, a third experienced *fluctuating* rolls, falling/rising year on year. For the majority (fifteen schools) however, the roll increased each year. Four schools experienced a decreasing roll each year and the remaining five schools exhibited some stability.

Table 9.4 summarises this information for both secondary and primary schools.

Table 9.4 Roll changes across three years

	Primary	Secondary
Rising	33	15
Falling	19	4
Falling rising (fluctuation)	30	2
Rising falling (fluctuation)	18	10
Stable	2	2
Stable rising	3	1
Stable falling	1	-
Rising stable	5	-
Falling stable	5	2
Total:	116	36

Perhaps the most notable evidence from these data is the lack of stability they exhibit. Managerially most difficult to handle must be rolls that fluctuate, making long-term planning uncertain. For some schools the fluctuation is not small, leading to problems of class size and staffing issues. For illustration, in the primary sector, one school's roll fluctuated from 260 in 1991, to 248 in 1992, increasing to 265 in 1993. Another school has experienced rolls of 227, 255 and 233 in these years. In the secondary sector, one school's roll changed from 962 in 1991 to 943 in 1992 and 973 in 1993. In another school, the roll fluctuated from 1,043 in 1991 to 1,130 in 1992 and 1,040 in 1993. For pupils in these schools, changes in the overall number may be having an effect on the curriculum and this affects the overall equity of the school system. The extent of this curriculum effect will, to some extent, depend upon the impact roll changes may have on budgets.

Roll change and school budgets

If we look at our more recent figures, and compare the 1992 roll with the 1993 roll, we find that, for our set of forty primary schools with *falling* rolls, the average number of pupils lost is twelve. The average size of *these* schools is 262 (1992 roll). We are able to illustrate the budget impact by reference to 1990/91 outturn data. From the set of seventy-one LEAs we have calculated the *average* age weighted pupil unit (AWPU) for ages three to ten (Bullock and Thomas, 1993b). This gives a mean AWPU value for the primary sector of £853 per pupil. Using our school-level budgetary data from twelve of thirteen LEAs (Bullock and Thomas, 1992; 1993b) we have calculated the mean formula allocation to primary schools with rolls greater than 260 and less than 265. The mean formula allocation for this set of twenty-five schools is £280,741. On the basis of this information we can suggest that a loss of twelve pupils would have represented a budgetary loss of £10,236, or a 3.65 per cent reduction in 1990/91.

Comments from two primary school head teachers express concern about the impact of a declining school roll:

worry about ability to afford staff from one year to next because of fluctuation of numbers beyond our control.

. . . constant worry about having to cut staff because of drop in pupil numbers.

Excluding the two amalgamations, sixty-six primary schools have *rising* rolls in 1993. The *average* number of additional pupils is fourteen. The average size of these schools is 262 (the set of schools with falling rolls has the same average size as the set with rising rolls). On the basis of the information outlined above, these additional pupils would have brought £11,942 to their schools in 1990/91, an increase in formula budget of 4.25 per cent.

In the set of eighteen secondary schools with *falling* rolls, the average number of pupils lost is twenty-five. The *average* number on roll in 1992 is 660. We have used the set of seventy-one LEAs to calculate an *average* AWPU for secondary aged pupils of £1,525 per pupil. From our set of schools in twelve LEAs, the average formula allocation to schools with between 640 and 680 pupils (twenty-three schools) is £1,111,838. From this we estimate that a loss of twenty-five pupils approximated to a loss of £38,135 in 1990/91, or a 3.43 per cent cut in formula budget

Twenty secondary schools experienced, on average, a *rising* roll of fifty-three pupils. The mean size of these schools is 833 (1992 NoR). From the set of schools in twelve LEAs, the average formula allocation to schools with between 813 and 853 pupils (numbering fifteen schools) is £1,413,746. Thus, an additional fifty-three pupils represents £80,825, a 5.72 per cent increase in formula budget.

The following two comments from secondary-school head teachers recognise the benefit of rising rolls, although both are cautious about their currently favourable position:

As a 'gaining' school with improved NoR for the last five years, I am most pleased with progress *but* I am always aware of the future and admission numbers become crucial. Reversal of trend could be disastrous.

To date, formula funding has worked well but we are an expanding school. The difficulty is doing long term planning when budgets come on an annual basis dependent upon pupil numbers which can vary so much at the top end of a 13–18 school.

Comments from head teachers on the second and third questionnaires illustrate some of these planning concerns:

pupil-driven funding does not make forward planning easy in areas where there is a high movement rate of families.

The only drawback is the uncertainty in Infant/First Schools of the number of pupils to be admitted the following year when we are so dependent upon pupil numbers.

The deputy head teacher at one of the schools we visited spoke of the direct impact fluctuating school rolls could have on the budget:

Formula calculations . . . that are so closely pupil numbers driven mean that we have little room to manoeuvre for any fluctuations in our pupils' numbers leading to a budget change, impinge quickly and directly on what we can do . . . The principle of LMS is sound but some of the practice is flawed, for example, we have a development plan for 3 to 5 years ahead but now in January 1993 we do not know what our budget for April is.

One head teacher quite simply commented that 'allowing schools to flounder financially due to AWPUs/pupil driven allocation is crazy!'.

Our data suggest that changes in pupil numbers may be quite considerable and certainly at a level where they have a significant effect upon budgets. For those schools where pupils are being lost, it may create difficulties for schools seeking to make plans which, for example, involve earmarking budgets for future developments. It is also possible that curriculum management becomes less predictable with consequences for learning, sometimes through the effect on class size.

Roll change and class size

Although extra pupils bring extra resources, the attractiveness of additional pupils is not straightforward. A head teacher responding to the third questionnaire details the impact of additional pupils at her secondary school:

The truly ridiculous situation arises where the numbers rise by a small amount, by just enough to necessitate an additional class in any given year group. The income from the few additional pupils does not give you enough to pay for an additional teaching salary – therefore you are in the position of trying to put parents off choosing your school! While this authority is well funded we have enough put aside to tide us over as small increases in numbers cause this problem – if the situation changes we will be in trouble! The only possibility for the school will then be to have large classes – and then parents will choose to go elsewhere. Is that parental choice?

At some schools, LM seems to have contributed to larger classes:

Pupil-driven funding is a nonsense – money comes seven months too late for a start. Critical numbers where decisions have to be made in employing an extra teacher will lead to larger classes until you reach a level where numbers allow you to employ an additional teacher – or could lead to mixed age classes to solve the problem.

A deputy head we interviewed commented that 'the pupil driven formula has resulted in increased class sizes: between twenty-five and twenty-seven to thirty to thirty-two in the Juniors and between twenty and twenty two to twenty four to twenty six in the Infants.'

One head wrote of the apparent conflict between reducing class sizes and enhancing the budget:

I feel somewhat confused. I welcome the freedom to take decisions, in principle. In practice we are about to take a dive. We are traditionally organised. We want to *reduce* the size of our roll, in order to reduce the size of our classes. When (not if) we do, we'll lose money and therefore part-time support staff. Our high standards will drop.

The potential for competition is seen by some as leading to school closures:

In some areas schooling will become a cut-throat business as schools with spare capacity attempt to market their services in direct competition with one another. Clearly the DES is expecting that some schools will not survive in the market place, they are expecting 'bankruptcies'. In effect, 'the weak will go to the wall', some schools will lose numbers to the extent that they will no longer be viable, some schools will close.

(Ball, 1990b: 65)

In order to explore this issue, in the 1992 and 1993 surveys, head teachers were asked to respond to the attitude statement *I believe LM is likely to lead to school closures*. Almost half of the primary school heads (49 per cent: one hundred and twenty-one schools) agreed with this statement in 1992. The level of agreement reduces to 43 per cent the following year. In the secondary sector (forty schools), 48 per cent agreed in 1992, increasing to 60 per cent in 1993. Clearly, there is quite a widespread belief that LM may lead to school closures, although the extent to which possible closures is directly related to competition for pupils is open to question. This becomes apparent when we examine changing rolls in the context of some data on competition and collaboration between schools.

Changing rolls, competition and co-operation

On the first questionnaire, head teachers were asked if the number on roll had, in their view, changed significantly since January 1990 and, if it had, to suggest an explanation. Of those providing a reason for a significant change, 268 heads – 61 per cent – put it down to demography (including population movement, bulge year, increased birthrate). In these instances, school budgets are being affected by what may be local circumstances outside the control of the school. Add to these the impact of the competitive pressures desired by the government and the scale of change can be expected to increase.

It has been argued that these reforms put schools in a quasi-market situation where they compete for pupils, and thus money. The theory behind these reforms was described by Simon as follows:

> competition will reinforce success and drive out or bankrupt the unsuccessful. What the schools in general do will improve, almost automatically. Above all, it is argued, standards will rise.
>
> (1992: 133)

He describes the Education Reform Act as an 'overall drive for a market economy' and sees the link between formula funding based on pupil numbers and open enrolment as a 'powerful weapon imposing what could become cut-throat competition between schools for survival' (1992: 146).

At the grass roots, however, schools may be developing local policies of agreement regarding pupil admissions. It is interesting that even the DfE/Coopers and Lybrand (1993) report on good management in small schools recommend that: 'governors and heads should consider the potential benefits that might accrue from co-operation with one or more local schools'. Although they do not identify agreements on pupil admissions, the level of co-operation they suggest might have the affect of dampening competition. They identify the following topics for co-operation: pastoral support for heads; sharing curriculum expertise; joint INSET sessions, using pooled GEST resources; sharing the services of the bursar; joint purchasing of goods and other services to obtain bulk purchase discounts; provision of expertise or services by secondary and large primary schools to small schools; combining arrangements for educational visits. Collaboration between schools is reported by others, for example, Hall and Wallace, who comment:

> Collaboration between schools and colleges is currently being promoted in at least a few areas as a local strategy which may subvert the competition

engendered by central government imposition of open enrolment and funding based on pupil numbers, within a context of surplus places.

(1993: 101)

They cite an example in an area of Bristol where all the secondary schools have agreed to transfer sixth-formers to a local college. They also buy services jointly, synchronise their timetables to allow for jointly arranged INSET and staff exchanges and do not compete for pupils.

In our third questionnaire to head teachers, we asked *Do you have any agreement, formal or informal, with schools in the neighbourhood regarding pupil admissions?* Exactly half of the primary school heads (sixty-one out of one hundred and twenty-two) indicated that they did have such an agreement. There were proportionally almost as many agreements amongst the group of secondary schools: nineteen out of forty-two secondary-heads had an agreement regarding pupil admissions.

Head teachers were also asked to comment on competition for pupils in their neighbourhood on the third questionnaire. From the one hundred and forty-seven responses it would seem that experience is varied. For some schools, competition is not an issue for reasons such as over-subscription for places (fifteen schools) and all the schools in the area being comfortably full (sixteen schools). To illustrate, such heads wrote:

Most schools are over-subscribed and therefore competition is not an issue

Competition is not at present a problem – too many children seeking places in schools

My school is usually over-subscribed. When a vacancy occurs it is offered immediately to those on the waiting list.

Another set of schools reported that there was no competition, or at least not yet (sixteen schools), whereas others experienced no overt competition, for a variety of reasons, including those related to the type of school (four schools): for example, 'this is a denominational school and caters specifically for Roman Catholics'; the operation of LEA admissions policies (six schools); locality (ten schools): for example, 'only school in town', 'rural area means generally that pupils go where the bus goes'.

Others (twenty-three schools) spoke of head teachers in the area having some kind of agreement whereby attempts are made to avoid transfer of pupils between schools and poaching activities. They made such comments as: 'informal cluster agreement for heads not to transfer without consulting other heads involved'; 'our agreement is not to poach'; 'informal agreement to stay with old catchment areas if possible'; 'we do not "tout" for business – there is a local agreement between heads on this'.

A number of other schools, however, were experiencing competition. For one group of these schools (twelve) it was present but 'not cut-throat', or 'significant though rarely overt', or 'friendly but very real'. Four spoke of *increasing* competition. Three specifically mentioned prospectuses and leaflets, one head saying: 'It is becoming increasingly intense with scarce resources now being spent on prospectuses, leaflets etc.' Five other schools felt they were losing pupils because of the activities of other schools, for example, admitting 'under-aged' pupils or making 'strenuous efforts to attract more pupils'. Other schools lost pupils because they had no nursery (three) or no sixth form (one). Eleven schools in particular commented on 'fierce', 'intense' and 'great' competition, making such remarks as:

> Cut-throat and great competition for able pupils in order to enhance the school's reputation and complete the 'success breed success' cycle.

> The whole situation is highly competitive. Heads do talk to each other but only just!

On both the 1992 and 1993 questionnaires, head teachers were asked to respond to the following attitude statement: *As a result of LM, we are actively seeking to attract more pupils*. We have comparative data on one hundred and twenty-four primary schools and forty secondary schools. In 1992, 43 per cent of primary head teachers agreed with this statement. This percentage drops quite considerably the following year: in 1993 only 31 per cent of primary heads agreed. Could this decline be connected to agreements with neighbourhood schools regarding pupil admissions? In considering this we compared the responses of the primary head teachers *with* agreements with the responses of those *without* agreements. Twice as many head teachers (42 per cent: 25/60) *without* agreements agreed that as a result of LM they were actively seeking to attract more pupils: 21 per cent (13/61) of those primary heads with agreements agreed with the statement. Although this does suggest that having an agreement with neighbourhood schools results in schools less actively seeking pupils, there remains a proportion of schools *with* agreements *actively* seeking pupils.

In the secondary sector, the proportion of head teachers agreeing with this statement has also declined: 63 per cent (25/40) in 1992, reducing to 53 per cent (21/40) in 1993. The number of schools is too small to make much of this decline. What can be said, however, is that the level of agreement is greater in the secondary sector.

This statement was also put to those interviewed on the school visits. We have the responses of thirty-nine head teachers, thirty-three deputy heads, sixty-seven teachers, twenty-nine chairs of governors and thirty-six administrative/clerical staff. In comparison with other groups, a greater proportion of teachers agreed that *As a result of LM we are actively seeking to attract more pupils*. However, 36 per cent of heads, deputy heads and chairs of governors disagreed with the statement.

From head teacher comments on the second and third questionnaire there can be no doubt the competition for pupils is very real for *some* schools. One head, for instance, comments that 'schools are competing for children/ pounds'. Heads talk of the need to attract parents:

> The pupil-driven element is causing strain between local schools. More parents choosing for what seems to be superficial reasoning to move children in/out of schools. More pressure on me to make our schools more attractive to parents – not based on sound educational philosophy, but on media pressure.

Others speak of the impact that competition for pupils has on relationships with other schools. One, for example, commented that it was 'dividing schools by making them compete for pupils'. Co-operation between schools had become more difficult in some places. Head teachers wrote:

> The competition for pupils has had a negative effect on co-operation between schools.

> Promoting competition – which may have sharpened our act but has lost in the process the old openness of sharing ideas etc.

> Not happy with the increased competition between schools but feel that a more collegiate climate between heads appears to be developing.

Two comments from head teachers indicate potential difficulties regarding relationships between schools arising from this competition for pupils.

> Generally, LMS is tending to increase competition between schools for pupils. In this area, one school in particular has adopted a very aggressive marketing policy, which has resulted in neighbouring schools attracting fewer pupils. These schools are now responding and I can see a 'dog eat dog' situation beginning to develop.

> I am accepting children from 'out of catchment' as my own catchment area does not have enough children. This in the future could affect relationships with colleagues in this 'market force' arena.

The strategy of admitting pupils at an early age in order to secure pupil numbers for the future is in evidence:

> I feel that there is competition between schools to attract more children. In Kent children are being admitted full-time at an increasingly early age to secure future funding. Once a school's roll begins to decline the most obvious result is loss of staff – creating a downward spiral.

> Governors feel comfortable class sizes are crucial in attracting 'customers', but how do we compete with schools who admit children into large groups when they are four years old? These classes are perhaps educationally unsound.

How these factors affect schools serving more disadvantaged communities is a concern voiced by two head teachers in those communities:

> I worry about the long-term effects on urban schools in deprived areas or schools with falling rolls. The emergence of 'sink' schools remains a possibility.

and

> It is causing wide discrepancies between schools and is affecting their ability to survive. Popular schools which are full are obviously in a stronger financial position than others, but this does not take account of any social factors or special conditions in those which may be in difficulty.

These legitimate concerns about the effect on disadvantaged communities are also illustrated in the local histories we document below but they also include cases which illustrate the more general complexity of the impact of changing rolls.

Local histories of changing rolls

Vignette 9.1: Inner-ring secondary

On our visits to thirty-seven schools, we found examples of the effect of changing pupil numbers on schools. In one secondary school for example, situated in the inner ring of a large city, the roll was falling to such an extent that closure was likely. Parents were exercising their powers of choice and choosing to send their children to schools outside the Inner Ring. The chair of governors commented that schools within the Inner Ring were 'not popular at present and are under-funded as a consequence'. The Head of History had 'grave misgivings about "teacher security" should a school fail to attract sufficient numbers'. He also commented: 'I have become much more aware of the importance of attracting parents to consider this school for their children. I feel that teachers need to work especially hard on this topic now that the school budget is influenced by the number of pupils on roll'. Others at the school recognised the importance of attracting parents. The deputy head spoke of the 'greater desire to please parents' and the need to 'respond to parental pressure' and 'publicise success'.

Vignette 9.2: Two inner-ring primary schools

At one primary school we visited, the head teacher told us of the changing pupil numbers. He explained: 'This school is in a redevelopment area – fluctuating/falling numbers will have immediate impact on staffing, LEA cannot give short-term support pending increase in numbers'. The fluctuating roll at this school seemed not to be the result of competition. This head teacher was one of a group of primary heads who, in recognition of the importance some parents attach to Standard

Assessment Tests (SATs), had prepared a joint statement on SATs to parents, signed by all the heads in this group. However, pressure of falling numbers led him to wonder how much longer this agreement will last.

A reduction in pupil numbers may result in a cut to staffing in a second primary school. The deputy head explained that a 'bulge year leaving at the end of the academic year 92/93 – resulting in projected staffing reduction – possibly one full-time post'. One of the teachers spoke of the 'possibility of redundancy due to drop in school roll'. The deputy head also commented on what he saw as the impact of linking school funding to pupil numbers:

> The notion of market forces determining the finance of schooling in my view is flawed, sets schools against school, and reduces the drive towards greater collaboration and co-operation between schools.

Vignette 9.3: Denominational factors

One primary school we visited illustrates the complexity of local situations regarding pupil numbers. It is the only Catholic school in the area and the only primary school in the town, the others being first schools. It is over-subscribed with large classes; one, for example, has thirty-seven pupils. In an effort to manage class sizes the school had recently fixed admissions to thirty. Despite the school being over-subscribed, to have done this is 'risky' since that school *loses* pupils at the age of nine to Middle schools which feed a more local secondary school. The reputation of the feeder high school for this school has improved and the numbers are more stable now. The feeder secondary is twelve miles away though. Possible losses of pupils at age nine makes staffing levels precarious. The head teacher spoke of 'an acknowledgement of our dependency on attracting children and parents. At present this does not pose a problem except that new staff may be offered temporary contracts' and 'staff are more aware of parents as customers and children as pots of gold. . . . The situation of funding the pupils is just another stress factor in the lives of the staff'.

Vignette 9.4: Competing for pupils (1)

The need to maintain pupil numbers formed a part of this school's Development Plan. 'Unfounded rumour and reputation' and 'marketing' have been identified as two of the schools 'weaknesses'. Two of the 'threats' are seen as 'marketing/competitive action by other schools' and the 'financial implication of falling rolls'. In the 'short term', 'marketing strategies' had been flagged as 'key development areas', and in the 'medium term', the 'opening of a play group' and 'number on roll'. The deputy and one of the teachers spoke of 'pressure'. The teacher commented: 'Our jobs are on the line each year dependent on pupil numbers – we are constantly under pressure'. The deputy commented: 'Pressure on maintaining numbers, mixed catchment area can make this a problem area, LMS makes problems more acute.'

The head teacher was clearly aware of competition between schools. The governors had agreed a policy to keep class sizes below thirty. The head recognised that small class sizes was a way to sell the school.

Vignette 9.5: Competing for pupils (2)

This secondary school had lost its sixth form under LEA reorganisation a few years ago. The school now loses pupils to a local Catholic school with a sixth form and to other schools in the next LEA with sixth forms. These latter pupils tend to come from more middle-class families living on the LEA border. To address a declining NoR situation, the deputy head had instigated an active marketing strategy. He outlined the school's advertising to parents: school prospectus, adverts on buses, the school's own newspaper, fliers, good primary links. He felt that 'advertising works' – the roll is now increasing . He commented: 'the government has drawn up the rules of the game and we must play it to our best advantage'. Clearly then, his approach to falling rolls is active advertising. One of the teachers recognised this and voiced some reservations: 'Marketing of the school is now an important part of things – are we losing sight of actually teaching children?' The head teacher viewed some of the 'marketing strategies' as beneficial for children, for example the enhanced links with primary schools. He commented: 'pupils in feeder schools have benefited through newly invented induction schemes designed to keep abreast of the competition initiated by neighbouring secondary schools.' His overall view of this changed situation was more caustic. He felt that the government and LM had 'poisoned the relationship between schools'. There was now competition for pupils and this school has producing glossies and fliers and advertisements on buses in response to other schools doing it.

Vignette 9.6: Planning problems

This primary school was experiencing slightly decreasing pupil numbers. Competition for pupils was not perceived as a real issue, although the school had lost about ten pupils. Some pupils had been lost to a nearby 'village' school where the PTR is better and the head teacher was seen as an active poacher. Others chose to attend the local private school. In addition, the nearby GM school, in the next LEA was actively poaching. The head said that although he did not intend to actively go out and advertise, he did rub his hands with glee when new pupils arrived as this meant £1,000 each.

The Chair of Governors spoke of the 'LM Problem' about numbers, class sizes and budgets. He explained that if seven pupils leave this reduces your budget by £7,000 but makes no real difference to class sizes or staffing levels. Slightly decreasing pupil numbers made long term planning difficult.

The secretary said that 'all staff . . . are aware that parents must be "courted" now'. She felt that it was 'not necessarily a good thing if we bow to them'. The people we spoke to were generally aware of the need to be nice to parents, to be aware of them as customers, because losing pupils meant losing money. One teacher commented: 'Parents are more aware of their role as customers and the need for schools to accommodate their wishes'. Another teacher said: 'pressure to maintain good relations with parents as clients. . . . Children are seen as financial assets with a price on their head – and there is despair when families leave the area because they affect the budget'.

Equity and changing pupil numbers

Our data on school rolls show that pupil numbers change and they can fluctuate to an extent that it affects school budgets. Although the reasons for declining or increasing pupil numbers are, in many cases, not the result of competition for pupils, there can be no doubt that competition does exist in some areas, and that at times it is 'cut throat'. However, we also found evidence of agreements between schools regarding the recruitment of pupils, strategies which may serve to undermine the government's emphasis on competition.

The effects on equity of roll change and related issues are complex. Declining numbers in a school will affect budgets and the curriculum that can be provided in the school. Paradoxically, growth in numbers can also have some detrimental effects if the growth leads to larger classes rather than more classes. Indeed, whatever may be the virtues of a more competitive environment, there must come a point at which the combination of demographic change and competition makes effective school planning almost impossible.

It could be argued, of course, that changes in roll represent parents making informed choices for their children's education. If that is the case, we see the problems of the trade-offs between the quasi-market allowing parents to seek out a better school against its impact on those who do not move. Scepticism as to whether such decisions are well-informed is represented by the comments of one primary school head teacher:

It puts children's learning resources, viz. teachers, into a 'market-place' situation. Long-term planning can only provisionally take place because the budget is not known from year to year. I deplore the whole scenario of children's learning being measured in pounds and pence. Popular schools, not necessarily good ones, should thrive and unpopular schools, not necessarily bad ones, will struggle.

It is view which illustrates one of the several difficulties in assessing the equity consequences of local management.

CONCLUSION: DIVERSITY AND EQUITY

We began this chapter with the proposition that a concern with equity must recognise injustices in the distribution of education and its benefits *between* and *within* social groups as well as between *individuals* with specific learning difficulties. There is already evidence of the effect of local management on these equity criteria and on the extent of diversity and the nature of equity in the school system.

On the funding of pupils by age, the emerging evidence is interesting less for its immediate effect on equity criteria than for the longer term consequence of a more transparent and public system for funding schools. In all likelihood, the change to formula funding served only to make public the diversity of funding levels between pupils of different ages as well as between LEAs. We are not persuaded that the change to formula funding led to any significant shifts in funding, with many LEAs trying to reduce the disturbance to schools by seeking to replicate as much of the status quo as possible. What may be more significant is the longer term effect of this greater openness. In this respect, the view of the Education Committee of the House of Commons may, with others, contribute to some shift in funding priorities towards the primary sector. Set against this is the current funding context where pressures for cuts may make LEAs hesitate before placing a disproportionate cut in spending on secondary schools in order to improve funding for primary schools. What may also occur, however, is a move towards a national formula for funding schools, a device which would go some way towards addressing equity-centred differences where the same social groups are seeking access to the national curriculum in different LEAs.

On the funding of pupils with additional educational needs, the evidence points to the complexity of arrangements in this area and its equity consequences for social groups and individuals. Our evidence shows LEAs pursuing quite different policies, some devising funding formulae which benefit schools with a high proportion of pupils with additional needs while comparable schools elsewhere are net losers in the change of funding. We also show very different levels of budget allocation to these areas. What our analysis also shows is the problem encountered by many LEAs in distinguishing between the needs of social groups as against individuals. In some cases, LEAs have included factors in their formulae which distinguish these categories but use the same criterion – free school meals – for allocating funds. We conclude that assessing the long term effect of the change in funding additional educational needs requires an investigation of the effect of local management over time.

Some commentary on this longer term effect is provided by the evidence we cite on changing pupil numbers. Our data suggest that the impact of local management is complex but tending to create greater difficulties in schools serving more disadvantaged communities. While it is a view that highlights our concern about the equity effects of the quasi-market elements of local management, we also observe the tendency for schools to seek out strategies of collaboration and the long term significance of such strategies merit careful monitoring.

Popular though local management undoubtedly is, above all with head teachers, the evidence of its effect on the school system raise some concerns. As our concluding chapters discuss, the efficiency and equity benefits of the current scheme of local management need careful scrutiny.

Schools at the centre?

Part III

Schools at the centre?

Chapter 10

Learning at the centre?

In the opening paragraph of this book we asked whether and how decentralisation matters to the 'real' world of teaching and learning in schools. We hope that at the heart of this book, therefore, has been a concern with that question and with evidence on how decentralisation is actually affecting teaching and learning. It provides the principal theme of our closing chapter, in which we review evidence from our comparative studies and the case study of England and Wales. We draw out the implications of our data recognising the diversity of policies of decentralisation, as well as equally important differences in the direction of change. Understanding diversity and difference are essential components for any reliable analysis of the impact of decentralisation and, in that respect, the first section provides a pre-condition for the evaluation of decentralisation in the second main section of the chapter. In that evaluation we attempt two things. Structured around the four criteria of autonomy, accountability, efficiency and equity, we review the national case study and the international material and reflect upon the evidence for an assessment of the state of decentralisation. We go further than this, however, and in the third main section consider how policies related to decentralisation might be developed to meet some of the conditions implied by the four criteria for developing and improving schools. It is here that we comment most critically on the concept of decentralisation as it is embodied in a practice which, typically, places institutions and institutional leaders at the centre of decision-making. We ask instead whether it is learners and learning which should be at the centre of policies of decentralisation and, if so, what this means for the development of policy and practice.

DIVERSITY AND DIFFERENCE

Diversity of responsibilities

Our review of national schemes and the case study of England and Wales serve to emphasise our initial contention that decentralisation is a concept which embraces a great diversity of responsibilities. While all the countries we have reported upon contain some elements of decentralisation, a summary using factors in the matrix introduced in Chapter 2 and applied in Chapter 5 shows this diversity.

Curriculum and assessment

Four countries – England and Wales, New Zealand, Australia and some States in the USA – have introduced policies which have centralised the curriculum to some degree. This has not always meant the national government specifying the curriculum, as in England and Wales, but has meant stronger guidelines from the national government, as in New Zealand, and a subsequent process of negotiation between the government and individual schools. In Australia, greater central direction has been at State level and has differed among the States. In parts of the USA, it has been concerned with setting goals in terms of standards of educational attainment which effectively shape the curriculum aims of schools. Set against this centralisation, Russia has introduced a greater degree of decentralisation of responsibility for the curriculum, albeit from a high level of national central direction while Poland has ended a central monopoly on textbooks. In Germany, where education is the responsibility of the regional government, North Rhine-Westphalia has revised its curriculum guidelines to 'a level of abstraction allowing a wide potential for practical application'. Elsewhere – in Uganda, Zimbabwe, Chile, China and in some districts of the USA – it is not apparent that the locus of responsibility for the curriculum has been significantly altered.

Human and physical resources

When we review the evidence on *resources*, there is a much clearer picture of decentralisation. Eight of the eleven countries – Australia, England and Wales, New Zealand, USA, Chile, China, Poland and Uganda – show some degree of decentralisation of responsibility for human and physical resources. This has either meant decentralisation to the school site or a shift of some responsibility from the national level to regional governments. In all of these countries decentralisation is, to some degree, partial. Even in the case of England and Wales, for example, the regional government (LEA) retains funds to provide for a number of services for locally managed schools. In the case of the much smaller number of schools which have left the LEA – grant maintained schools – there still remain a limited number of services provided by the LEA and the national government retains control over capital expenditure. It should also be noted that, in order to ensure that its policies of decentralisation were introduced as and when it wished, even in this area of responsibility there was some centralisation. On salaries and conditions of service, it is a body appointed by, and reporting to, the Secretary of State which recommends changes in these areas and it is the Secretary of State who makes the final decision on these matters. The complexity of simultaneous centralisation and decentralisation is further emphasised by the Secretary of State requiring the *School Teachers' Review Body* (Cm 2466, 1994) to make recommendations on teachers' pay and conditions which make the national guidelines so flexible as to allow individual school governing bodies enormous latitude to define local pay and conditions. This can include teachers being appointed to salary levels which are higher – or lower – than would be predicted from the national scales of pay. Australia also exhibits this complexity with respect to the regulation of teachers' employment. While introducing decentralisation of responsibility for physical resources, States retain and exercise the right of directing starting teachers to particular schools. Of the remaining three countries, it is not apparent that Russia and Zimbabwe have altered their policies. In the case of Germany, we do not have evidence of change although we are aware that some Länder – certainly Hamburg – are reviewing their policies in this area. The evidence we have considered points, therefore, to a pattern of decentralisation in this area of responsibility. What we must also recognise, however, is that this can occur with quite different changes in other areas of responsibility and, as we shall review later in this section, with differences in the orientation of changes as between, for example, emphasis on markets or professional responsibility.

Finance

The set of responsibilities we have classified as *finance* include the sources of finance and the mechanisms used to allocate funds to schools. Changes in responsibilities here show a marked difference according to the wealth of countries. Those countries with low levels of national income – Chile, Poland, China, Russia, Uganda and Zimbabwe – have all, with the exception of Poland, made changes that allow families and other non-governmental agencies to contribute directly to the cost of schools. In Chile contributions from families may be used to off-set costs for municipalities or, in the private schools, to increase the salaries of teachers. Schools in China can be part-financed through non-tax contributions from the local community as well as from local business, while Russia has not only decentralised some of the financing responsibilities to districts but has introduced laws allowing private sponsorship of schools. Uganda and Zimbabwe both have systems where reliance is placed upon some contributions from parents. In the case of Poland, some of the costs of school premises and learning materials have been decentralised to municipalities. Set against this, we have no evidence of significant changes in the sources of funding in the five wealthier countries we have surveyed. England and Wales and New Zealand represent cases, however, where the regulations as to how schools are funded have been centralised to provide for a more uniform approach. In England and Wales, these changes allow the government to establish funding arrangements which rely on recruitment of pupils, an important element in creating a competitive environment. The centralisation of rules on funding in both these countries again illustrates the way in which decentralisation can be accompanied by greater centralisation.

Access

The responsibilities we have classified as *access* include decisions with respect to regulating admissions and decisions about the information schools must provide about themselves, although, for the latter, the information we have secured from our literature searches has been comparatively limited. In the cases of China, Germany, Poland and Russia, we have not been able to identify changes in policy direction in this area. This also appears to be the case in Australia where admissions policies place great emphasis on equity and in many States in the USA, the use of bussing to ensure racial mix is a clear indicator of the continued importance of equity. This contrasts with the decentralisation of decisions on admissions in Chile, England and Wales and New Zealand. In these countries, there is a focus on competition and some concept of parental choice, although as admissions rules are increasingly decentralised to schools, it is the schools and not parents who arbitrate choice. Also, in each of these countries there is more published information, the government requiring schools to provide information on factors such as retention rates, academic achievement and financial resources. Set against these, decisions on access in Uganda and Zimbabwe reflect the resource context of each system. In Uganda, levels of primary school attendance are low and access is more a function of community and family resources than specific policies on admissions. This is also the case in Zimbabwe, which has high levels of primary enrolment, while the right of admission to secondary school depends on an ability to meet the cost of fees.

In reflecting upon the diversity of responsibilities we have summarised, it is essential to recognise the difference between comparisons of *change* in the distribution of the responsibilities we have examined and the *substantive* distribution of responsibilities. We illustrate this by reference to the curriculum. We have observed, for example, how policies for the curriculum have become increasingly centralised in England and Wales, New Zealand, Australia and parts of the USA while, by contrast, Russia and Poland have introduced greater decentralisation. However, these changes do not tell us about the actual *balance* of responsibilities, and it can be the case that those countries which are centralising may still have a more decentralised distribution of responsibilities than countries such as Russia, which are moving from a highly centralised system to one that is somewhat less controlled from the centre. We should also recognise that the provision of set texts from the national government provides for powerful central control. Despite these caveats, we suggest that the direction of change is, none the less, an important indicator of developments in education and, in this respect, what is apparent is the widespread nature of decentralisation of responsibilities for the management of human and physical resources, our evidence pointing to this in eight of our eleven countries. These changes seem to be part of Beare's (1993) 'mega-trend' and should be distinguished from policies with respect to other responsibilities which must be met in providing education in schools. Thus, any decentralisation of finance is essentially a function of lower levels of national wealth and the budget crises faced in these countries. Where governments have sought to re-orient schools towards competition, notably in England and Wales and New Zealand, policies on finance have been subject to greater centralisation. Equally, and in so far as our data are sufficient, policies on the curriculum and access appear to reflect government concern to exert more or less control over professional groups. This theme emerges in the next section where we examine the orientation of change.

Difference in orientation

The diversity of responsibilities we have summarised is reflected in differences in the orientations of national systems and in the *direction* of policy change. These have been indicated in the organisation of Chapter 5, in which we group countries into two main sets, the first representing policy changes which can be interpreted and understood as having a direct impact on educators, while the second may be understood as a decentralising of authority from one level of government to another. In the following discussion we endeavour to interpret the direction of these changes by drawing upon the analysis of 'mixed economies' introduced in Chapter 3.

Changing professionalism

Policies of decentralisation, which we classify as being primarily concerned with changing the role of professional educators, fall into three sub-groups. In the first of these we locate the changes introduced in England and Wales and New Zealand where the key element in understanding change is the challenge they embody to the primacy of educators in decision-making. The centralisation of the curriculum, the introduction of pupil-led funding and more open enrolment policies which place an emphasis on competition, together reduce the discretion of educators in areas where, in both systems, professionals have traditionally had primacy. Against these changes, in both systems their role in managing human and physical resources has been increased. However, since this must be undertaken in partnership with lay governing bodies at the school level it represents a reduction in professional discretion at the level of LEA officials and an insistence that school principals are not given the discretion to act on their own judgement but must persuade their governors. In terms of our analysis of the 'mixed economy' of education, these changes represent reductions in the place of the 'college' in decision-making and a greater emphasis on 'command' and 'market'. The deprofessionalisation we observe in these changes compares with the redefinition of professionalism in Australia. The stronger role of the States in the curriculum indicates a shift away from the 'college' towards 'command' but, in decentralising responsibilities over resources to school principals, as compared with the governing bodies of England and Wales and schools' councils in New Zealand, we see an enhancement of the 'college'. What is not apparent in the changes in Australia is any orientation towards 'market'. This is also the case on the basis of evidence we have cited of changes in States in America. State policies to be more directive on the curriculum have been introduced with decentralisation of responsibility over resources, which has typically been to the school principal. By contrast, evidence from one of the German Länder contrasts with all of these countries and exemplifies an enhancement of the traditional conception of professionalism. The increased role of educators in decisions over the curriculum is 'college' in orientation and, it would appear, represents an important statement about the trust which remains in the ability of educators to fulfil their obligations.

Regional decentralisation

The second set of countries are organised around the principle of regional decentralisation. In other words, if we are to understand change in these countries it is more about changing the responsibility relationships between tiers of government and less about re-structuring the role of educators. As with our analysis of the first set of countries, we suggest there are three sub-groups of change. Chile and Russia represent cases where there is a stronger orientation to 'market' in the funding of schools. The concept of an educational voucher is evident in Chile and, in a more limited way, is also evident in the funding changes in Russia. Alongside these changes, there is some limited flexibility over the curriculum in Chile, largely in terms of the selection of texts, while in Russia a more substantial level of decentralisation to schools from the previously highly centralised system. In both cases, these appear to represent a greater orientation to 'college' where educators have a somewhat greater role in curriculum decisions. We also observe in Russia the establishment of more local political authority as the role of municipalities is increased, a democratising change which we would identify as indicating some orientation towards the 'collective'. With respect to the orientation towards 'markets', some of these changes have parallels with those of England and Wales and New Zealand. We see them as distinct, however, both because of differences over the direction of change in responsibility for the curriculum and the comparatively limited discretion over resources given to individual schools. These similarities and differences reinforce our view of the need for a careful analysis of national education policies if we are properly to understand their nature, direction and orientation. The comparisons also show how certain orientations, such as the 'market', can be used in different ways. Thus, in England and Wales or New Zealand, they have been used to reduce professional control and increase parental choice of schools, but in a way which has coincided with a centralisation of the curriculum. By contrast, the greater decentralisation of curriculum and finance in Russia points to a system that also has in place the essentials for a stronger 'market' orientation for the curriculum.

Decentralisation in China represents a case of change which is essentially concerned with a clear re-structuring of responsibility between tiers of government, the 'command' of central administration being replaced with 'command' at the lower level of regional and municipal administration. Alongside this, the information we have on greater diversity in sources of funding is less easy to interpret. The growing emphasis on contributions from local communities and business could be understood as appealing to community interest in education and a commitment to its support, an orientation which in drawing upon some conception of altruism, locates these changes as 'collective'. It may be, however, that some of the contributions from business may be more directly linked to the conditions of employment in the company where parents gain additional support for their children and, if that were the case, the appeal is more to self-interest and a 'market' orientation. In the case of Poland, the decentralisation of funding premises re-structures the 'command' of central administration with the 'command' of local administration. The reliance on more local funding, drawing upon an historically close association between schools and municipalities may represent an appeal to principles of local 'collectivity'.

The role of non-government and parent sources is more evident in the changes that have occurred in Uganda and in Zimbabwe. In Uganda and in Zimbabwe, resources for schools draw upon the local community as well as upon parents and, in this respect, provision represents an important statement on the readiness of communities to express a 'collective' support for education. In Zimbabwe, the charging of fees for primary schools is a new departure and shows the perceived need for the system to appeal to 'market' self-interest to attract resources to compensate for very limited national resources for education.

The regional re-structuring which we have represented here would seem to arise from rather different policy imperatives. In the cases of Chile and Russia, there appears to be a concern to decentralise responsibility for some elements of educational finance but also to alter the configuration of other relationships: the changes in curriculum and towards pupil-based funding point to a 'market' orientation, which is part of the wider policies of government in these countries. In the remaining four countries, China, Poland, Uganda and Zimbabwe, the decentralisation is largely about issues of financial responsibility and has little to do with the curriculum and wider issues of educational purpose. In the case of Poland there is also a concern to increase democratic control of education in municipalities. Each exemplify again, however, the differences to which we must be alert in the study of decentralisation. In addition to the diversity in what is or is not decentralised is difference in the orientation of change embodied within reform. These diversities and differences provide a suitably complex background against which we proceed to our evaluative analysis of these changes.

EVALUATING DECENTRALISATION

In Chapter 4 we proposed four criteria as essential elements in evaluating the impact of decentralisation – autonomy, accountability, efficiency and equity – and we then applied these to our analyses in Chapters 5–9; in this section we draw upon and develop those earlier analyses.

Autonomy and decentralisation

In Chapter 4 we defined autonomy as a concept concerned with autonomy of agency and critical autonomy, and we proposed that it should be interpreted in relation to the individual learner, the educator and the institution. This differentiation recognises that the provision of education may be changed in ways which might alter the autonomy of an individual learner in one direction while altering the autonomy of educators or institutional leaders in the same or different directions. This becomes apparent when we examine the pattern of change in the countries we have examined in this book.

Autonomy and resources

Our review shows that in eight of the eleven countries responsibility for the management of human and physical resources is being decentralised. In four countries this is to the school site and in four it is to a lower level of government. Where such decentralisation is to the school, it would appear to provide the conditions for a greater degree of autonomy for institutional leaders. This would seem to be supported by the evidence from the case study of England and Wales. In Chapter 6 we note that over 90 per cent of head teachers welcomed the responsibility and the flexibility provided by the delegation embodied in LMS and the chapter as a whole shows how head teachers have been able to use their new powers with respect to decisions over a whole range of human and physical resources. The enhanced power of head teachers, however, sits alongside an erosion of the employment position of teachers and non-teaching staff, Chapter 6 also reporting the increase in the number of teachers on temporary contracts. We can only conjecture whether or not this contributes to how teachers exercise their autonomy in work but it is scarcely likely that these uncertainties increase their sense of control over their lives. It may be, of course, that institutional leaders increasingly include teachers and others in decisions over resources and, where this is the case, it may add to teachers' experience of autonomy. As to learners, however, it is not apparent that this component of decentralisation contributes directly to their autonomy, although how resources are actually deployed within schools may create conditions for learning which are more likely to support the development of the autonomous individual. Assessing whether or not this is the case would require a study of change in the nature of teaching and learning in schools and also demand an analysis of the factors contributing to any observed changes. The difficulty of undertaking such analysis is compounded by what are often simultaneous changes to national policies on the curriculum.

Curriculum autonomy

Decentralisation over human and physical resources must be set against changes in the curriculum. The four countries which have decentralised responsibilities over human and physical resources to the school site – England and Wales, New Zealand, Australia and parts of the USA – have centralised control over the curriculum to some degree. That is, institutional autonomy over human and physical resources has been increased while autonomy has been reduced in areas traditionally associated with the professional identity of educators. This paradox is not apparent in the remaining seven countries. In Chile, China, Poland, Uganda and Zimbabwe regional decentralisation over resources has been accompanied by no apparent change to the curriculum. Russia and the German Länder studied have decentralised some responsibility over the curriculum while leaving control of human and physical resources unchanged.

The paradox of simultaneous centralisation and decentralisation apparent in four of the eleven countries merits comment. In these cases, schools and their leaders are seen as capable of making decisions on how best to match resources to educational priorities but it is for governments or their appointed agencies to define those educational priorities. Moreover, the paradox is the greater because it appears to be part of a wider contradiction in which each of these governments is broadly committed to 'market' solutions for economic development. In principle, the decentralisation of control over resources can be viewed as consistent with the 'market' principle of decisions being decentralised to small operating units and to individuals. Yet, the centralisation of control over the curriculum would appear to be contrary to the market principle and more consistent with the principles underlying planned economies. The logic that explains this paradox is to be found in the increasingly tense relations arising between governments and professional educators over the latter's contribution to the perceived failures of school systems to make an adequate contribution to economic growth. Faced with what has clearly been viewed as a high risk strategy of allowing market relations to determine the curriculum, governments have opted for an approach where they assume that they 'know' the nature of an economically relevant curriculum and can use their powers to insist that this be taught in schools. In marked contrast to the virtues of 'privatisation' espoused by the government in England and Wales, as illustrated by John Major's (1989) description of it as 'quite simply the best way to ensure that service to the consumer naturally comes first', the curriculum has been systematically nationalised, apparently following the principle that the minister in Whitehall 'knows best'.

Finance and autonomy

The limits of the 'market' are no less evident when we review the nature of change over finance. The comparative analysis on this issue shows a clear distinction between rich and poor. The six poorer countries have all introduced policies which have decentralised some responsibilities over the funding of education. These have included schemes for increasing family contributions or increasing revenue sources from regional and local governments. To the extent that market principles involve moving some of the costs of education directly onto families, all these countries exhibit this trend in some degree. With respect to the principle of autonomy, changes here generally point to increasing limits on learners gaining access to educational opportunities. For institutions and their leaders, autonomy must also become constrained as they become increasingly preoccupied with obtaining resources to sustain their viability.

The position of the five richer countries is quite different. In three – Australia, USA and Germany – there is no evidence of major change in finance. In England and Wales and New Zealand, the principal change has been in the centralisation of regulations about the funding of schools, a move which has allowed these governments to create funding mechanisms in which schools rely heavily on pupil recruitment, an important component in creating competition between schools. With respect to the principle of autonomy, this is a potentially significant change. The pressure on pupil recruitment, linked with the need to achieve success on an externally specified curriculum, must further serve to limit institutional autonomy in deciding the nature of the curriculum. Whether this leads to less diversity in approaches to teaching and learning is an important empirical question in terms of the principle of autonomy.

In none of these countries is there any compelling evidence of a privatisation of the funding of schools, taxation remaining the source of funding. We might note, however, that a study of the wider education system might well show an increasing emphasis on family subsidy of education as the cost of supporting students through higher education is transferred from the public purse.

Autonomy and access

Our comparative study provided only limited information on changes in the rules regulating access to schools. In six countries information was limited but pointed to little change. In Uganda and Zimbabwe, the two poorest countries, access is increasingly determined by ability to pay, a change which excludes many from the opportunities schools can offer for developing the autonomy of learners. In Chile, New Zealand and England and Wales, changes in rules relating to access all emphasise greater attention to published information on school and pupil performance. While this clearly reduces the autonomy of institutions and their leaders, who must make available the information required of them by government, it is less clear what it means for learners. It may be, for example, that the nature of the curriculum activity required by government contributes more to the development of learner autonomy than that previously required by schools. Indeed, whether greater direction of schools by government increases or diminishes the autonomy of learners must remain a question capable of only an empirical answer.

The evidence we have been able to collate on decentralisation and its consequences for the general principle of autonomy illustrates the complexities of these changes. With respect to the decentralisation of responsibilities over human and physical resources, our analysis suggests an increase in the autonomy of institutional leaders but a recognition that its consequences for those employed in schools may be less certain; the consequences for the autonomy of learners must depend upon how resources are managed in practice. As to changes in the curriculum, institutional autonomy would appear to have been reduced in four countries and increased in two, while the consequences for learners are unclear. On finance, the overall perspective appears negative: for the six poorer countries, these changes point to greater limits in autonomy for institutions, their leaders and learners; for the richer countries, the change appears negative for institutions and their leaders. Finally, on access, institutional autonomy is reduced while its consequence for learners remains unclear. Taken as a whole, the impact of decentralisation – and centralisation – on the general principle of autonomy appears uncertain and problematic. The clear outcome of greater autonomy for institutional leaders with respect to decisions over human and physical resources must be understood in the context of some reduction in autonomy – for institutions, leaders and learners – in other areas but, above all, we must recognise the uncertainty of evidence of its effect on the autonomy of learners, perhaps the most prized objective of all in developing and improving the quality of education.

Accountability and decentralisation

In our consideration of accountability in Chapter 4 we indicated that our focus in this study would be on the accountabilities and mutual obligations owed by stakeholders within educational systems. In a government-financed system this could include the accountabilities of educators to appropriate levels of government as well as to parents, pupils and members of the wider community. We also recognised the concept of professional accountability, whereby educators interpret and judge their actions against some concept of a professional mode of behaviour. The extent to which our study has been able to explore these different facets of accountability differs between countries, reflecting the extent and quality of the data we have collected.

It is clear that the processes of decentralisation – and centralisation – are re-structuring accountabilities in several countries. In England and Wales and in New Zealand, there has been a clear challenge to the autonomy of professional educators and a strengthening of their accountabilities to other stakeholders. This has occurred in two ways. In England and Wales the centralisation of the curriculum, accompanied by national testing of pupils and regular inspection of schools, provides performance information which can be used as means of holding schools to account by government agencies. It also provides information to parents and pupils when making their school choice, decisions which affect school budgets and, therefore, the jobs of teachers. In New Zealand, more central specification of the curriculum, the schools' charter, performance information and open enrolment act in similar ways, although it has a less direct effect on jobs. Chile also exemplifies some of these changes, more performance information on schools allied with choice between government and private schools altering accountabilities in ways which increase the information available to government for monitoring. In England and Wales and New Zealand such information is also used by parents in exercising choice between schools. In each country, therefore, accountabilities have been structured to strengthen the position of government, community representatives and parents as 'consumers'. In Australia, by comparison, accountability has been altered by creating a greater role for school councils as part of decision-making on the management of human and physical resources. Our information on Australia does not show how this form of accountability is working in practice, but evidence on community representation is available from the case study of England and Wales. Thus, in Chapter 7 we noted that some school governing bodies were probably not sufficiently critical and prone to 'rubber stamp' the decisions of head teachers. It is evidence of the difference between establishing a new structure of accountability and it providing the new relationships expected by the government – an example of a more general issue of policy statements and legislative enactment leading to outcomes which differ from intentions. This issue is apparent in the USA.

There is certainly ample comment from the USA of concern about the quality of education and demands for re-structuring (Chubb and Moe, 1990; Lieberman, 1993; Jacobson and Berne, 1993). In practice, however, substantive changes appear modest. The most substantial change has been the delegation of responsibility for human and physical resources to the school site, but this has often been done in a way which gives the school principal greater authority, a change in accountability relationships which increases the authority of principals as against officers of local school districts. There is some parallel here with change in the German Länder where accountabilities have not only been slightly modified but, in doing so, have increased the authority of educators.

In four of the remaining countries – China, Poland, Uganda and Zimbabwe – arrangements for funding schools provide a key indicator of likely changes in accountability. In China, the greater emphasis on the funding of schools from lower levels of government and from local commercial organisations can be expected to make them more concerned with what schools are doing. This might also be expected in Poland. In Uganda and Zimbabwe, making families and local communities more responsible for funding provision might also be expected to lead to educators being held more accountable for their work. In all of these cases, however, we should be alert to cultural difference and aware that assumptions about parents holding schools to account in one society (England and Wales) may conflict with norms and expectations in other societies. In Russia, the clearest change in accountability has been the delegation of responsibility for inspection of schools to regional levels of government. While this means that the relationship between institutions and the *level* of government has been altered, it does not necessarily alter the nature of that accountability in practice. However, we should recognise that Russia also has made modest changes in the degree of curriculum centralisation, a change which would appear to increase the autonomy of educators and, therefore, demand more of their concept of professional accountability.

The nature of much of our information on changes in accountability in these countries demands caution with respect to our conclusions. In the context of that caveat, it appears that in three countries – England and Wales, New Zealand and Chile – the accountabilities of educators have been increased through a combination of greater national monitoring and parental choice of schools. In Australia, greater accountability has been through the introduction of school councils, while the USA, the German Länder and Russia show no great change in accountability. In the USA there is evidence of accountability change in some States and no change in others, despite much rhetoric in the USA on the need for change (Koppich and Guthrie, 1993). Finally, we *conjecture* that the greater reliance on local and family funding of schools in China, Poland, Uganda and Zimbabwe is likely to make educators in those countries more accountable to local communities. Set against this outline of accountabilities is evidence of its practice in England and Wales. In Chapter 7 we note the apparent weakness of the role of school governing bodies as observed from our questionnaire data and interviews on school visits. We also observe the weak position of local authorities as agents of accountability, much of our evidence pointing to schools perceiving local authorities as being accountable to them rather than the converse. Evidence such as this points to the need for caution in assuming that policy declarations and legislative enactment become practice: there is no escape from empirical enquiry if we are properly to understand how policy changes alter practice.

The analysis serves to illustrate the complexity of decentralisation as a phenomenon. There is no single pattern of change in the accountability relationships of educators with other stakeholders; some systems show clear evidence of greater accountability while others show a readiness to demonstrate increased confidence in the role of educators and less concern that they be more answerable for their work. In the next section we will consider whether such diversity is also apparent with respect to efficiency.

Efficiency and decentralisation

A concern with efficiency demands as great a concern with 'what is got out' as well as 'what is put in'. With respect to the relationship between these, a brief extract from an earlier quotation captures its essence: 'if two schools which are comparable in every respect are equally effective in terms of performance, the one that uses the smaller amount of resources is the more cost-effective' (Mortimore and Mortimore with Thomas, 1994: 22). In applying this perspective to education, it is essential to recognise that measurement cannot rely on a calibrated scale but requires informed judgement based upon a range of quantitative and qualitative information. This is far from easy to apply in practice but, since the resources available for education are scarce, a concern for assessing the efficiency of resource must be of great importance. It is all the more significant, therefore, that when we examine decentralisation the absence of clear evidence on its efficiency effects is striking.

This absence is partly a consequence of the nature of the data available to us on several countries. The accounts we have presented have been concerned more with describing the structural changes entailed by decentralisation and less with providing accounts of their impact on practice. Indeed, with the exception of England and Wales, the most sensible conclusion is that we know too little about the impact of the changes to comment on their efficiency. In the case of these countries what we are able to do, however, is comment on the conditions which need to hold in order for the policy changes to generate efficiency gains. Thus, in New Zealand, Chile and Russia, all countries which have placed greater emphasis on inter-school choice, efficiency gains might be expected if the assumptions of quasi-markets are borne out empirically. In Australia and the USA, the assumption which must hold is that educators at the school site are better at matching resources to needs than administrators located elsewhere; in making this assumption, it is important to recognise that additional administrative costs (operating inefficiencies) arising from decentralised management need to be taken into account (Coopers and Lybrand, 1988). In the case of Germany, the assumption which must hold is that increasing the responsibility of educators over the curriculum leads to improved educational outcomes. As to China, Poland, Uganda and Zimbabwe, the assumption is that placing greater demand for school funding on local communities and/or families will lead to raised expectations about performance and that, in this more accountable environment, schools will respond more effectively in relation to a given level of resources.

Testing the assumptions related to these different circumstances is far from easy, as becomes apparent when we examine the evidence available from the England and Wales case study. In Chapter 8 we examined the efficiency consequences of decentralisation by exploring evidence of the impact of local management of schools on learning. We did this by reviewing evidence of its effects on three factors associated with effectiveness in schools and, by implication, efficiency. These are: purposeful management and leadership, the nature of participation in decision-making and the extent to which schools focused upon the practice of teaching and learning. On the first of these factors, our data show local management affecting planning, management and decision-making in schools but the extent to which this brought benefits to a school appears to depend upon the financial situation of the school and the management style of the head teacher. As to the second factor, the survey showed some schools securing high levels of staff participation, although this depends upon the areas of decisions with some areas, notably on staffing, being the preserve of senior staff and governors. When we examined what these mean for children's learning, however, the evidence is mixed. Among head teachers of smaller primary and secondary schools, there is little consensus that children's learning is benefiting from LM or that standards of education have improved as a direct result of LM, conclusions which may reflect the poorer financial position of these schools. This compares with head teachers of larger schools and, for heads as a whole, our data showing them becoming more positive as their experience of local management grows.

It may be that the most convincing evidence of the impact of local management is on the opportunities which it has provided for managing the environment and resources for learning, both factors which can act to support the quality of learning in schools. What remains elusive, however, is clear-cut evidence of these leading through to direct benefits on learning, an essential component if we are to conclude that it is contributing to higher levels of efficiency. How the changes contribute to equity is the focus of our next section.

Equity and decentralisation.

In analysing the equity effects of decentralisation, we argued in Chapter 4 that our concern is the distribution of educational benefits between social groups, within social groups and upon individuals with specific needs. As with our assessment of the efficiency effects of decentralisation across the eleven countries, assessing equity requires us to make predictions about the direction of change using the evidence of the policies we have described; only in the case of England and Wales are we able to complement that analysis with empirical data.

Our analysis suggests that policies which emphasise equity are not a priority for several nations. In England and Wales the emphasis on competition must place some threat to equity as those with 'market' power and competition use it to their advantage. This threat is also evident in New Zealand, despite equity statements contained in school charters. In Chile, the opportunity for private schools to attract State funding is likely to lead to greater inequality while, in Russia, the readiness to allow market-led provision suggests that equity has a low priority. In China, reliance on richer communities and on locally funded 'centre' schools contributes to inequality as does the reliance on municipalities in Poland. Increased reliance on community and parental funding in Uganda and Zimbabwe is likely to have similar effects. This leaves Australia, USA and Germany, and here there is little evidence that changes are having a direct effect on the equity of provision. In these, as in all the other countries we have surveyed, however, it is essential that we are cautious in drawing conclusions without more data which allow a greater scrutiny of changes in practice. This becomes apparent when we examine some further evidence on the equity consequences of the changes in New Zealand and in England and Wales.

The information we have drawn upon in Chapter 5 sets out the nature of the structural changes in eleven school systems. An examination of the effects of these changes in practice shows the complexity which can arise. In New Zealand, for example, a study on the impact of competition pointed to the lack of evidence that the greater market orientation of the system was leading to greater inequality (Lauder *et al.* 1994). Our case study of England and Wales is also interesting for the way in which it highlights the complexity of practice with respect to the effect of decentralisation on groups and on individuals with specific needs. In Chapter 9 we show how the transparency of rules and information on funding has led to schools in the same LEA serving comparable intakes being funded on the same basis. The information has also led to national debate as to whether the funding of children of the same age in different parts of the country should be equal. The data on additional educational needs shows how some LEAs were able to interpret national guidelines in ways which favoured schools with a high percentage of AEN pupils while other LEAs moved in the opposite direction. This uneven national pattern is mirrored also in the competition arising from decentralisation in England and Wales, our data showing how some schools have developed policies of collaboration to resist what are seen as the negative effects of competition; we also show how competition is seen as having a negative effect on the ability of schools to treat disadvantaged groups fairly.

The more detailed information on England and Wales shows how important caution is in our assessment of the actual effects of policy changes. Despite that however, it is notable that in eight of the eleven countries, policies on some aspects of equity do not appear to have priority in the specification of contemporary changes in education. The complexity on this issue does merit emphasis, however. As the case of England and Wales shows, in changing the funding basis of schools, the national government's guidelines force a degree of equity which was not obviously apparent earlier. Thus, the requirement that all children of the same age in a single LEA be funded equally applies an equity principle of like treatment for members of the same group. This is accompanied by the application of a second equity principle, which means that schools with pupils who differ on some other criterion, such as level of family poverty, can get additional resources. It is also possible for individuals with distinct needs to be given additional resources. This does not mean we should ignore concerns that the competitive nature of the changes in England and Wales will lead schools to favour recruitment of more advantaged pupils. We recognise this as a real concern, though we note our evidence of schools collaborating in order to off-set what they regard as the negative threats of competition. Evidence such as this serves to emphasise the complexity of change and the need to take account of how policies are interpreted in practice before we can draw firm conclusions on their long terms effects, a matter which informs our concluding discussion.

DECENTRALISATION AND LEARNERS

If learning is at the heart of education, it must be central to our final discussion of decentralisation. It means asking whether, in their variety of guises, the changes characterised as decentralisation have washed over and around children in classrooms, leaving their day-to-day experiences largely untouched. In asking this question we must begin by recognising that structural changes in governance, management and finance may leave largely untouched the daily interaction of pupils and teachers. In other words, we must not assume that the decentralisation of resource decisions has any real effect on pupils' learning in classrooms: rather than assume a beneficial or a negative impact, we need to consider the evidence. It invites caution and this becomes apparent in remarks drawing predominantly on the experience of England and Wales.

Having reviewed the data on the efficiency of decentralisation in England and Wales, we concluded that the most convincing evidence of its impact relates to the opportunities provided for managing the school environment and the resources for learning. These are both factors which act to support the quality of teaching and learning in schools, and their value should not be discounted. Yet they are not likely to be highly significant factors in determining quality. That is, while the decision to spend a little more or less on books as against teachers (or carpeting a classroom as against purchasing a computer) gives opportunity for decision makers in schools to match resources to needs, they are changes at the margins of expenditure; at best, therefore, they can be expected to have a marginal change on the overall experiences and achievements of pupils. This is not to discount the potential benefits of decentralising the management of resources but to retain a perspective of how much it might be expected to achieve. We note and share similar comments by Levacic (1995) who recognises gains on the impact side of resource management but is more cautious in the conclusions about the effectiveness of local management in terms of learning.

It may be that the quasi-market competition between schools together with the public monitoring of school inspections will be more influential, forcing schools to undertake a more self-critical review of their activities. If that were to be the case, it would illustrate the effect of the new accountabilities arising through competition, the role of governing bodies and more public monitoring of schools. Yet some of the evidence we provide on these accountabilities is far from clear-cut. Certainly, the role of governing bodies as agents of accountability would appear to be rather weak and, with respect to the effects of quasi-markets, there is some evidence of competition being subverted by agreements among schools to collaborate and to avoid competition strategies; although, as with other research findings, we fully recognise that there is also a good deal of competition. This still leaves the effect of formal and publicly reported inspections as a further element of an elaborate range of accountabilities and it is, indeed, difficult to assume that none of these will affect schools and their performance. Whether the overall effect is positive – or as positive as it might be – on the standard and quality of learning depends upon how decentralisation affects the autonomy of learners, educators and institutions.

As we have argued, LMS in England and Wales increases the autonomy of head teachers over resources and diminishes the employment position of other staff, and the nationalisation of the curriculum limits the professional autonomy of teachers. Whether or not this is desirable is *the* fundamental question about re-structuring in England and Wales. Asked bluntly, has the creation of a national curriculum acted generally to raise standards and expectations among teachers? If too many teachers had expectations that were set too low, more central direction may act to alter those in ways which bring benefits to pupils, all the more in view of the more intensive monitoring from national assessments and the cycle of school inspections and public reporting. In responding to this we place the concept of autonomy, as outlined in Chapter 4, at the centre.

If one of the purposes of education is developing and sustaining principles of autonomy and critical autonomy, allowing teachers to practise those principles in work would seem to be part of the more general reason for developing them in the first instance – what is the purpose of nurturing these principles at school if they are to be set aside in the world of work? However, we do not interpret this as a licence for teachers to proceed without regard for the view of others as to what should be taught. The accountability of teachers to stakeholders arises both as a consequence of a democratic and professional practice but also as one of the means by which members of the wider society sustain their autonomy and critical autonomy: the active citizen will have concerns about what schools teach. This means a model of curriculum, however, which relies more upon dialogue and negotiation rather than statutory imposition, although we may need statutes which facilitate dialogue and create frameworks of governance which bring together stakeholders. There may also be general principles and guidance on programmes of study available from national and local governments. Above all, however, we need to ensure that policies and practices are concerned with nurturing the autonomy and critical autonomy of learners, and it is not obvious that contemporary policies of decentralisation – perhaps in all eleven countries reviewed – give these enough attention. Decentralisation has focused essentially upon changes in resource choices giving all too little attention to what it means for processes of teaching and learning.

In making this observation about the limits of decentralisation as manifested in the eleven countries we have reviewed, our purpose is less to diminish the phenomenon than to place it in a wider context. The decentralisation of responsibilities over human and physical resources which characterises the direction of change in eight of the eleven countries is certainly part of 'mega' policy trend, but our data and our analysis suggest that it is unlikely to have a 'mega' impact on the standard and quality of learning. Policy-makers and educators need to turn away from the seductive but false promise that structural reforms can bring about significant changes in learning. The standard and quality of learning relies upon daily interactions between teachers and learners: how teachers define their curriculum, how they engage in their pedagogy and how they negotiate these with learners and their wider communities are far more significant in their consequence than the degree of control and marginal choice exercised over human and physical resources. A concern with issues of teaching and learning requires a stronger focus upon the professional development of teachers as educators and more attention to the neglected relationship between the pedagogies used in schools and their forms of organisation; these do not appear to be a significant part of the concerns of policy-makers. For example, the challenges for pedagogy and organisations that arise from the new technologies are but one arena where the relationship between teaching, learning and organisation need to be examined if schools are to make best use of these new conditions. It would be an irony if the policies of decentralisation that are being enacted were to neglect the potential for decentralised learning – and new partnerships in that learning – arising from new technologies. Yet, the danger of the type of decentralisation we are experiencing is not that it is undesirable in itself but that it may too often deflect the energies of school principals into administering resources – even to finding resources in poorer countries – and away from the more demanding task of an educational leadership which places the autonomy of learners at the centre.

If the standard and quality of learning is to be at the centre of education – and it is surely the key test of decentralisation – it is not apparent that the policies and practices of decentralisation we have discussed in this book are adequately geared to its achievement.

Notes

1 Although there are differences in the National Curriculum and local management arrangements for England as against Wales, these are minor in the context of a comparative international study and for these reasons they will be treated as one country.
2 Throughout this Report, a *small* primary school is taken to be one with fewer than 200 pupils. In the secondary sector, a *small* school is taken to be one with fewer than 700 pupils on roll. The DfE/Coopers and Lybrand report on good management in small schools states that 45% of all primary schools in England and Wales have 200 or fewer pupils. They comment: 'There is no agreed definition of what constitutes a small school. This guide takes as a working definition schools with fewer than 200 pupils' (1993: 1).
3 Historic budgets were calculated for each school using the formula:
   [(budget share – formula) / (level of transitional protection for 1990/91 / 100)] + formula
4 The asterisks indicate level of confidence (that the association is not due to chance):
       * means confidence at the 0.05 level
       ** means confidence at the 0.01 level.
   The closer the correlation is to 1, positive or negative, the stronger the association between the two variables.
5 Primary: r=0.50**; Secondary: r=0.40**
6 All schools: r=0.04. Primary: r=0.03. Secondary: r=-0.26

References

Arnott, M.A., Bullock, A.D. and Thomas, H. (1992) *The Impact of Local Management of Schools: A Source Book* The University of Birmingham

Audit Commission (1989) *Losing an Empire, Finding a Role: The LEA of the Future* London: HMSO

—— (1991) *Management within Primary Schools* London: HMSO

—— (1993) *Adding Up the Sums: Schools' Management of their Finances* London: HMSO

Audit Commission/Ofsted (1993) *Keeping Your Balance: Standards for Financial Administration in Schools* London: Ofsted

Ball, S. (1990a) *Markets, Morality and Equality in Education* Hillcole Group Paper 5. London: The Tufnell Press

—— (1990b) *Politics and Policy Making in Education: Explorations in Policy Sociology* London: Routledge

Barry, N. (1987) 'Understanding the Market', in M. Loney *et al.* (eds) *The State or the Market* London: Sage pp. 161–71

Beare, H. (1993) 'From the Director: the Policy Megatrands', *International Directions in Education* Commonwealth Council for Educational Administration 1 (1)

Berger, J. (1990) 'Market and State in Advanced Capitalist Societies', in A. Martinelli and N.J. Smelser (eds) *Economy and Society: Overviews in Economic Sociology* London: Sage

Blaug, M. (1970) *An Introduction to the Economics of Education* Harmondsworth: Penguin

Boyd, L.W. (1994) 'National School Reform and Restructuring: Parallels between Britain and the United States', Paper prepared for the BEMAS annual conference, Manchester: UMIST

Bradach, J.L. and Eccles, R.G. (1989) 'Price, Authority and Trust: From Ideal Types to Plural Forms', in *Annual Review of Sociology* [In Thompson *et al.* 1991 pp. 277–92]

Buchanan, J.M. (1969) *Costs and Choice* Chicago: Markham

—— (1978) (ed.) *The Economics of Politics* London: IEA

Bullock, A.D. and Thomas, H. (1992) *Pupil Numbers and Schools Budgets: An Examination of Formula Allocations to Schools of Different Size* Birmingham: University of Birmingham

—— (1993a) 'Pupil-Led Funding and Local Management Funding Formulae', in M. Smith and H. Busher (eds) *Managing Schools in an Uncertain Environment: Resources, Marketing and Power* Sheffield: Hallam, pp. 38–53

—— (1993b) 'Comparing School Formula Allocations: An Exploration of Some Problems', in G. Wallace (ed.) *Local Management, Central Control: Schools in the Market Place* Bournemouth: Hyde Publications, pp. 14–29

—— (1994a) *The Impact of Local Management on Schools: Final Report* Birmingham: University of Birmingham

—— (1994b) *The Funding of Schools After the 1988 Education Reform Act* Unpublished Report: University of Birmingham

Burgess, R., Hockley, J., Hughes, C., Phtiaka, H., Pole, C. and Sanday, A. (1992) 'Case Studies: A Thematic Look at Issues and Problems', in *Resourcing Sheffield Schools* Sheffield: Sheffield City Council pp. 31–6

Caines, J. (1992) 'Improving Education Through Better Management: A View from the DES', in T. Simkins, L. Ellison and V. Garrett (eds) *Implementing Educational Reform: The Early Lessons* Harlow: Longman pp. 14–31

Caldwell, B.J. and Spinks, J.M. (1988) *The Self-Managing School* Lewes: The Falmer Press

Carnegie Forum on Education, Task Force on Teaching as a Profession (1986) *A Nation Prepared: Teachers for the 21st Century* New York: Carnegie Forum on Education and the Economy

Carroll, L. (1865) *Alice's Adventures in Wonderland* London: Cathay Books

Chitty, C. (1989) *Towards a New Education System. The Victory of the New Right* Lewes: The Falmer Press

Chubb, J.E. and Moe, T.M. (1990) *Politics, Markets and America's Schools* Washington, DC: The Brookings Institute

Colclough, C. (1993) 'Primary Schooling for All: How can it be achieved in Africa' Paper prepared for the International Symposium on the Economics of Education, 19–21 May 1993, Manchester

Cm 2466 (1994) *School Teachers' Review Body, Third Report 1994* London : HMSO

Coopers and Lybrand (1988) *Local Management of Schools: A report to the DES* London: HMSO

DES (1977) *Local Authority Arrangements for the School Curriculum* London: HMSO

—— (1988) *Education Reform Act: Local Management of Schools* Circular 7/88 London: HMSO

—— (1991) *Local Management of Schools: Further Guidance* Circular 7/91 London: HMSO

—— (1992) 'Pupil–Teacher Ratios for each LEA in England', Statistical Bulletin 2/92, February

DfE/WO (1992) *Choice and Diversity: A New Framework for Schools* London: HMSO

—— (1992) *The Implementation of Local Management of Schools: A Report by HM Inspectorate 1989–92* London: HMSO

—— (1994) *Local Management of Schools* Circular 2/94 London: HMSO

DfE/Coopers and Lybrand (1993) *Good Management in Small Schools* London: DFE Publications Centre

DfEE (1996) *A Guide to the Department for Education and Employment* London: DfEE

Doyal, L. and Gough, I. (1991) *A Theory of Human Need* London: Macmillan

Drury, D. and Levin, D. (1993) *School-Based Management: The Changing Locus of Control in American Public Schools* Draft Final Report for the US Department of Education Washington: Pelavin Associates Inc

Evers, C. and Lakomski, G. (1991) *Knowing Educational Administration* Oxford: Pergamon Press

Fallon, M. (1990) 'More Choice For Parents, Bigger Budgets For Schools, Says Fallon' *DES News* 390/90

Feyerabend, P. (1978) *Science in a Free Society* London: New Left Books

Forth, E. (1993) 'Schools Minister Welcomes Report on Schools' Financial Management' *DfE News* 204/93

Fowler, F.C., Boyd, W.L. and Plank, D.N. (1993) 'International School Reform:

Political considerations', in S.L. Jacobson and R. Berne (eds) *Reforming Education: The Emerging Systemic Approach* California: Corwin Press, pp. 153–68

Gatawa, B.S.M. (1994) 'Zimbabwe: System of Education', in T. Husén and T.N. Postlethwaite (eds) *The International Encyclopedia of Education* Second Edition pp. 6814–21

Glennerster, H. (1992) *Paying for Welfare: The 1990s* London: Harvester Wheatsheaf

Golby, M. (1992) 'School Governors: Conceptual and Practical Problems' *Journal of Philosophy of Education* 26 (2) 165–72

Haenisch, H. and Schuldt, W. (1994) *The Effectiveness of Schooling and Educational Resource Management: The North Rhine-Westphalian Project* Landesinstitut für Schule und Weiterbildung

Hall, V. and Wallace, M. (1993) 'Collaboration as a Subversive Activity: A Professional Response to Externally Imposed Competition Between Schools' *School Organisation* 3 (2) 101–117

Halsey, J. (1993) 'The Impact of Local Management on School Management Style' *Local Government Policy Making* 19 (5) 49–56

Higgins, K.E. (1993) 'The Local Education Authority: A Disappearing Phenomenon?' *Local Government Policy Making* 19 (5) 15–20

Hirst, P.H. and Peters, R.S. (1970) *The Logic of Education* London: Routledge & Kegan Paul

HM Inspectorate (1992) *The Implementation of Local Management of Schools* London: HMSO

HM Chief Inspector (1994) *The Annual Report of Her Majesty's Chief Inspector of Schools* London: HMSO

Holmes Group, The (1986) *Tomorrow's Teachers* East Lansing: USA

Hough, J.R. (1981) *A Study of School Costs* Windsor: Nelson NFER

House of Commons (1994) *Second Report of the Education Committee, Session 1993-94*, H.C. (93–94) 45 London: HMSO

Huckman, L. (1991) 'Decision Making in Primary Schools With Special Reference To LMS' Paper presented at the BERA Conference, 1991

Humphrey, C. and Thomas, H. (1985) 'Giving Schools the Money' *Education* 165 (19) 419–20.

—— (1986) 'Delegating to Schools' *Education* 168 (24) 513–14.

Jacobson, S.L. and Berne, R. (eds) (1993) *Reforming Education: The Emerging Systemic Approach* California: Corwin Press

Komorowska, H. and Janowski, A. (1994) 'Poland: System of Education' in T. Husén and T.N. Postlethwaite (eds) *The International Encyclopedia of Education* Second Edition pp. 4542–9

Koppich, J.E. and Guthrie, J.W. (1993) 'Examining Contemporary Education-Reform Efforts in the United States', in H. Beare and W.L. Boyd (eds) *Restructuring Schools: An International Perspective on the Movement to Transform the Control and Performance of Schools* London: Falmer Press pp. 51–68

Lauder, H., Hughes, D., Waslander, S., Thrupp, M., McGlinn, J., Newton, S. and Dupuis, A. (1994) *The Creation of Market Competition for Education in New Zealand* The Smithfield Project. First Report to the Ministry of Education, 1990–93

LEAP (1990) *Locally Managed Schools* Milton Keynes: LEAP

Lednev, V.S., Ryzhakov, M.V. and Shishov, S.E. (1995) 'Federal Components of the State Educational Standard for Primary, Secondary and High Comprehensive School: General Provisions' Moscow

Lee, T. (1991a) *Additional Educational Needs and LMS: Methods and Money 1991–2* Bath: Centre for the Analysis of Social Policy, University of Bath

—— (1991b) 'Formula for Uncertainty' *British Journal of Special Education* 18 (3) 100–2

—— (1992a) 'Finding Simple Answers to Complex Questions: Funding Special Needs Under LMS', in G. Wallace (ed.) *Local Management of Schools: Research and Experience* BERA Dialogues Number 6. Clevedon: Multilingual Matters pp. 68–81

—— (1992b) 'Local Management of Schools and Special Educational Provision', in W. Swann (ed.) *Learning For All* Milton Keynes: Open University Press

Leeds City Council (1990) *The Leeds Scheme for Local Management of Schools*

Le Grand, J., Propper, C. and Robinson, R. (1992) *The Economics of Social Problems* Third Edition London: Macmillan

Lehmann, R.H. (1994) 'Germany: System of Education' in T. Husén and T.N. Postlethwaite (eds) *The International Encyclopedia of Education* Second Edition pp. 2470–80

Leibenstein, H. (1966) 'Allocative efficiency and X efficiency' *American Economic Review* (56) 392–415

Levacic, R. (1992) 'Local Management of Schools: Aims, Scope and Impact' *Educational Management and Administration* 20 (1) 16–29

—— (1995) *Local Management of Schools. Analysis and Practice* Milton Keynes: Open University Press

—— and Glover, B. (1994) *OFSTED Assessment of Schools' Efficiency: An Analysis of 66 Secondary Inspection Reports* Milton Keynes: Open University Press

Lieberman, M. (1993) *Public Education: An Autopsy* Cambridge, MA: Harvard University Press

Lockheed, M. (1995) 'Effective Schools in Developing Countries: A Short and Incomplete Review' Keynote address presented at the ICSEI 1995 Congress, Leeuwarden, Netherlands, 2–6 January 1995

Louden, L.W. and Browne, R.K. (1993) 'Developments in Education Policy in Australia: A Perspective on the 1980s', in H. Beare and W.L. Boyd (eds) *Restructuring Schools: An International Perspective on the Movement to Transform the Control and Performance of Schools* London: Falmer Press pp. 106–35

MacGilchrist, B., Mortimore, P., Savage, J. and Beresford, C. (1995) *Planning Matters: The Impact of Development Planning in Primary Schools* London: Paul Chapman

Macpherson, R.J.S. (1993) 'The Reconstruction of New Zealand Education: A Case of "High Politics" Reform' in H. Beare and W.L. Boyd (eds) *Restructuring Schools: An international perspective on the movement to transform the control and performance of schools* London: Falmer Press pp. 69–85

Major, J. (1989) *Public Service Management: Revolution in Progress* Management Lecture organised by The Audit Commission, June

Marren, E. and Levacic, R. (1992) 'Implementing Local Management of Schools: First Year Spending Decisions', in T. Simkins, L. Ellison and V. Garrett (eds) *Implementing Educational Reform: The Early Lessons* Harlow: Longman in association with BEMAS pp. 136–50

Miller, D. (1989) *Market, State and Community. Theoretical Foundations of Market Socialism* Oxford: Oxford University Press

Mortimore, P., Sammons, P., Stoll, L., Lewis, D. and Ecob, R. (1988) *School Matters: The Junior Years* Wells: Open Books

Mortimore, P. and Mortimore, J. with Thomas, H. (1994) *Managing Associate Staff: Innovation in Primary and Secondary Schools* London: Paul Chapman

Mueller, D.C. (1979) *Public Choice* Cambridge: Cambridge University Press

National Commission on Education (1993) *Learning to Succeed* Report of the National Commission on Education London: Heinemann

National Commission on Excellence in Education (1983) *A Nation at Risk: Imperative for Educational Reform* Washington, DC: Government Printing Office

Nikandrov, N.D. (1994) 'Russia: System of Education', in T. Husén and T.N.

Postlethwaite (eds) *The International Encyclopedia of Education* Second Edition pp. 5098–5107

Novak, M. (1991) *The Spirit of Democratic Capitalism* London: IEA

Nussbaum, M.C. and Sen, A. (1993) eds *The Quality of Life* Oxford: Clarendon Press

Odaet, C.F. (1994) 'Uganda: System of Education', in T. Husén and T.N. Postlethwaite (eds) *The International Encyclopedia of Education* Second Edition pp. 6493–501

OECD (1994) *Effectiveness of Schooling and of Educational Resource Management: Synthesis of Country Studies* Paris: OECD DEELSA/ED (94) 17

Ofsted (1995a) *The Annual Report of Her Majesty's Chief Inspector of Schools 1994/95* London: HMSO

—— (1995b) *Guidance on the Inspection of Secondary Schools: The Ofsted Handbook* London: HMSO

Patten, J. (1993) 'Survey Proves Popularity of School Governorship' *DfE News* 57/93

Peters, R.S. (ed.) (1967) *The Concept of Education* London: Routledge & Kegan Paul

Picot, B., Rosenergy, M., Ramsay, P., Wise, C. and Wereta, W. (1988) *Administering for Excellence Effective Administration in Education (The Picot Report)* Wellington: Government Printer

Plant, R. (1990) 'Citizenship and Rights' in *Citizenship and Rights in Thatcher's Britain: Two Views* London: IEA Health and Welfare Unit

Plowden Report (1967) *Children and Their Primary Schools* London: HMSO

Raab, C.D. (1992) 'Parents and Schools: What Role for Education Authorities?' in P. Munn (ed.) *Parents and Schools: Customers, Managers or Partners?* London: Routledge pp. 148–68

Rae, K. (1994) *Ano Te Hutinga O Te Harakeke – The Plucking Still of the Flaxbush: New Zealand Self-Managing Schools and Five Impacts in 1993 from the Ongoing Restructuring of Educational Administration* A paper prepared for the International Congress for School Effectiveness and Improvement, Melbourne, 3–6 January 1994

Ranson, S. (1990) 'From 1944 to 1988: Education; Citizenship and Democracy', in M. Flude and M. Hammer (eds) *Education Reform Act 1988: Its Origins and Implications* London: Falmer Press pp. 1–19

Robinson, P. and Smithers, A. (1991) *Teacher Turnover* University of Manchester: School of Education

Rodríguez, C. (1994) 'Chile: System of Education', in T. Husén and T.N. Postlethwaite (eds) *The International Encyclopedia of Education* Second Edition pp. 738–46

Sallis, J. (1987) '1986 Education Act' *The CASE Governors Pack* Newcastle: CASE

—— (1991) *School Governors: Your Questions Answered* London: Hodder and Stoughton

Saltman, R.B. and von Otter, C. (1992) *Planned Markets and Public Competition. Strategic Reform in Northern European Health Systems* Milton Keynes: Open University Press

Sammons, P. (1991) 'Measuring and Resourcing Educational Need: The Impact of LMS and "Formula Funding" on Resource Allocations To Inner London Schools' Paper presented at the BERA Conference, 1991

Secada, W.G. (1989) 'Education Equity Versus Equality of Education: an Alternative Conception', in W.G. Secada (ed.) *Equity in Education* Lewes: The Falmer Press pp. 68–88

Sen, A.K. (1977a) 'Rational Fools: a Critique of the Behavioural Foundations of Economic Theory' *Philosophy and Public Affairs* 6, Summer, 317–44. Page references as in Sen, A.K. (1982)

—— (1977b) 'On Weights and Measures: Informational Constraints in Social Welfare Analysis' *Econometrica* 45 October, 539–72

—— (1982) *Choice, Welfare and Measurement* Oxford: Blackwell

Shackle, G.L.S. (1973) *An Economic Querist* Cambridge: Cambridge University Press

Sharpe, F.G. (1995) 'Towards a Research Paradigm on Devolution' *Journal of Educational Administration* 34 (1) 4–23

Simon, B. (1992) *What Future for Education?* London: Lawrence and Wishart

Smith, M.S. and O'Day, J. (1991) 'Systemic School Reform', in S. Fuhrman and B. Malen (eds) *The Politics of Curriculum and Testing* Bristol: Falmer pp. 233–67

Smithers, A. and Robinson, P. (1991) *Staffing Secondary Schools in the Nineties* Manchester: University of Manchester School of Education

Steffy, B.E. and English, F.W. (1995) 'Radical Legislative School Reform in the United States: An examination of Chicago and Kentucky', in D.S.G. Carter and M.H. O'Neill (eds) *Case Studies in Educational Change: An International Perspective* London: The Falmer Press pp. 28–42

Teng Teng (1994) 'China, People's Republic of: System of Education' in T. Husén and T.N. Postlethwaite (eds) *The International Encyclopedia of Education* Second Edition pp. 750–5

Thomas, G. (1990) *Setting Up LMS: A Study of Local Education Authorities' Submissions to the DES* Milton Keynes: Open University Press

—— (1991) *The Framework for LMS: A Study of Local Education Authorities Approved Local Management of Schools Schemes* Milton Keynes: Open University Press

Thomas, H. (1996) 'Secondary Headteachers' Perspectives on Locally Managed Schools', in J.D. Chapman, W.L. Boyd, R. Lander and D. Reynolds (eds) *Dilemmas of Decentralisation, Quality, Equality and Control in Education* London: Cassell

—— and Martin, J. (1996) *Managing Resources for School Improvement: Creating a Cost-effective School* London: Routledge

Thomas, H. and Bullock, A.D. (1992a) 'School Size and Local Management Funding Formulae' *Educational Management and Administration* 20 (1) 30–8

—— (1992b) 'Local Management Funding Formulae and LEA Discretion', in T. Simkins, L. Ellison and V. Garrett (eds) *Implementing Educational Reform: The Early Lessons* Harlow: Longman pp. 216–25

—— (1994) 'The Political Economy of Local Management of Schools', in S. Tomlinson (ed.) *Educational Reform and Its Consequences* London: IPPR/Rivers Oram Press pp. 41–52

Thompson, G., Frances, J., Levacic, R. and Mitchell, J. (eds) (1991) *Markets, Hierarchies and Networks. The Coordination of Social Life* London: Sage Publications in association with The Open University

Thurmaier, K. and Swianiewicz, P. (1995) *Decentralization in Poland: Shifting Primary Education Administration to Local Self-Governments*

Times Educational Supplement, The (1991) 'Everyday is market-day', 25 October, p. 11

Titmuss, R.M. (1970) *The Gift Relationship* London: Allen and Unwin

Tomlinson, J.R.G. (1989) 'The Schools', in D. Kavanagh and A. Seldon (eds) *The Thatcher Effect : A Decade of Change* Oxford: Oxford University Press pp. 183–97

Tsang, Mun C. (1993) 'Financial Reforms of Basic Education: the Chinese Experience' paper prepared for the International Symposium on the Economics of Education, 19–21 May 1993, Manchester

United Nations Development Programme (1990) *Human Development Report 1990* Oxford: Oxford University Press for the UNPD

Warwickshire County Council (1990) *LMS Scheme* Warwick: County Hall

Welsh Office (1988) *Education Reform Act: Local Management of Schools* Circular 36/88 Cardiff: Welsh Office

Wiseman, J. (1978) 'The political economy of nationalised industry', in J.M. Buchanan (1978) (ed.) *The Economics of Politics* London: IEA pp. 71–92

Wragg, T. (1988) *Education in the Market Place: The Ideology Behind the 1988 Education Bill* NUT, Hamilton House, London: The Jason Press

Wylie, C. (1995) 'The Shift to School-based Management in New Zealand – The School View', in D.S.G. Carter and M.H. O'Neill (eds) *Case Studies in Educational Change: An International Perspective* pp. 61–80

Yeung, Yun Choi and Bannister, B.J. (1995) 'The Administration of Compulsory Education in China: Lessons from Guangzhou' *Journal of Educational Administration* 33 (4) 59–68

Zabalza, A., Turnbull, P. and Williams, G. (1979) *The Economics of Teacher Supply* Cambridge: Cambridge University Press

Index

'able' governors, availability of 131–2
access: autonomy and 213; distribution
of responsibilities 15–16; diversity of
responsibilities 206–7; international
perspectives 52–70 *passim*; scope of
decentralisation 8, 13–15
accountability 2, 3, 117–37, 220;
assessing impact of decentralisation
41, 43–4, 213–16; decision-making
structures 119–21; development
planning and 142; dialogue of
decision-making 121–6; dialogues of
44, 117–19; information for 119,
126–30; international perspectives
52–70 *passim*; and LEA 118, 132–3,
137; quality of 130–3; paradox of
132–3; roles, relationships and
governor involvement 133–6
additional educational needs (AENs)
30, 46, 173–83, 198, 218; advice and
guidance 174–5; and equity 183;
framework for re-distribution 173–4;
level of funding 179–83; problems of
definition and eligibility criteria
175–9
additional teaching staff 91
administration: head teachers' time 127;
meetings focused on 159–60
administrative/clerical staff 95–9;
budget administration 82–3; changing
role 96–8; increased number of hours
95–6; recognition 99; re-grades and
salary enhancements 98; *see also* non-
teaching staff
admissions 30, 206; competition, co-
operation and changing rolls 190–4;
scope of decentralisation 7, 8, 13–14;
see also access

advertising 196
age, pupil: early admission 193; and
funding 168–73, 184, 198, 218,
219
age-weighted pupil units (AWPUs)
169–72, 187
agency, autonomy of 37–8, 41–2
Aggregated Schools' Budget (ASB) 12,
169, 175
allocative mechanisms 17–31; as ideal
types 20–9; mixed economies 20,
29–31
allowance posts 92
altruism 18–19, 26–7, 28–9, 29
appointments 86–8; influence of salaries
88–9
assessment 204; distribution of
responsibilities 15–16; international
perspectives 52–70 *passim*; scope of
decentralisation 7, 8, 9–10
Audit Commission 76–7, 82, 83, 141
Australia 54–5, 71, 204–19 *passim*
autonomy 2, 3, 72–116; access and 213;
of agency 37–8, 41–2; assessing
impact of decentralisation 41, 41–3,
210–13; budget management 73–85;
collective resource allocation 27–8;
components of delegated
management 72–3; critical 37–8, 41–2;
curriculum 42, 43, 211–12;
decentralisation and learning 220–1;
delegation in practice 115–16; finance
and 3, 72, 73–85, 212; impact of new
staffing responsibilities 101–6;
international perspectives 52–70
passim; non-teaching staff 93–101;
role of LEA 106–15; teaching staff
85–93